The Secrets of the Tarot

Barbara G. Walker

The Secrets
of the Tarot

Origins, History, and Symbolism

Photography by Werner P. Brodde

1817

HARPER & ROW, PUBLISHERS, San Francisco
Cambridge, Hagerstown, New York, Philadelphia
London, Mexico City, São Paulo, Singapore, Sydney

For information on a complete set of Tarot cards based on the artwork by Barbara G. Walker contact U.S. Games Systems, Inc. 38 E. 32 Street, New York, New York 10016.

Grateful acknowledgment is made for the use of excerpts from:

"The Waste Land" from Collected Poems 1909–1962, by T. S. Eliot, copyright 1936, by Harcourt Brace Jovanovich, Inc.; copyright © 1943, 1963, 1964, by T. S. Eliot; copyright 1971 by Esme Valerie Eliot. Reprinted by permission of Harcourt Brace Jovanovich, Inc. and Faber and Faber Ltd.

"The Oracles" from The Collected Poems of A. E. Housman. Copyright 1922 by Holt, Rinehart, and Winston. Copyright 1950 by Barclays Bank Ltd. Reprinted by permission of Holt, Rinehart, and Winston, Publishers and The Society of Authors as the literary representative of the Estate of A. E. Housman, and Jonathan Cape Ltd., publishers of A. E. Housman's *Collected Poems*.

Designed by Leigh McLellan

Library of Congress Cataloging in Publication Data

Walker, Barbara G.
  THE SECRETS OF THE TAROT.

  Bibliography: p.243
  1. Tarot.   I. Title
BF1879.T2W33   1984   133.3'2424   84-47737
ISBN 0-06-250927-6

87 88 10 9 8 7 6

Contents

Part I. History's Mysteries

Part II. The Greater Secrets

Part III. The Lesser Secrets

Part I

History's Mysteries

Madam Sosostris, famous clairvoyante,
Had a bad cold, nevertheless
Is known to be the wisest woman in Europe,
With a wicked pack of cards. Here, said she,
Is your card, the drowned Phoenician Sailor,
(Those are pearls that were his eyes. Look!)
Here is Belladonna, the Lady of the Rocks,
The lady of situations.
Here is the man with three staves, and here the Wheel,
And here is the one-eyed merchant, and this card,
Which is blank, is something he carries on his back,
Which I am forbidden to see. I do not find
The Hanged Man. Fear death by water.
I see crowds of people, walking round in a ring.

—T. S. Eliot, *The Waste Land*

1

Part I

History's Mysteries

The Sacred Tarot

Tarot cards were the ancestors of modern playing cards. Tarot suits of cups, wands, pentacles, and swords evolved into the symbolically related hearts, clubs, diamonds, and spades. The modern deck of fifty-two cards is a shortened version of the standard Tarot deck of seventy-eight cards. Of the twenty-six lost cards, only one now remains: the Joker, or Fool, who usually doesn't play. His card is not much liked. A common saying calls anything suspicious "a joker in the deck."

Why were twenty-six cards—a third of the deck—removed?

This is an important question, because twenty-two of the twenty-six lost cards used to be the most significant ones. They were the suit of trumps, called Major Arcana or Greater Secrets. Today's card players are obliged to designate one of the other suits "trumps" for trick-taking games, because the real trump cards were abolished. Who abolished them?

It seems the original enemies of the cards' Greater Secrets were Christian clergymen. Their objections were based on more than some vague notion that card games were frivolous. One scholar writes, "Preachers have never liked playing cards, and it can be said that the story the cards tell is very much opposed to the basic tenets of Christianity."[1] The issue was a religious one. Cards apparently conveyed a heretical message detested by the church.

Here is the starting point for historical inquiry. What was that heret-

3

ical message? Who interpreted the cards' arcane symbols, and how? What did the "games" mean? Why did church fathers think these little pasteboard pictures so threatening as to call forth the most resounding ecclesiastical thunders?

No doubt the thunders were serious. St. Bernardino of Siena said the Tarot was an invention of the devil, and the Major Arcana was the devil's breviary, "in which various figures are painted, just as they are in the breviaries of Christ, which figures show forth the mysteries of evil."[2] Another churchman claimed the devil invented the cards "that he might the easier bring in Idolatry among men." The trump cards seem to have been the "idols" referred to; the trump suit was called "rungs of a ladder leading to the depths of hell."[3]

In 1376 the cards were forbidden in Florence. In 1378 they were banned in Germany. In 1381 they were condemned in Marseilles. In 1397 they were forbidden in Paris and the city of Ulm.[4] In 1441 importation of cards was prohibited in Venice. In 1450 a Franciscan friar denounced the cards in northern Italy. In 1452 Cardinal John Capistran caused "a great heap of packs of cards" to be burned in the marketplace of Nuremberg, as if they were living witches.[5]

A century earlier, the monk John of Brefeld apparently learned a sympathetic interpretation of the cards. He made the tactical error of writing that, in them, "the state of the world as it is now is most excellently described and figured." Other clergymen overruled this opinion, calling the cards a devil's book and a secret scripture of Gnostic heretics.[6]

When the cards first became popular in Europe, "the state of the world as it is now" included many pockets of opposition to the entrenched religion, widespread disillusionment with the church, and a tendency to seek alternate faiths. Europe was poised on the brink of the Renaissance. An influx of new ideas from Eastern lands had stimulated intellectual curiosity, and revived the old Indo-European paganism that once gave both East and West their common heritage of language, culture, and religion. These new ideas percolated through all levels of society, so that not only intellectuals, but even illiterate peasants were beginning to question the church's right to control their minds.

Church-sponsored Crusades had sent many of Europe's rude barbarians to the Eastern centers of what was, at the time, a higher civilization. Crusaders didn't find streets paved with silver, as they had expected; but they did find their Saracen adversaries adept in such interesting subjects as art, mathematics, algebra, alchemy, astronomy and astrology, and many mystical philosophies. These shook the warriors' or pilgrims' Christian faith in a church that was still proclaiming itself to be the world's only legitimate source of "truth."

The Saracens had used cards for gaming and divining since at least the eighth century. The Spanish word for cards, *naipes*, derived from Saracenic *naib*.[7] Another cognate was the Hebrew *naibi*, "sorcery."[8] Sorcery was a Judeo-Christian blanket term for alien religious observances, in accord with the biblical rule that all "gods of the heathen" were devils (Deuteronomy 32:17).

It seems many Europeans thought the figures on the cards really were pagan deities. Eastern peoples long used pasteboard picture-cards as unbound sacred books, to show the attributes of goddesses and gods, and to teach religious doctrines to children and other illiterates while they played games.[9] The same principle was well known in pre-Christian Europe.

Ancient *ludi* or "sacred games" had been redefined by the church as frivolity and carnival clownishness, giving rise to the word *ludicrous*; but the original purpose of their dances, masks, costumes, and processions was to reveal gods to their worshipers. A "pageant" once meant a series of mystical revelations in the sacred drama. Its component *paginae* became medieval "pages": movable floats or stages in the mystery play, each showing a tableau of divine persons or symbols. Such plays still appear in the Orient, demonstrating the Eastern origin of many European figures in traditional miracle drama and literature, *commedia* and pageant—as well as their formerly sacred connotations.[10]

Not only Oriental symbols, but also much similar material from Occidental paganism found its way into Renaissance games and Tarot cards. The trump cards so disliked by churchmen took their title from the holy pageant known to the ancient world as a *triumph*. Sacrificial processions and sacred games in pagan Rome were under the charge of a high priest called a *triumphator*.[11] The central figure in a triumph was usually an apotheosized hero, sacred king, emperor, or a man impersonating a god—like Jesus in Jerusalem's annual triumphal procession on the Day of the Palms, which was originally held in honor of the Goddess Ishtar and her dying-god consort Tammuz (Ezekiel 8:14).

In one of Rome's most venerable rites, a triumphal procession circumambulated the city, calling on the Lares (ancestral ghosts) and the Goddess variously named Ceres, Car, Carmenta, or Carna, "Maker of All Flesh," whom Ovid described as "a Goddess of the olden time," and Plutarch called "Fate presiding over human birth."[12] Her priestesses, the *carmentes*, sang hymns called *carmen*, which passed into Old English as *cyrm*, meaning a sacred song, then became the "charm" supposedly spoken or sung by witches.[13] The *carmentes'* triumphal procession ended with the cry of *Triumpe*, which became *triumphi*, Italian *trionfi*, English "trump."[14]

This shows a specific link between the Tarot's Major Arcana cards and the idea of a sacred procession in which, traditionally, deities displayed their *exuviae*, or "attributes."[15] These displays included images, masks, costumes, songs, dances, and stylized postures that later descended into the repertoire of carnival clowns—who resembled the Fool leading the Tarot procession of trumps. Clowns performed "antics," derived from Italian *antico,* Latin *antiquus,* meaning "ancient, venerable."[16] In England, the Fool's dance was an "antic hey," a figure-eight step based on the international holy infinity sign, which had a peculiar significance in the Tarot, as we shall see. Songs that accompanied such dances called for the "antic hey" figure in the chorus, for example, "Hey, nonny nonny," or "Hey, Derry-down."

The Goddess Carna was once the presiding deity of Carnival, which still conceals remnants of the old religion under pretended clownishness. Pagan rivals of the Christian savior continued to be sacrificed, incarnate in beasts or effigies, as Green George, Lord Baal, the May King, the Lord of Misrule, Prince of Fools, Carnival King, and other relics of the ancient King of the Games *(rex ludorum),* actually sacrificed at the end of his temporary kingship. His death became less literal, but he still suffered a mock execution each year in the role of sacred king of the revels.[17] If Christian priests scented heresy in the effigies hung "between heaven and earth," crucified on trees, sent to hell, and resurrected to bear away the sins of the people, they were slyly told it was "only a game."

Games of cards, wheels, and dice boards had always been popular media for religious instruction in the East. Worshipers of Vishnu placed a portrait of each of their god's ten incarnations on the court cards of their suits.[18] Cards in sequence imitated holy processions, in which certain divine images were carried, and masked, costumed human beings impersonated supernatural entities for the edification of the faithful. Sequential cards also copied the "instructive picture gallery" that was placed along corridors leading to the central Holy of Holies in Oriental temples.[19] Each picture meant a new revelation in the process of initiation. For those who couldn't make the pilgrimage to the temple, holy pictures could be painted on cards for private meditation.

This important Oriental concept was copied by Europeans in several ways. A Christianized version became known as the Stations of the Cross. Mystery cults in general led the novice through a series of "stations" in the temple, where he could meet supernatural beings (either holy images, or costumed temple personnel). He received instruction, and symbolically repeated the life story of the savior-god in order to become "one" with him, and thus achieve the same resurrection. In Egypt, a worshiper of Osiris became "an Osiris." In Greece, a worshiper of Dionysus similarly acquired "grace" or *enthusiasm,* the state of "having the god within." The idea of salvation depended on merging the self with the god, by sacramentally eating him, by imitating him, by memorizing his myth and teachings. Christianity copied the idea, but devotees of the older Eastern savior-gods had it first—as Renaissance travelers had just begun to realize.

Crusaders, traders, and pilgrims returning from the Holy Land brought more than ideas and merchandise back to Europe. Their ships brought Oriental black rats, which brought their own fleas, which in turn brought the scourge of the fourteenth century: bubonic plague. A modern reader can hardly picture the devastation wrought by this pestilence. Whole villages and towns were wiped out. Entire districts were abandoned. Crops went untended, and famine followed the Black Death. By the end of the century, the population of Europe had been reduced by at least 50 percent.

Under such agonizing conditions, many people openly doubted the goodness of a God who—as the pope himself said in a bull (a papal letter)—deliberately sent these horrors "to afflict the Christian people for their sins." A law professor wrote, "The hostility of God is stronger than the hostility of man."[20] The church failed to rise to the crisis. Clergymen fled plague-stricken districts in "panic fear and neglect."[21] The dead rotted in the streets, unshriven and unburied. According to the superstitious notions of the day, omission of the last rites automatically damned plague victims to an eternity of torture in hell, deserved or not. Survivors bitterly resented this injustice to their relatives.

French clergymen made the mistake of advertising the cult of St. Roch as a sure defense against the plague. They said no sickness could enter a house bearing on its door the letters V.S.R. (Vive Saint Roch).[22] The mocking letters stood on the doors of many houses left empty, their inmates all dead, a monument to crude superstition.

The people's impressions of ecclesiastical and divine indifference to human suffering brought back the old Gnostic image of the demon-god. A thousand years earlier, Manicheans and other Gnostic sects of the primitive church called Jehovah an evil demiurge who made the material world to entrap souls, as he had sent the serpent to entrap Adam and Eve. They quoted Isaiah to show that God himself admitted having created evil (Isaiah 45:7), and argued that subordinate demons tormented mankind only by God's will and permission. The orthodox church actually agreed with the heretics on this point, but never carried the argument to its logical conclusion: that a deity who ruled demons must be an arch-demon. This Gnostic view became popular as the Renaissance gathered momentum.

In practice, the real divinity of the Renaissance seems to have been the Christianized version of the Great Mother, whom the pagan worshipers of Juno, Diana, and Ceres used to address as Mother of God, Blessed Virgin, and Queen of Heaven. Mary, the new Great Mother, won the hearts of the people where the patriarchal deities failed. "The vitality of Christ's own Church has often seemed to depend on her rather than him." She alone had mercy on the suffering. Germanus said she could turn away God's "threat and sentence of damnation . . . therefore the Christian people trustfully turn to you, refuge of sinners."[23] A Franciscan wrote: "When we have offended Christ, we should go first to the Queen of Heaven and offer her . . . prayers, fasting, vigils, and alms; then she, like a mother, will come between thee and Christ, the father who wishes to beat us, and she will throw the cloak of mercy between the rod of punishment and us, and soften the king's anger against us."[24]

Old woodcuts showed God the Father shooting the arrows of plague, inflation, and war at the world, while human beings pleaded with the Virgin to claim kinship with them and save them from God's wrath.[25] In despair, men reverted to that "strong unconscious trend towards mother-worship" that has been discerned even in male-dominated societies where manifestations of the Goddess were officially denied.[26] Mary herself was denied by the early church, but accepted after the fifth century when it became clear that not even converts would tolerate the loss of their divine Mother. Strong indications of Goddess worship may be seen in the feminine imagery of the Tarot, hinting at one of the reasons for its success.

Aside from its half-suppressed Great Mother, the Renaissance church offered little comfort. In 1360 the pope admitted that many wealthy abbots and priests took up arms against their own flocks, to "participate in rapine and despoliation, even in the shedding of blood."[27] St. Bernard wrote that nearly every prelate sought to empty the pockets of his parishioners, rather than to subdue their vices.[28] St. Catherine of Siena wrote so bluntly of the priests' sins that, even now, "the English translation published under official Roman censorship discreetly and silently suppresses her all too candid descriptions."[29] The friar Raymond Jean publicly declared, "The enemies of the faith are among ourselves. The Church which governs us is symbolled by the Great Whore of the Apocalypse, who persecutes the poor."[30] He was burned at the stake.

Pierre de Bruys was also burned for declaring that praying to the cross was a pointless procedure; that "God is no more in the church than in the market-place"; and that priests lied when they claimed bits of bread were Christ's body, given to people for their salvation. In thirteenth-century Paris, reformers charged that priests accused "honest matrons" of heresy and condemned them to death, only because the same matrons had refused to consent to the priests' lascivious proposals.[31] Bohemians publicly burned papal bulls at the pillory in Prague, after stringing them around the neck of a prostitute who mocked them with lewd gestures.[32] Konrad of Megenburg wrote a popular satire in which "Lady Church" denounced her own priests as hypocrites, whoremongers, and shameless worshipers of Lady Avarice-and-Vain-glory.[33]

Dreadful Crusades of extermination were waged by Christian Brethren of the Sword and Teutonic Knights against the pagan populations of Prussia, Livonia, Courland, and the Polish Wends. Lithuanians were "converted" by military force in the fourteenth century.[34] Every man, woman, and child among the Stedingers of the Weser river valley was put to the sword for worshiping non-Christian deities, and consulting wise-women.[35] Two centuries of warfare and atrocities still failed to bring dissenting Balkan countries into the fold. As late as the eighteenth century, the monk Spiridon complained that many Bulgarians still worshiped their ancient Thunder-god Pyerun instead of Jesus.[36] Well over a million Cathari in the cities of southern France were massacred by papal decree, for contesting the official theology and refusing to pay their tithes to Rome.[37] Whole subnations like the Basques, or the people of Navarre, were declared heretics and witches in toto.[38] Innumerable sects banded together to oppose the church, such as the Brothers and Sisters of the Free Spirit, the Poor Men of Lyons, the Waldenses, Hussites, Fraticelli, Spiritual Franciscans, Dolcinists, and many others who paid with their lives for holding unorthodox views.

By the thirteenth century, it was becoming increasingly clear that despite the church's apparently complete conquest—chiefly by violence —orthodox authority was being challenged on every side by rebellious heretics. Even though the papacy had reached a pinnacle of worldly power, and the Crusaders were slaughtering thousands of unbelievers at home and abroad, the native populations of Europe stubbornly resisted the alien God who vilified their ancestral deities as demons, and condemned their own natural thoughts and feelings as sins.[39]

Churchmen applied more and more pressure to the mutinous masses by threatening them not only with death, but with damnation to a crueler hell than any other religion had previously envisioned. An extraordinary sadism surfaced in these official visions of hell. St. Thomas Aquinas and other theologians insisted that the righteous (like themselves) would watch joyfully from heaven as the damned writhed in eternal torture, having no pity on the sinners. St. Bernardino of Siena said heaven couldn't be perfect without "due admixture of groans from the damned." Moreover, the vast majority would go to hell, and only a few would deserve heaven. Raymond Lull was declared a heretic for criticizing the "mercy" of a Christ who would consign nearly all human souls to such an eternity of torment.[40]

Instead of cleaning its own house, the church resorted to violent suppression of its critics; thus the Inquisition was born. "God's Gestapo" held Europe in a reign of terror for nearly five centuries, the greatest persecution known to history, exceeding even the twentieth-century

9

Holocaust in Germany. The Inquisition ravaged all Christendom by its war on heresy.[41] Historian Charles Lea called the inquisitorial system "a standing mockery of justice—perhaps the most iniquitous that the arbitrary cruelty of man has ever devised."[42] It created a police state in every village and hamlet on the continent, excepting only the Scandinavian countries which paid no attention to Christianity until the eleventh century, and subsequently refused to admit the church's judges and torturers.[43]

In such circumstances it was inevitable that alternative religious or mystical beliefs should cloak themselves in secret codes, carefully guarded, and made known only to trusted initiates. Paganism still flourished in the fourteenth century as the faith of the *pagani* or "country folk"; but the menace of persecution turned its rites and ceremonies into *occulta*, "hidden things." The German word *Heiden*, meaning both "hidden" and "heathen," shows the increasing concealment of the people's deities.[44]

Churchmen never doubted the reality of these deities. "The orthodox believed in the existence of Thor and Odin as firmly as the heathen did; the only difference was that, while to the latter they were gods, to the former they were demons."[45] Even though many of their devotees were exterminated as sorcerers and witches, yet the peasantry feared to abandon the religion of their ancestors.

Women especially clung to the old religion, because it gave them spiritual status as priestesses of the Goddess. All-male Christianity gave them no such status. Far from honoring the ancient laws of mother-right, medieval clerics blamed women for the existence of sin, and even denied that women had souls.[46]

Women therefore maintained the rites of their Goddess, the Mother of nature, the moon, the earth, the waters; they continued even after the theological significance of the rites became garbled, or forgotten. Martin of Braga condemned all women for keeping traditional ceremonies: "Decorating tables, wearing laurels, taking omens from footsteps, putting fruit and wine on the log in the hearth, and bread in the well; what are these but worship of the devil? For women to call upon Minerva when they spin, and to observe the day of Venus at weddings and to call upon her whenever they go out upon the public highway, what is that but worship of the devil?"[47] As late as the fourteenth century, there were still unofficial priestesses who annually "conjured the Rhine" to prevent floods.[48]

Some pagan rituals were thought so essential to public welfare that they persisted in spite of every effort to suppress them, and eventually had to be adopted—or at least tolerated—by churchmen. "A thousand years ago . . . old and young assembled in woods or on plains to bring gifts to their gods, and celebrated with dances, games, and offerings the festival of spring. . . . These celebrations have taken Christian names, but innumerable old heathen rites and customs are still to be found in them."[49]

Among these rites and customs are: May poles, Halloween masks, Christmas mistletoe, holly, ivy, pine trees, and Yule logs; Easter eggs brought by the Moon-hare; Harvest Home feasts; Lent fasts; Midsummer bonfires; mystery plays, carnival processions, well-dressings, and circle dances. Some became children's games, nursery rhymes, and maze dances like "Troy Town." The fairy-ring dance, which circled widdershins (counterclockwise) around the Goddess's Holy Rose, contributed its chant as "Ring-Around-A-Rosy" in English, *"Ringel-Ringel Rosenkranz"* in German.[50] Hobbyhorse and broomstick dances were once performed by adults, not children, in honor of the Mare-goddess Epona. Pagan sacred symbols also reappeared in children's party games like bobbing for apples and pinning the tail on the donkey. Blindman's buff was once a sacrificial ritual.

Religious instruction via games and other visual aids obviously was intended for the illiterate, who couldn't study scriptures. For these— the overwhelming majority of people in ancient or medieval Europe— the only readable "books" were pictures, which is why Gothic cathedrals were covered with graphic representations of heaven, hell, doomsday, saints, devils, and all the rest of the church's messages. Similar messages seem to have been conveyed through the pictures on cards.

Card packs were often called "books" by the same clergymen who denounced them.[51] Some authorities mentioned mysterious Elf-books, given by "the fairies" to people they loved, "which enabled them to foretell future events."[52] Elf-books evidently were packs of divinatory cards.

The fact that Tarot cards were, and still are, used for divination strongly suggests that they were once considered holy. "Divination" comes from "divine" for the very reason that only sacred things were supposed to have prophetic powers. Literate Christians often used the Bible for divination, because of its sacredness. They would open the book at random and touch some words, then draw a prophecy from the text. St. Augustine himself recommended divination from the scriptures "in all cases of spiritual difficulty."[53]

This particular kind of divination required that one should (1) own a Bible, and (2) know how to read it. Neither case was very common at the beginning of the Renaissance. Few Europeans could read or write. Even a majority of the clergy were illiterate. A candidate for the priesthood was not required to learn to read, only to memorize a catechism.

11

General education was not attempted in Europe until the nineteenth century; but even in the 1890s, only a third of the population could read.[54]

Since Bibles were written in Latin before the Reformation, a person wishing to read one would have to be literate not only in his own language, but in a foreign language too. Even then, a layman couldn't read the Bible because he was forbidden to do so by ecclesiastical law. Pope Gregory the Great long ago made it illegal for laymen to read Scriptures, lest they might find something contradictory to the official theology.[55] Up to the Reformation, any person owning a Bible written in the vernacular was subject to burning at the stake.[56]

But the Judeo-Christian Bible was only one source of sacred material. There were pagan scriptures, cabalistic books, alchemical treatises that were really thin disguises for mystical philosophy. There were idols and icons of many kinds. Holy images and literature came to Europe from the East, and were incorporated into Grail myths, heraldry, and cults of courtly love.

Perhaps cards were credited with occult powers for the very reason that the "bibles" of the East were often arranged like card packs, with their unbound pages stacked together and secured with string. Such "bibles" were known as Books of Life. This same term was applied to packs of cards in Europe.[57] Among the Slavs, a divinatory card reader was called *Vedavica*, literally "one who reads the Vedas," referring to the sacred books of India.[58]

Oriental sages never thought games incompatible with religion. They disseminated religious ideas through cards, dice, and colorful board games like the still highly popular Tantric Buddhist "Game of Rebirth."[59] Similarly ancient card games were found in the West. One of the oldest was ombre, from Hispano-Moorish *hombre*, "the Game of Man," which resembled the Hindu game *ganjifa*.[60] Taylor's *History of Playing Cards* said " 'The game of man,' a modification of the earlier game of primero, is of all modern games that which most resembles the ancient Tarot."[61]

Another early card game was Faro, "the Game of Kings," named after Egyptian pharaohs by the gypsies, who pretended to be their descendants.[62] These people were called "Egyptians" ('Gypties) because, on their first recorded appearance in Germany, they claimed to be exiled noblemen from Little Egypt. Gypsies well knew that Europeans were impressed by any reference to Egypt, which they associated with magic and mystery.

The gypsies' real homeland was India, whence they began to migrate westward about the ninth century, carrying their typically Hindu sacred booklets as card packs. Gypsies have always been linked with

Tarot cards, which they used not only as a source of income from for-tune-telling, but also as their "Bible of the occult beliefs."[63]

Gypsies played a leading role in disseminating occult beliefs connect-ed with the cards. Many of the gypsies' beliefs centered on the religious figure that Christian authorities most disliked: the Great Mother, still worshiped in India as the Goddess of a Hundred Names.[64] In Egypt she was credited with a thousand names. She was "that powerful being . . . whether known as Isis, Parvati, Devaki, Kali, Bhavani, Artemis, Athena, Minerva, Diana or Madonna, who are all . . . *unam eandemque* (one and the same)."[65]

Her portrait still appears on the "last trump"—the culminating card of the Tarot's Major Arcana—as the World Mother, or cosmic Shakti, to whom all foregoing revelations point. Gypsies knew her as Ma, or Mat-ta, or Laki (Lakshmi), or Kali, or Sara, or Tara. The last was a primor-dial Mother Center-of-the-Earth known to ancient Celts by the same name, Tara, or Taranis; to the Semites as Terah; to the Romans as Terra Mater. An annual carnival in Athens was dedicated to her and bore her name: Taramata, "Mother Tara."[66] The mysterious word Tarot, whose origin has never been traced, may have been derived from the name of this Goddess who ruled men's fates.

Twenty-one incarnations of Mother Tara are still associated with sa-cred divinatory dice-boards of Tantric Buddhism. A board of twenty-one squares is officially "the Twenty-One Taras." Another board of fifty-six squares is "for determining the successive regions and grades of one's future rebirths."[67] These magic numbers, 21 and 56, are the numbers of the Tarot's Major Arcana and Minor Arcana, respectively. A full deck includes only one card more, the numberless Fool, who "do-esn't count" because he is always Zero.

Numerical grouping of the cards probably originated, like the figures of the I Ching, with combinations of throws of the rods or dice used for oracles. Twenty-one is the total number of possible throws with two dice. Fifty-six is the total number of possible throws with three dice. Together they make seventy-seven, or seven elevens, the prime magic number of dice games.

The Zero card may have been added to the deck by astrologically minded occultists, to make the zodiacal total, the sum of all the num-bers of the twelve zodiacal signs. One $+ 2 + 3 + 4 + 5 + 6 + 7 + 8 + 9 + 10 + 11 + 12$ equals 78, the number of cards in a full deck. The Tarot was often given astrological significance. German horoscopes or "Nativity Calendars" in the sixteenth century were created with pictures directly copied from the Major Arcana.[68]

Gypsies were familiar with the Tantric belief that the female principle preceded the male principle, and the supreme deity was the Goddess, not the God.[69] The whole universe sprang from her genital hub, commonly symbolized by the lotus—a female symbol appearing in many sacred mandalas. The highest-ranking Tantric lamas used a special "lotus dice-board" as both a game and a divining instrument. Each petal of the lotus bore a number corresponding to prophecies written in a manual, like the I Ching books, compiled by "The One who sees all actions"—possibly the Goddess herself.[70]

The primacy of the female principle in Tantrism may explain why the feminine-numbered Major Arcana Tarot cards were trumps or Greater Secrets, while the Lesser Secrets added up to a masculine number. Among the trump cards, important figures were more female than male —including a female pope.

Fifty-six, the number of the Lesser Arcana, was associated with male gods. India even had a god who personified the number and bore the name of Fifty-Six.[71] Buddha shared some attributes of this god. When the Enlightened One was born, he took fifty-six steps, fourteen in each of the four cardinal directions (seven forward and seven back), forming a cross.[72]

The same cross can be made of the four Tarot suits of fourteen cards each, which total fifty-six. In the East and West alike, the cross was generally assimilated to phallic gods and the masculine principle. Fifty-six was a natal number of the Sun-god born to Mother Earth (Tara). His rays formed a cross as he died to re-enter her subterranean tomb-womb and be born again.

Fifty-six was also the number of years in the ancient astronomical Great Year. Lunar and solar cycles coincided once every 56 years in ancient calendars. This was usually mythologized as a periodic wedding of the Moon-goddess and Sun-god, represented by the numbers 18 and 19—the same numbers assigned to the Moon card and Sun twins of the Tarot. These stemmed from the observation that the full moon of the midwinter solstice moves from maximum north declination to minimum north declination in 18.61 years, which had to be multiplied by 3 to correct for its fraction, producing the cycle of 56 years. The 56 "Aubrey holes" at the Stonehenge temple evidently served as an eclipse-predicting computer for the Great Year:

> If the priests . . . had used a simple 19-year interval, they would have been right for perhaps two intervals, and then after a third interval would have been off by a full year. A rigid 19-year cycle would have soon drifted into hopeless error. The only regular-interval alternative, an 18-year cycle, would have been twice as bad. The smallest time unit that would have remained accurate for many years would have been the triple-interval measure, 19 + 19 + 18, or a total of 56 years . . . Stonehenge moon phenomena repeated every 56 years with good uniformity.[73]

The question of calendars was a sore one in the Middle Ages. Europe actually followed two incompatible systems of time-reckoning. The church insisted on the solar Julian calendar of 12 months, while common folk kept to the old pagan lunar calendar of thirteen 28-day months, supposedly derived from the menstrual cycles of the Goddess, manifested in the phases of the moon. Mutual conflict between the two calendars is shown in the two different versions of the nursery rhyme: (1) "How many months be in the year? There be thirteen, I say," and (2) "How many months be in the year? There be but twelve, I say." The standard time period of nursery rhymes, fairy tales, ballads, and other remnants of paganism is "a year and a day," meaning the lunar year of 364 days (thirteen 28-day months) plus one more day to make 365.

The ecclesiastical calendar retained the seven-day lunar weeks—which is why they no longer fit the months—but broke up the thirteenth "moon" (Anglo-Saxon *monath* meant both "month" and "moon"). The extra days were added to the other twelve months. Thirteen was once a sacred number because of the thirteen annual lunations; but the churchmen imputed evil to it. In honor of the Goddess called "threefold Moon, Queen of Fate," thirteen priestesses used to dance in the widdershins direction, following the retrograde motion of the moon around the wheel of the ecliptic.[74] Such a group came to be called a "coven" of witches, and the lunar Goddess acquired the title of Coventina, "Mother of Covens."[75] The connection between femaleness and the number 13 is reflected in the Tarot: each Tarot queen is the thirteenth card of her suit.

After the defeat of the lunar calendar, 13 became the "devil's dozen." Friday the Thirteenth was called the unluckiest of days because it combined the Goddess's sacred number with her sacred day, named after one of her Teutonic forms, Freya. In Latinate languages, the day is named after Venus. The ancients ate fish on Friday because fish, too, were sacred to the Sea-goddess and were thought to arouse the passion of love through her influence.

Ironically, the church's main festival of Easter was derived from another of the Goddess's many names, Eostre, a Saxon form of Astarte. Despite the institution of the solar calendar, the death and resurrection of the Christian savior-god like those of the pagan ones was, and still is, determined by the moon. Easter is one of the "movable feasts" that follow the pre-Christian system of dating—though the faithful are not told that it bears the name of the Great Goddess.[76]

Another difference between Christian and pagan calendars was that the former reckoned the solar day from midnight to midnight, whereas the latter reckoned the lunar day from noon to noon. Therefore, pagan festivals preceded their Christianized counterparts by twelve hours, being celebrated on the Moon-day, or Eve, of the solar date. For instance,

15

May Day was a new Christian form of the old feast of May Eve or Walpurgisnacht (Beltane to the Celts). All Hallows' Day or All Souls' Day was a new Christian form of Hallow-Eve, the Celts' Samhain, Feast of the Dead. Even Christmas Eve was dedicated to the Goddess rather than the God. In medieval England, Christmas Eve was Modranect or Matrum Noctem, "the Night of the Mother."[77] The pagan habit of calling each night a day was still prevalent in Shakespeare's time, when people said good-night by wishing each other "good den"—literally "good day."

Hindu tradition said it was the Goddess who first gave birth to time itself, and to all methods of measuring it: the year, the month, the season, the lunar day, the days of the week, twilight, night, and dawn, the trinity of Aeons, and the methods of keeping time in music. A great manifestation of Mother Kali was her Wheel of Time, Kalanemi.[78] From her name, the universal Indo-European concept of "Kalends" descended. The earliest calendars were lunar and feminine.

In the tenth century, when gypsies were beginning to move west, the most revered religious text in their native India was the Kalacakra Tantra, dealing with the Wheel of Time. This scripture is still "the most important tantric cycle in Tibet, coming at the head of the tantric section of the sacred canon."[79] Some of the gypsy tribes who reached Persia in the tenth century called themselves Kalenderees, or people of the Time-goddess Kali.[80]

Gypsies were such devoted worshipers of Kali that they professed to find her again in Europe, disguised as the famous black Virgin Giving Birth, in the pre-Christian crypt under Chartres Cathedral. In Roman times this Goddess-dominated crypt was revered as the womb of Gaul. Gypsies identified its antique image as their Black Mother, whom they called Sara-Kali or Queen Kali. Ignoring Christians who insisted that the image was Mary, the gypsies said her crypt was "the womb of your mother . . . the source of the spring of life which flows over the gypsy race . . . the mother, the woman, the sister, the queen, the *Phuri Dai*, the source of all Romany blood."[81]

Among the gypsies were "occult couples" trained like priests and priestesses of Kali to perform the Great Rite *(Maharutti)* known in India as *maithuna*, in the West as *karezza* or *coitus reservatus*—that is, coitus indefinitely prolonged, without male orgasm. Like Kali's *sadhakas*, who imitated her divine consort Shiva in his eternal union with the Goddess, gypsy men were taught that "occult coition is a means of increasing psychic powers." Love-power generated by controlled sex was thought necessary to the training of a sage. Gypsies said, "If one really wants to possess the power of love, he should always give more than he takes."[82]

When gypsies worshiped the Christian Virgin, they did so in the same way that Hindus worshiped Kali. They offered the heads of sacrificed fowls, piled up in front of her church.[83] As it was said of Kali, "To the Goddess is due the lifeblood of all creatures—since it is she who has bestowed it . . . hence beheading is the form of sacrifice, since the blood drains quickly from the beheaded beasts."[84] The same ancient rationale produced the Jews' "kosher killing."

Sara-Kali was lightly Christianized by a few legends claiming that she accompanied the three Marys from the foot of Jesus's cross, on their sea voyage to a landing place at Saintes-Maries-de-la-Mar. Others, however, said Sara-Kali was a gypsy queen living in France before the Marys arrived.[85] Gypsies claimed all French cathedrals were arranged so as to mirror, on the earth, the stars of the constellation Virgo, home of Queen Kali in heaven.[86]

Gypies understood the Hindu concept of the Goddess as a trinity of Virgin, Mother, and Crone, governing all creation, preservation, and destruction (or, birth, life, death). A typical gypsy prayer to her alluded to these functions:

> Thou destroyest and dost make everything on earth; thou canst see nothing old, for death lives in thee, thou givest birth to all upon the earth for thou thyself art life. . . . Thou art the mother of every living creature and the distributor of good; thou doest according to thy wisdom in destroying what is useless or what has lived its destined time; by thy wisdom thou makest the earth to regenerate all that is new . . . thou art the benefactress of mankind.[87]

Gypsies didn't believe in heaven or hell. Like their Hindu ancestors they believed in cyclic reincarnations on the Goddess's eternal Wheel of Time.[88] About his own death, a gypsy said, "Naked, I shall return to the womb of my mother. . . . The earth is our mother, and so is woman. The secret of life comes from the ground."[89] Gypsies espoused the Tantric philosophy that viewed death as the indispensable counterpart to life, and symbolized it in the destroying Crone who must be as much adored as the beautiful Virgin or the kindly Mother, even though she was a hideous deity of disease and dissolution. Tantric poets said no man could truly know the Goddess until he knew her death aspect, as his "tearer and devourer."[90] She "devours all existence." At doomsday she would destroy the whole universe, to re-create it for the next cycle. At the end she would be clothed in "a red mass of blood" while she devoured the gods she once gave birth to.[91]

Similarly, the gypsy Goddess as a bringer of disease and death was clothed in red. In this aspect she was Bibi, the Crone who "has the power to cause all kinds of disease, especially at the beginning of a new month when there is a full moon." Gypsies said conception also occurred at the full moon; no woman ever became pregnant without the moon's help.[92] This death-and-resurrection motif, with the dead soul going to the moon to be recycled, is one of the common themes of mystery religions all over the world.

As the "compendium of gypsy philosophy and religion," Tarot cards set forth the cyclic concept of life and death in a symbol system that could be read by the illiterate.[93] To communicate through such a system, some general agreement on the meaning of symbols had to be reached. Modern psychologists maintain that a certain amount of such agreement is genetically built into the human mind, as basic archetypes found in all times and all cultures, as well as in individual dreams and visions. Modern interpreters of the Tarot find in the archetypal concept a credible rationale for deriving valid insights from the cards. The language of the unconscious consists of symbols rather than words; and the cards' symbol system is thought capable of guiding thought into the mind's hidden depths.[94]

Symbol systems founded on archetypal figures have been used by many secret religious fraternities, especially in the Orient, where learned lamas still believe in an international code that provides the meaning of occult doctrines. Some scholars have thought the hieroglyphics of Egypt and Mexico arose from similar esoteric symbol codes. In the ancient world, there were Druidic, Pythagorean, Orphic and Platonic fraternities who conveyed their doctrines by means of symbolic figures.[95] As we know, there were many symbolic paths for the secret teaching of heretical religious ideas in medieval Europe: not only the pageants and mystery plays, but also carnival games and costumes, ornamental designs on the *paginae* even of Bibles, and various figures incorporated into the very fabric of churches were among these symbolic paths. Certainly the gypsies, like other non-Christian groups, needed a secret vehicle for the exchange of their ideas on spiritual matters, especially in a Europe where only one religion could be openly professed, while all others were subject to persecution.

Tarot interpreters surely would have found secrecy an advantage, in a period of European history that was plagued by the church's secret police, alert for any whisper of heresy, and ready with their racks and thumbscrews to turn a whisper into a scream. Gypsies suffered along with other "witches" under the Inquisition, whereby they were arrested whenever possible.[96] Gypsies were known as Diana's Foresters, or Minions of the Moon, meaning witches. Sometimes they were called fairies, or "fays"; one of the most common gypsy surnames to this day is Faa.[97] In 1500 the Diet of Augsburg ruled that any Christian could kill any gypsy without legal penalty. It came to be a gypsy proverb that the gypsies had two enemies: the devil, and Christ.[98]

Witch-hunters could never quite pin down what was heretical about Tarot symbolism, since pictures don't explain themselves as clearly as words do. Like the Bible, the Tarot passed through the hands of many interpreters who kept revising its "canonical" meanings. The process still goes on today. Part of the charm of Tarot cards lies in their fluid adaptability to any creative exposition, verbal or symbolic.

In the nineteenth and early twentieth centuries, for example, it became fashionable to relate the Tarot to the Jewish Cabala, linking its twenty-two Major Arcana to twenty-two letters of the Hebrew sacred alphabet, with great emphasis on the Tetragrammaton or magical "secret name of God," Yod-he-vau-he (YHWH).[99] In earlier times, however, the Tarot and the Cabala came from separate roots, converging only insofar as all mystical systems tend to overlap. Renaissance thinkers needed such systems, and therefore devised or adapted many of them.

"Under the autocratic regime of persecuting Christianity during the Middle Ages of Europe, Christian dogma was indeed accepted nominally by great intellects, but it was accepted under duress."[100] The thinkers' real thoughts had to be concealed by carefully guarded language or by allegorical, allusive expression. There could hardly be found any more appropriate medium of such expression than the ancient myth-forms that nearly all people could understand, each according to his or her own background, insight, or education. Both the learned and the vulgar could comprehend symbols like those of the Tarot, just as both could comprehend their own dreams. Tarot symbolism was as firmly rooted in the archetypes as any dream. The cards' pictures evolved not from beliefs that were forced on the people, but from beliefs that they wanted.

It seems clear that Tarot symbols expressed some form of the primordial cyclic, matriarchal nature-religion that Christianity consistently fought. This archetypal feminine-centered faith was still widely popular in the East during the twelfth and thirteenth centuries. In Europe it kept struggling for recognition even though the church was devoted to its extirpation. The Tarot may have been one of its underground channels. In Nuremberg, scene of some of the worst witch persecutions, card painters were women.[101] Many women manufactured cards also at Tournai, in Belgium, a famous center of arts and crafts.[102]

Tarot symbolism was especially viable. It was broadly applicable, and it was popular. It could be appreciated on many levels from the shallowest to the deepest. Gypsies could use it for simple fortune-telling, to bilk the gullible; they adapted the Tarot to their repertoire of tricks, collectively called *hakkni panki*, which passed into English as "hanky-panky."[103] Yet philosophers could use it too, finding in the cards an almost ecstatic form of mystical enlightenment. Gerard Encausse wrote, "The game of cards called the Tarot, which the Gypsies possess, is the Bible of Bibles. It is the book of Thoth Hermes Trismegistus, the book of Adam, the book of the primitive Revelation of ancient civilizations."[104]

Subsequent chapters will investigate various revelations of the Tarot in terms of archetypal symbolism and probable meanings of a secret Gnostic initiation, as it might have been conceived by Renaissance folk. Tarot number systems, arcana figures, and traditional layouts continually point to the premise that the cards' deeper meanings were of a religious but non-Christian nature. To meditate on some of these meanings can indeed help foster a new freedom of thought.

Elementals

The oldest theory behind cartomancy (divination by cards) is that a mystic power of Fate guides the shuffling and dealing of the cards, so the resulting layout will yield a meaningful message when properly interpreted. The same theory underlies many other kinds of divination. Seers have always read apparently random patterns in tea leaves, coffee grounds, lees of wine, animal entrails, bones, stones, seeds, sand, ashes, and thrown dice, as well as the yarrow sticks of the I Ching. Some kinds of divination evolved highly complex symbol systems.

One of the most elaborate divinatory rationales governed the shuffling of cards. Shuffling represented the process of creation itself: mixing and ordering the elements of the universe. The elements were in the cards, as four mixable suits.

From the earliest civilizations, people everywhere believed all organic and inorganic matter was made of combinations of four elements in various proportions: water, fire, earth, and air. The idea was already well developed in Sumeria, the oldest known literate culture.[1] It was equally prevalent among the Chinese, Hindus, Aztecs, American Indians, Egyptians, Greeks, Romans, and barbarian tribes of every continent.[2] These same elements were signified by the Tarot suits, so that mixing the cards was viewed as formation of the shape of things to come. Cartomancers derived their symbol system partly from Stoic philosophers who worshiped, and named their sect after, the same elements

21

THE HOLY MOUNTAIN

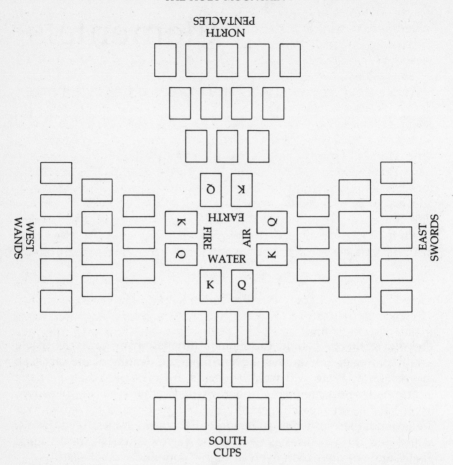

(stoicheia), "whose infinite variety of combinations gave rise to all perceptible phenomena."[3] But the idea was much older than the Stoics.

Tarot cups stood for the "female" water element. Tarot pentacles stood for the "female" earth element. These two suits were associated with matters of love and money, respectively—as also shown by their modern counterparts, hearts and diamonds. Tarot wands stood for the "male" fire element. Tarot swords stood for the "male" air element. These two suits were associated with matters of power and death, respectively—as also shown by their modern counterparts, clubs and spades. A club is a weapon, and so is a spade, for it was derived from the Spanish *espada*, "a sword." The peaceful elements were seen as female; the warlike ones as male.

Coincidentally perhaps, modern suit colors agree with an immeasurably ancient Tantric conception of femaleness as the active, creative power—qualities often associated in the Orient with redness—and of maleness as passive and destructive, the qualities associated with black. These ideas of male and female characteristics were deliberately reversed by patriarchal thought. The reversal is still a hidden tenet of Western conventional wisdom.[4]

According to the earliest idea of the creative Logos (Word), the Goddess imposed order on primal chaos by forming the elements out of her magic syllables: Va, water; Ra, fire; La, earth; and Ya, air. They were joined together by the mother-syllable Ma, meaning "Intelligence," or "the Mother."[5] Tantric Buddhists still say the elements are ruled by her.[6] They were in and of herself, even in the condition of primordial formlessness, which passed into Hebrew tradition as *tohu bohu*. Sages addressed the Goddess: "Thou art Earth, Thou art Water, Thou art Fire, Thou art Air, Thou art the Void . . . and Thou art the Supreme Divinity."[7] At doomsday, when this universe came to its end, she would again resume her infinite dark formlessness, until she decided to create again.[8]

Kali's necklace of skulls or jewels was inscribed with the letters of the sacred Sanskrit alphabet, which she invented to pronounce the mantras of creation. Half the letters were male, "fiery" and "airy"; half were female, "watery" and "earthy." It was said the mantras with a preponderance of female-elemental letters were benevolent; mantras with a preponderance of male-elemental letters were "cruel," as is still suggested by the clubs and spades, wands (or rods) and swords.[9]

The Goddess arranged her necklace so the male and female elements alternated, neither predominating over the other. This represented her "correct order," a model for the magic circle (*chakra*) of her male and female worshipers, which in turn served as a model for many other circles, such as the once-sacred round dances of European pagans. Though secularized, traditional folk dances still show this arrangement of the sexes. Another offshoot was the classic egg-and-dart frieze of Greco-Roman architecture, which alternated female and male symbols and was known as the Frieze of Venus and Mars. An Egyptian hieroglyphical forerunner showed alternating male-and-female shapes as obvious genitalia.[10]

To the Greeks, too, the Goddess's necklace meant "correct order," *Kosmos*, a word used by Homer for feminine ornaments. The first manifestation of order at creation was *Diakosmos*, "Order of the Goddess." She drew forms from the matrix "eternal, immense, uncreated, from which all is born," that is, herself as universal womb.[11] The Bible calls this matrix "the Deep"—Hebrew *tehom*, derived from Sumerian Tiamat, Egyptian Temu, Greek Themis, all of which were names for the primal Goddess. Judeo-Christian tradition carefully concealed the feminine

23

gender of "the Deep," ignoring earlier Scriptures that said the spirit hovering over the dark waters was the Mother of the Gods.[12]

The concept of the water-womb was well developed in Orphic, Pythagorean, and Stoic lore. Thales of Miletus said water was the *Arché*, the first of the elements, having "mastery" over the others because it brought them forth. Though Europeans tended to emphasize the masculine elements, they said "Only Earth and Water bring forth a living soul."[13]

Symbols of the Tarot suits seem to have come directly from Tantric imagery, where four-armed Kali flourished her elemental cup, scepter, ring (or wheel), and sword—the two left hands holding the female symbols, the two right hands holding the male ones. Greeks assigned their own versions of these elemental symbols to their own Fate-goddess, Nemesis, to whom even the Heavenly Father bowed down in fear. She carried a cup, a wooden wand, a wheel, and a sword.[14]

Thus the Tarot suit signs were always connected with the signs of the four elements—the original four, in which all the world believed, up to the nineteenth century when the real elements began to be discovered.

But why was it supposed in the first place that these four substances, and no others, were the basic building blocks of the whole universe?

Despite the universality of the belief, a realistic answer to this question has never been offered. Yet it isn't difficult to formulate one. What might it be that these four disparate things have in common—a connection that would have been readily seen by every primitive group, everywhere in the world, at an early stage of culture?

The connection is this: among primitive groups, with the sole exception of cannibals, water, fire, earth, and air represent the only possible means of disposing of the dead. A corpse may be cast into water, burned, buried, or exposed to carrion birds, as was the custom in North America and in ancient Persia, and is still the custom of the Parsees. In each case the dead body was returned to an "elemental" condition, preparing for rebirth.

Since the sea was much identified with the primal Mother, boat burials were common among coastal peoples. Welsh bards used to sing funeral dirges called *marwysgafen*, "giving-back-to-the-sea-mother."[15] Vikings regarded the sea as the Mother of their race, and sent their dead back to her. The Norseman's word for death meant "to return to the Mother's womb."[16] A burial ship was *ludr*, a boat, a coffin, or a cradle; it was seen as all three.[17]

In Egypt, dead kings entered the sun boat and sank with it into the waters in the far west, as Osiris did when he became Father Ra (who might have personified the Hindu fire-element Ra). Osiris could pass through the subterranean womb to the east and be reborn with the sun at dawn. In the month of Athyr (Hathor), Egyptian women threw images of Osiris into the Nile or the sea, to send him to the yonic gate of the Goddess in the far west, Ma-Nu, symbolized by a vase or goblet of water.[18] Here the water element was very early associated with "cups."

There may have been a link between Ma-Nu (Mother-Fish) and the Vedic Manu, who resembled the Mesopotamian flood heroes: Sumerian Ziusudra, Babylonian Ut-Napishtim, Hebrew Noah. Flood heroes generally rode out the great inundation that destroyed one creation and made way for the next. Like Osiris, they passed through the primal womb of chaos in a boat. The ark of Manu placed him within the Mother (Ma), so he became the embryonic fish (Nu). The same Nu, "Fish," was both a letter of the sacred Hebrew alphabet and the Semitic form of Noah, whose "ark" was derived from the Sanskrit *argha*, Manu's boat.

Gods of the sun, fire, and lightning—traditionally connected with the suit of wands—were often mated to the Goddess of the abyss, since fire and water elements made a male-female pair. There was once a theory that the blood of living creatures was made of seawater infused by fire from heaven, which turned it warm and red, though it still tasted of the sea. The fire-god lost his life when he descended into the abyssal womb for this fertilization. Vedic sages said the phallic god "came" as a bolt of lightning and was "quenched" by the Goddess's all-encompassing yoni, as a lightning bolt is quenched in the sea.[19] Hence the belief, especially prevalent in Rome, that the feminine water element is dangerous to men.[20]

The same sexual magic of fire and water passed virtually unchanged into the Christian ritual of consecration of the baptismal font, which was called "the immaculate womb of Mary," that is, *maria*, the seas. A burning candle was plunged into the water of the font, which was then declared *igne sacro inflammata*, fecundated by the holy fire.[21] Holy fire was a common, ancient metaphor for sexual passion in general—before Christianity proclaimed that sex was not holy, but rather the prime medium of transmission of original sin from generation to generation.

The fiery hero reborn, from the same waters that swallowed him, in Tantric tradition was Padma-sambhava, "he who takes his being from the Lotus," also known as "the lake-born *vajra*."[22] Like the Tibetan *dorje*, a *vajra* was both a phallic scepter or wand, and a lightning bolt.[23] The lake-born virility-god foreshadowed the Celtic Lancelot, born of the Lily Maid (Virgin Lotus), or the Lady of the Lake. An older version of his name was Lanceor (*lance d'or*), the Golden Lance, meaning a lightning bolt.[24]

The other pair of elements, earth and air, usually meant Mother Earth and Father Heaven. The sword was his phallic symbol in the Tarot as well as in mythology. Her symbol was the *omphalos*, a yonic "mount" at the center of the world, marked by a sacred stone with its inscribed pentacle, wheel, or cross. The ubiquitous Hindu lingam-yoni (heaven-penis in the earth-vulva) had a Celtic counterpart in the famous Sword in the Stone, which had to be drawn out by any man aspiring to heroship, such as Perceval, Arthur, or Galahad.

Even in recent times the sword was still viewed as a phallic symbol. In Scandinavian wedding customs, plunging a sword into the main beam of the house was said to be "proof of the virility of the bridegroom."[25] To throw a sword into the feminine water element signified fertilization and reincarnation, which explains King Arthur's dying wish to have his sword cast into the Lady's lake.[26] Only then could the Triple Goddess come, in the form of "three fairy queens," and take Arthur in the sun boat to her paradise in the west.

Mother Earth, the heavenly swordsman's usual mate, was represented as the giver of every kind of riches. Teutonic tribes who knew her as Freya or Frigg titled her Gefn, "the Giver." Her name meant "wealth."[27] The Greeks' Great Mother Rhea was known as Pandora, "All Giver," or sometimes a female Pluto, whose name meant "wealth."[28] Rome's Terra Mater (Mother Earth) was the source of all *material* wealth. Her older Sabine counterpart was Ops whose name supplied the origin of the word "opulence." Heavenly Father Jove could not aspire to the title "Lord of Riches" until he became the consort of Ops, and took her name; he was Jove Opulentia.[29] A medieval name for Mother Earth was Habondia, or Dame Abunda, the Lady of Plenty.[30] The gypsies followed sound mythological precedent in their word for money, good fortune, or luck: "earth."[31]

As the Tarot suit of the earth element, pentacles always represented money matters. Another name for the suit was *denarii* or "coins." Even when it became the suit of diamonds, it still stood for richness and earth. The gem's very name Dia-Mond means "Earth Goddess."

According to Celtic mythology the earth-womb was sometimes a mountain of diamond or crystal. An effort to imitate this mythic image was found at the New Grange burial mound, which was once covered with quartz fragments, so it would sparkle in the sun like a diamond.[32] Such a grave mound was a "tomb," from the Latin *tumulus*, which also meant "swelling" or "pregnancy"—a relic of pagan belief in rebirth from Mother Earth's womb.[33] Similarly in Hebrew, the word *hara* meant both "mountain" and "pregnancy," evidently derived from the Vedic Earth-goddess Hariti.[34]

Romans firmly believed in Mother Earth. Roman tombstones bore the phrase *Mater genuit, Mater recepit*—the Mother bore me, the Mother took me back. A Roman wrote in the third century A.D., "Holy Goddess Earth, Nature's mother, who bringeth all to life, and revives all from day to day, the food of life Thou grantest in eternal fidelity. And when the soul hath retired we take refuge in Thee. All that Thou grantest falls back somewhere into Thy womb." Another devotee said of Mother Earth, "the Goddess is the beginning and end of all life."[35]

Tacitus said all the barbarian tribes of Europe regarded Mother Earth as "the all-ruling deity, to whom all else is subject and obedient."[36] Heathen funerary prayers were even copied into Christian epitaphs, such as *Suscipe Terra tuo corpus de corpora sumptum*—Accept, O Earth, this body that was taken out of your body.[37] In like manner, Hindu priests addressed a dead man, "Go, seek the Earth, that wise and kind mother of all. O Earth, rise up and do not hurt his bones; be kind and gentle to him. O Earth, cover him as a mother covers her infant with the skirts of her garment."[38]

Everywhere in the world, burial was conceived as a return to the same womb that gave life. American Indians said all people and all animals emerged in the beginning from the yonic hole of the earth, "just like a child being born from its mother. The place of emergence is the womb of the earth."[39] Like gypsies, American Indians believed that after death they would re-enter the Mother's body and be born again.[40]

Medieval scholars believed in four classes of elemental spirits, which were pre-human races, having emerged long ago from the mountainous womb of the Mother on her four primordial rivers of paradise. They were water spirits called undines; fire spirits called salamanders; earth spirits called gnomes; and air spirits called sylphs. Psellus's *Compendium Maleficarum* listed all of them as demons and witches: "The first is the fiery, because these dwell in the upper air and will never descend . . . the second is the aerial, because these dwell in the air around us. . . . The third is terrestrial . . . some dwell in the fields and lead night travelers astray; some dwell in hidden places and caverns. . . . The fourth is the aqueous, for these dwell under the water in rivers and lakes. . . . They raise storms at sea, sink ships in the ocean, and . . . are more often women than men."[41]

Medieval writers tried to classify different nations according to the elemental spirits they worshiped, following classical authors who said, for example, the Egyptians worshiped water, the Persians worshiped fire, and so on. Yet most scholars agreed that human beings combined all the elements in themselves, so that "within the small compass of his body he [man] might bestow under the requirements of Nature the whole energy and substance of the elements."[42] Again this idea could be traced back to the worship of Kali, who gave water to create the bloodstream, fire for vital heat, earth for flesh, and air for breath.[43] Even the Bible agrees that flesh is "clay," and the soul is "breath" (Ezekiel 37:9). Among patriarchal Brahmans, a father pretended to give his newborn child its soul by breathing in its face three times.[44]

The human "temperament" came from Latin *temperare*, to mix the elemental "humors" in the body. The mixture was never quite even. A

27

predominance of blood gave a *sanguine* or bloody temperament; of phlegm, a *phlegmatic* or earthy one; of bile, a *melancholic* or watery one; of ether, an *ethereal* or airy one.[45] Similarly, mixtures of suit cards in Tarot layouts were considered indicative of elemental character. The court cards of the four suits represented persons of appropriate temperament. In the trump suit, the Goddess Temperance was shown mixing *(temperare)* the elements in her vessels, which also drew symbolism from the Tantric notion of sexual union as a merging "like pouring of water into water."[46]

At some point there was an attempt to Christianize the Tarot suits as emblems of the four Grail Hallows, which were listed in the twelfth century as (1) the Holy Grail, Christ's chalice of the Last Supper; (2) the lance with which the mythical St. Longinus pierced Christ's side; (3) the paten or platter from which the disciples ate the paschal lamb; and (4) King David's legendary Sword of the Spirit. However, the Grail Hallows themselves were quite un-Christian, having begun as monkish revisions of Celtic pagan elemental symbols, the Four Treasures of the Tuatha Dé Danann, "People of the Goddess Dana," that is, Danish colonists of Iron Age Ireland. Their Four Treasures were (1) the Cauldron of Regeneration; (2) the Spear of Lug; (3) the Stone of Fal, or Stone of Sovereignty, an omphalos in the sacred grove of Tara; and (4) the Sword of Nuada.[47]

The so-called signs of the four evangelists were also stolen from pagan elemental symbolism. The serpent stood for water, the lion for fire, the bull for earth, and the eagle (or angel) for air. In Egypt they were four animal-headed spirits who guarded the four corners of temple or tomb, called the Four Children of Horus.[48]

Similarly, the Bible's four rivers of paradise were copied from the elemental streams which, in Tantric tradition, flowed from the Goddess's body: (1) water, (2) wine (or blood) for fire, (3) honey for earth, and (4) milk for air. These determined ancient India's idea of elemental colors: blue for water, red for fire, yellow for earth, white for air—in other words, what are known as the primary colors, from which all other colors are made by mixing.[49] It is interesting to note that the Bible placed two of these elemental streams in Palestine, the land of "milk and honey," whereas the other two came from the body of the Savior, who when pierced gave forth blood and water (John 19:34). And his blood was also wine.

The Vedic gods lived on Mount Meru, a four-sided pyramid built of elemental forces when the universe was young. The south face of the mountain was made of blue lapis lazuli or sapphire, representing the water element, whose sacred river flowed from its summit, the "Navel of Waters . . . guarded by a majestic and beneficent Goddess."[50] The west face was made of ruby, and its river was fire (lava), or blood, or wine. The north face was gold, and its river was honey—a substance sacred to the Earth Goddess in every ancient tradition. It was a Hindu marriage custom to daub the bride's genitals with honey as she began her "honey-moon."[51] Loved ones are still called "honey," and marriages are still solemnized with the ancient earth symbol, a ring of gold. The east face of the holy mountain was made of silver, crystal, or diamond, Its river was milk, the food of infants, and also of toothless elders approaching death. Here began the popular Indo-European fairy-tale notion of the journey to death (or paradise) as a climb up a crystal mountain to a pinnacle of rebirth (the Fairy Queen's palace).[52]

Some said this magic mountain of the gods lay among the peaks of the Himalayas, which is why Germanic Aryans continued to call the heaven-mountain *Himmel*.[53]

For centuries, Eastern sages built a symbol system relating the elements and the heaven-mountain to the four stages of life, both individual life and the life of the universe, which passed through four great eons called *yugas*. This was the basis for Greek philosophers' notion of the four world ages. Tarot suits might well have been used as visual aids to explain this ancient symbol system.

Tantric sages said the first age of life is ruled by the water element (Venus), and known as Sambhoga, the age of love, pleasure, emotional attachments: the period of childhood, when each human being is socialized by affection and sensual contact, chiefly with the mother. Hindu gods lived in eternal bliss "on the lap of the Mother," for their mountain home had a feminine gender, as most Himalayan peaks still have—the real name of Mount Everest, for example, is Chomo-Lung-Ma, Goddess-Mother of the World. Gods' magic blood, which kept them young forever, was blue because it came from the spring of Sambhoga. Therefore "bluebloods" once meant "gods," and later became a synonym for aristocrats. In portraits, Hindu deities are still commonly painted blue. Porphyry wrote that the creator of the visible world, like Hindu gods, had a dark blue complexion.[54] The Tantric tradition continued to influence medieval alchemists, who believed in a blue elixir of immortality, the *quinta essentia* or "fifth element."[55] This wonderful "quintessence" was supposed to control the other elements, like the Philosopher's Stone; so it was sometimes equated with the Tarot's fifth suit, the Major Arcana.

The second age of life, ruled by the fire element, was Nirmana, the process of building: the restless, self-developing, power-seeking activity of early adulthood. The Tarot suit of wands (fire) still carries the same connotation of power-seeking, empire-building, mercantile activity, establishment of a family and a niche in the world. The suit of wands was said to be governed by Mars and identified with the "sacred fire" of sexual drives.

The third age of life, ruled by the earth element, was Artha, "wealth": the same root word that gave "earth" to other Indo-European languages, and the Goddess variously named Ertha, Hretha, Heartha, Urtha, Erda, and so on. This was the age of full maturity, material success, golden harvest, the glowing autumn of life; a river of honey symbolized the sweetness of fulfillment. Artha has an obvious connection with the Tarot suit of pentacles, governed by Mother Earth (Terra Mater), the giver of riches. Every card of the suit was in some way concerned the money and property. To own "earth," or real estate, was the ultimate basis of all wealth under feudalism; so the gypsies' identification of money with earth was not at all unreasonable.

The fourth age of life, ruled by the air element, was Moksha, "Liberation," or the Art of Dying. In old age, the enlightened one would commence mystical preparations to send the soul soaring free on the air, like a bird.[56] In fact "bird" used to be synonymous with a dead ancestor, which is why the Greeks and Romans took so many omens and auguries from flying birds. They thought all birds were ghosts bearing messages from the spirit world. A person who learned the power of Kundalini, "serpent power," could understand the language of birds: this was much used in Greek myth and in medieval fairy tales. Egyptian hieroglyphics gave the *ba*-soul the form of a bird, and the Great Goddess as a death-crone the form of a vulture, bearing the flail of authority.[57] As the Grandmother of the Gods, she carried souls into the upper airs. Isis as a vulture displayed in each claw the *ankh* or Cross of Life.[58] Thus, the Tarot suit of swords or "air," governed by Jupiter, traditionally spoke of death or disaster, but with the implication of change or transformation from one stage to another.

The sages pictured time on an endless cycle around the holy mountain. On both the individual and the cosmic scale, the end of one cycle was the beginning of the next. Many cycles were divided into four parts in addition to the cycle of human life. There were the Four Ages of mankind; the four seasons; the four quarters of the moon, the earth, and the zodiac; the four winds and four cardinal directions—and the four suits of the Tarot.

It's no coincidence that the fifteenth-century card game of Triumphs (Trumps), played by European nobility and condemned by the clergy, identified the four suits with qualities very like the Tantric life-stages of Sambhoga, Nirmana, Artha, and Moksha: namely, Pleasures, Virtues, Riches, and Virginities.[59] "Virtue," deriving from the Latin *vir*, "man," once connoted phallic symbolism, like the scepter and wand. "Virginity" could refer to the ascetic life recommended for sages in the period of Moksha.

Such sages were believed to acquire *siddhi* ("magic power") by constant meditation. Among other things this meant knowledge of the elements, and how they combined and recombined in different patterns to create different forms from matter. A completely enlightened sage could not only determine his own form in the next life; he could even control transformations of matter, such as converting base metals into gold.[60] This trick was performed by legendary Hindu *mahatmas* and by King Midas, though the latter failed to control it properly. With these precedents, medieval alchemists ceaselessly and passionately searched for the secret. Only a few gave up seeking the fact, and remained content with the symbol, taking the Philosopher's Stone as a metaphor for mystical enlightenment.

This did not mean the "enlightenment" of Christianity. It meant Gnostic mysticism, which amalgamated the Stoic doctrine of the elements with the Tantric vision of the holy mountain, where both male and female principles governed each element. Each of the four elemental gods was paired with his Shakti Goddess, without whom he was powerless to act, for the very definition of Shakti was "Power."

Tarot suits could be laid out in the formation of the holy mountain, showing each face with its two deities (King and Queen) at the summit, atop rows of three, four, and five cards. This "elemental" design could be used for fortune-telling, but it also explained graphically a rather subtle philosophical system. Comprehension of the system was necessary, in the Gnostic view, to *apolytrosis*, "liberation," an idea almost identical to the Tantric sages' Moksha.[61]

Worship of the elements didn't stop with the passing of classical civilization. The ethical system and mystical beliefs of Stoicism remained, tied to the *stoicheia* or "elements," in which everyone believed, including churchmen. The symbols were embedded in the Tarot.

Christian mystics studied the classical writers and tried to pour their beliefs into the mold of contemporary orthodoxy; but the fit was poor. As one historian put it, "Stoic ethics are self-sufficing; they proceed from nature, so to speak, and do not rely upon grace; they have no need of a doctrine of Redemption. . . . There is nothing in common between them and Christianity save the elements it once borrowed from them."[62] However, Gnostic sects maintained the pagan traditions, especially in Sicily, Spain, and the south of France, where many *coffrets gnostiques* (Gnostic reliquaries) and other nonorthodox cult objects have been discovered.

The Stoic idea of ultimate dissolution of the universe into its component elements figured prominently in medieval doomsday myths, which even included the ancient opinion that doomsday would be brought on by the Goddess's disgust at men's and gods' cruel, destructive behavior. The whole cycle of romances focusing on the Goddess as Minne, "Love," carried a strong suggestion that neglect of her worship would bring on a catastrophe of nature (or of the spiritual climate) symbolized by the Waste Land, *La Terre Gast*. It had already happened in the barren land called Arabia Deserta, according to the Eastern mystics; Islam had deserted the Mother, so the Mother had "deserted" the earth. When they saw that dessicated country, Crusaders were inclined to believe the mystics' explanation. Troubadours threatened the same dire fate in Britain and continental Europe when worship of the Goddess declined: "A wrong against a feminine being and a plundering of nature were perpetrated. . . . The origin of the trouble was looked upon as an offence against the fairy world, i.e., actually against nature."[63] The offenders were Christians, who diabolized and persecuted rival religions. It is interesting and perhaps significant that Christian salvation was supposed to save individuals from the horrors of doomsday, and only a select few individuals, at that—for Thomas Aquinas and other theologians insisted that the vast majority of human beings would be damned—whereas the heathen salvation was supposed to save the whole earth.[64] The old, familiar heathen/Stoic/Gnostic view did seem more generous.

SYMBOLS ASSOCIATED WITH THE HOLY MOUNTAIN

Elements	Water (female)	Fire (male)	Earth (female)	Air (male)
Faces of Mt. Meru	South Lapis-lazuli, sapphire	West Ruby	North Gold	East Diamond, crystal, silver
Sacred rivers	Water	Wine, blood	Honey	Milk
Tantric primary colors	Blue	Red	Yellow	White
Seasons	Spring (sowing)	Summer (growth)	Autumn (harvest)	Winter (death)
Ages	Childhood	Youth	Maturity	Old age
Tantric life stages	Sambhoga (Pleasure)	Nirmana (Building)	Artha (Riches)	Moksha (Liberation)
Tarot life areas	Love	Power	Wealth	Death
Tantric symbols	Cup	Scepter	Ring	Sword
Tarot symbols	Cups	Wands	Pentacles	Swords
Playing-card suits	Hearts	Clubs	Diamonds	Spades
"Triumphs"	Pleasures	Virtues	Riches	Virginities
Elemental spirits	Undines	Salamanders	Gnomes	Sylphs
Roman deities	Venus	Mars	Terra Mater	Jupiter
Celtic "Treasures"	Cauldron of Regeneration	Spear of Lug	Stone of Fal	Sword of Nuada
Moon sabbaths	New moon	Waxing quarter	Full moon	Waning quarter
Greek World Ages	Gold	Silver	Bronze	Iron
Zodiacal signs	Pisces Cancer Scorpio	Aries Leo Sagittarius	Taurus Virgo Capricorn	Gemini Libra Aquarius
Body components	Fluids	Heat	Solids	Breath
Humors	Bile	Blood	Phlegm	Ether
"Evangelical" signs	Serpent	Lion	Bull	Eagle (angel)
Grail Hallows	Holy Grail	Spear	Paten	Sword of Spirit
Pagan-Christian festivals	May Eve (Beltane)	Lammas Eve (Lugnasad)	Halloween (Samhain)	Candlemas (Imbolg)

Wheels of Becoming

Everyone who has ever studied mathematics knows the symbol for infinity, a horizontal figure eight (two tangential circles), sometimes called a lemniscate. Along with the rest of our Arabic mathematical signs, this actually came to Europe through the Middle East from India.[1] Like all numerical symbols, it was originally numinous or holy. We are familiar with its connotations in ancient sacred dances, as the figure-eight "hey" traced on the earth by stepping in a circle clockwise, then in another circle counterclockwise.

The infinity sign carried a peculiar significance in the Tarot. It first appeared as a broad-brimmed hat or halo over the head of the Magician (Trump #1), a male figure leading the first decade of cards. It next appeared as an identical broad-brimmed hat or halo over the head of the Goddess of Strength (Trump #11), a female figure leading the second decade of cards. It appeared for a third time on the deuce of pentacles, formerly the "key" card of the Minor Arcana, which bore the card-maker's signature, like the ace of spades in modern decks.

It was customary to encircle the two pentacles or coins with the mystic world-symbol of two serpents swallowing each other's tails, or one serpent swallowing its own tail. The direction of the serpents' coiled bodies showed that one circle was to be drawn clockwise, the other counterclockwise. The word deuce, medieval *dusius*, came from the Latin *deus*, "god"; so one might expect the deuce of the earth-elemental

35

WHEELS OF BECOMING

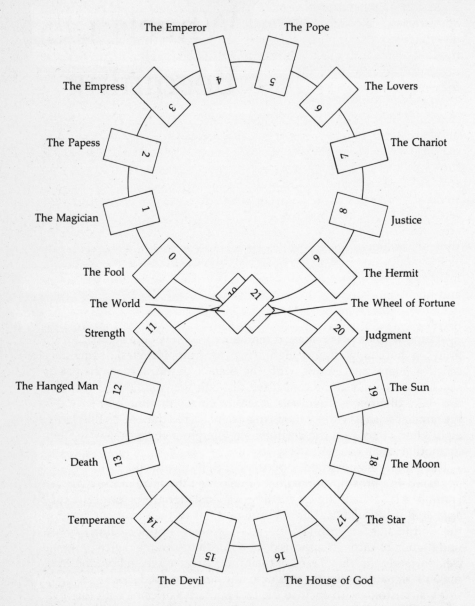

suit to convey an important message in addition to the cardmaker's name.[2]

The serpents seemed to be demonstrating a card layout of two joined circles, the first "male" (the Magician), the second "female" (Strength). A clue to its meaning is provided by the Tantric symbolism of the infinity sign. The first clockwise circle followed the sun, and represented the Right-Hand Path of the god Shiva; that is, a daytime world of outward appearances. The second counterclockwise circle followed the moon, like the widdershins circle dances of European witches. It represented the Left-Hand Path of Shiva's eternal beloved, Kali: the night world of mystery, fate, the soul, and "true inner meanings," called Vamacara, the Way of the Goddess.[3]

All over the Indo-European culture complex it was generally accepted that movement toward the right hand, in the "solar" direction, invoked male gods, whereas movement in the other "lunar" direction invoked manifestations of the Goddess. Egyptians said the left hand stood for the Goddess Maat, Mother of Truth; the right hand stood for her consort Thoth, patron of magicians. Babylonians prayed, "Let my goddess stand at my left hand! Let my god stand at my right hand!"[4] Hindus represented Existence as a two-sexed entity whose right side was male and whose left side was female. Idols of Kali and Shiva sometimes showed the two deities thus combined in a single figure.[5] The infinity sign meant infinity for the very reason that it symbolized their union: male and female, matter and spirit, reason and inspiration, conscious and unconscious functions forever inseparable.

This sign, three times pointed out by traditional Tarot designs, has been called the first key to the secrets of the Major Arcana.[6] It must be noted that some of the Tarot decks designed after 1900 arbitrarily exchanged Trumps #11 and #8, so Strength with her lemniscate hat no longer led the second circle of cards. Apparently, this was the original idea of the Golden Dawn Society, to make the Major Arcana fit an astrological system.[7] Earlier designs always put the feminine bearer of the infinity sign in the number 11 slot, as she initiated the second, left-hand, widdershins circle.

When the trumps are laid out in the shape of the infinity sign, the cards of the first, solar circle face outward, toward the world of material concerns; the cards of the second, lunar circle face inward, toward the spiritual realm of inner meanings. Each card in the first circle corresponds to a card in the second. Numbers of matching cards add up to twenty, the fingers-and-toes number that was held sacred by Indo-Arabic numerologists.[8] There is one exception. The two cards showing rounded mandalas, the Wheel of Fortune and the World, cross each other in the center of the design. The World (#21) or Last Trump lies on top, completing the sequence with her 20 and with her 1 signaling a new birth.

This arrangement reveals several heretical views that were current in the fourteenth century. The figure of the Pope (#5) in the material world is seen to correspond to the Devil (#15) in the spiritual world. The two figures display similar poses, and each has a pair of worshipers at his feet. Here is a symbolic presentation of the Gnostics' opinion that the Roman church was "the Synagogue of Satan" and its pope was the Antichrist.[9]

The Papess (#2) however corresponds to the Moon (#18) in the spiritual realm, as if a female pope were still associated with the lunar religion. A crescent moon usually appeared on the Papess's card. Clergymen seemed to regard the Papess with special distaste, so much so that in some later packs she was replaced by the Goddess Juno, or even by a man.[10] Most modern packs call her the High Priestess.

Some knowledge of the Renaissance period is needed to interpret the connection of the Emperor (#4) with the #16 Trump, variously called the Lightning-Struck Tower or the House of God. The organization of the medieval church was sometimes known as the Proud Tower. A much-repeated Gnostic prophecy foretold its destruction by Lucifer, whose name means Light-bringer, and whose weapon was the same lightning wielded by the elder gods. It was said in the fourteenth century that both Italian and French Gnostics "worship Lucifer and believe him to be the brother of God, wrongly cast out of heaven."[11] Under an oppressive theocracy the Gnostic sects yearned for the predicted coming of a deity of light to blast the Tower, as the card showed. Oddly enough, the very same scene was carved in stone on a panel of Rheims Cathedral, as if executed by one of the Gnostic brotherhoods of Free Masons who slyly inserted many pagan concepts into the fabric of churches.[12]

On both the Tarot card and the cathedral, two figures were shown falling from the Tower's crown as the lightning bolt struck it. If one figure was intended to be the pope, the other could only have been the Emperor (Trump #4), suggesting a catastrophic downfall of both church and state. In fact, there was a popular belief that soon a people's revolution would overthrow the established church together with "a great monarchy"—presumably the Holy Roman Empire.[13] Afterward there would be a new age of social equality and peace among all classes. The coming of the new age may have been signaled in Tarot symbolism by the Naked Goddess pouring out her blessings on land and sea, on the card following the Tower's destruction, Trump #17, the Star. Her earthly manifestation in the other sphere was the Empress (#3).

Thus, it seems the Tarot symbolism called for a return to the feminine principle, at least in part. This was actually attempted in the cult of Mary, who like the Empress was identified with the Star, as Stella Maris, "Star of the Sea." Mary was also addressed as an Empress, and "Lady of all the world," as well as a new version of the ancient Triple Goddess, according to the *Speculum beatae Mariae:* "Queen of heaven where she is enthroned in the midst of the angels, queen of earth where she constantly manifests her power, and queen of hell where she has authority over all the demons."[14] It was the Marian cult that brought the rosary into Christian use about the twelfth century; but the rosary was copied from Kali's "rose-wreath" *(japamala)*, the necklace of mantras, used for many centuries in the East to keep track of repetitive prayers.[15] Kali's rosaries also formed the infinity sign as a sacred mandala for meditation.

Though churchmen's hostility to the Major Arcana must have been based on implications of heresy, there was more to the Tarot message than simple opposition to Christian patriarchy. The infinity sign was not invented in Europe to vex the clergy. It was invented by Eastern mystics to represent the eternal "cycles of becoming" *(sangsara)* governed by the Goddess's karmic wheels. The solar and lunar paths eternally circling, merging one into the other, referred to the typical Eastern doctrine of eternal rebirth, or transmigration of souls.

The theory was that each living creature spent a period in the daylight world, on what was called the sublunar sphere, then another period in the otherworld awaiting a new birth. The corollary belief was that all flesh is alike in essence, and so is all spirit. Forms change, but the basic material of life is forever the same.

Pre-Christian religions generally espoused this doctrine. The writings of Pythagoras taught, "The spirit wanders, comes now here, now there, and occupies whatever frame it pleases. From beasts it passes into human bodies, and from our bodies into beasts, but never perishes."[16] Plato's *Republic* spoke of Greek heroes in the underworld, choosing their bodies for the next incarnation. The same "heroic" privilege was extended to Tantric "enlightened ones" in the Intermediate State. Greek mystics spoke of the *kyklos geneseon*, "cycles of becoming," as much as their Hindu counterparts did. The rebirth doctrine was common in ancient Greece, and it was a lofty philosophical principle among cultured Greeks who were initiates of the Mysteries.[17]

Among the most popular Mysteries were those of Orphism, which continued long into the Christian era, often as a preferred alternative to the Mysteries of the Christian church. Orpheus and Christ were sometimes worshiped side by side in the same chapels.[18] As a savior figure, Orpheus was an older *Christos* (Anointed One) who had suffered martyrdom, descended into hell, and rose again from the dead bearing esoteric secrets of the afterworld to impart to initiated followers. The most important Orphic manual, *The Descent into Hades*, described the geography and personages of the underworld so the Enlightened Ones would know how to deal with them, and how to achieve a blessed rebirth.[19] Initiated ones partook of a sacramental communion feast that assimilated them to the deity himself, and enabled them to share his resurrection. Orphic sacramentalism flowed into all the later mystery cults including Christianity, which copied its baptismal and communion ceremonies. The history of Western religion owes much to Orphism, though the debt was never acknowledged.[20]

Christian churches shamelessly copied their Orphic rivals before the latter were finally suppressed as "devil worship." Origen, counted one of the fathers of the church, at times even considered a saint, declared the doctrine of metempsychosis to be a secret teaching of the Christian church as much as it was of the Orphic temple; it was imparted to an inner circle of Christian initiates, above the level of common congregations who heard only the exoteric teachings. Origen was revered in his time as a great sage acquainted with all the innermost secrets of Christianity. But three centuries after his death, the official theology repudiated the doctrine of metempsychosis, finding the promise of heaven and the threat of hell more effective in controlling the credulous. In 533 the Second Council of Constantinople decreed that "Whomsoever shall support the mythical doctrine of the pre-existence of the soul and the consequent wonderful opinion of its return, let him be anathema." Origen suffered a postmortem excommunication because his beliefs were declared heretical.[21]

Nevertheless, secret fraternities maintained pagan and Gnostic beliefs, including the belief in transmigration of souls, for a thousand years after the church claimed to have eliminated them.[22] Even the Talmud adopted Gnostic views, stating that the soul of Adam transmigrated into David, then into the Messiah.[23] Confused Christian theologians actually represented Christ as "the second Adam" on the basis of such Gnostic traditions.

Some of the common vehicles of instruction in the pagan Mysteries were wheel-shaped mandalas on which various mystic figures imparted their secrets, like the circularly arranged deities of the Intermediate State on Tantric icons.[24] Oriental "life-wheels" represented the stages of existence on such mandalas, and were also utilized as revelations of the larger universe.[25] Such Oriental icons bore a strong resemblance to Tarot trumps laid in a circle.

In the year 1837, an Orphic mandala dating from the fifth century A.D. was unearthed in Rumania. It was a golden bowl with sequential figures in relief around its circumference, showing the progress of an initiation. First appeared the priestess who kept the temple door, and drew aside the veil for the novice to enter—much like the Tarot Papess who sat before a veiled gateway. There was a meeting with the Great Goddess, Demeter, who resembled the Tarot Empress. She was accompanied by her underground alter ego, Persephone, whose name means "Destroyer," and who served as the Greek version of Kali's death aspect.[26] Persephone escorted the Orphic initiate into her nether world, as he recited the formula, "I come a suppliant to the Holy Persephone, that of her grace she receive me to the seats of the Hallowed."[27] The Goddess promised him blessedness, and after initiation he was privileged to say, "I have sunk beneath the bosom of Persephone, Queen of the Under-world."[28]

To descend into the underworld, halfway around the circle, the novice saw the figure of the Goddess of Fortune, just as the Tarot path going from the first sphere to the second would pass the Wheel of Fortune at the crossing. Then came the god Agathodaemon holding the poppy stalk of the sleep of death; then the Lord of the Abyss holding a Luciferian lightning bolt. That the Tarot cards should show figures of Death and the Devil in this area of the sequence was surely no coincidence. It was for these very meetings, to learn about the dread lords of the underworld, that the whole pantomime was enacted.[29]

Apuleius wrote that during his initiation into the Mysteries of Isis he entered the land of death and encountered a similar series of chthonian figures: "I approached the limits of the dead: I trod upon the threshold of Proserpina and I was carried beyond the spheres of the elements. I saw the sun shining brilliantly at midnight, and approached the Gods of the Underworld, and those from On High; and I worshiped them face to face." As Persephone was the dark underground aspect of Demeter, so Proserpina was the dark underground aspect of Juno, the Empress of Heaven (who was also Isis); she was sometimes entitled Juno Inferna.[30] After meetings with underground deities, the Orphic initiate as well as Apuleius returned to the upper world, "reborn" in a new spirit, like one freshly baptized—or like the joyously dancing Sun children of the Major Arcana.

In the center of the Orphic bowl, a freestanding, three-dimensional figure of the Great Goddess represented the power that governed all cycles, supernal and infernal. She was the ultimate revelation, as the dancing Naked Goddess of the World card was the ultimate revelation of the Tarot trumps.[31] Her Tarot card was sometimes called the Universe, derived from the old Latin name of the Triple Goddess, Uni, the One in Three, in turn a cognate of Indo-European *yoni*. Uni meant the totality of the Capitoline Triad of Fates, originally consisting of Juventas the Virgin, Juno the Mother, and Minerva the wise Crone—a female creator-preserver-destroyer trinity as Kali and Demeter also were.[32]

To meet the deities, to undergo initiation and enlightenment, people everywhere used to enter underground temples or sacred caves, and pass through a dramatization of the same descent into hell pioneered by Orpheus, or Osiris, or Yama, or Shiva, or Attis, or any of several dozen other savior figures, including Jesus. "According to the old religion, an initiation ceremony allowed the candidate to descend into an underground chamber, simulate death, undergo great trials, and experience a rebirth into a new life. The early Christian church continued this custom, calling such pagan shrines 'purgatories.' "[33]

The Welsh saga of Peredur depicts a Druidic initiation ceremony of this type, taking place in the "magic castle" of Caer Sidi—from Celtic *sidh*, reminiscent of the Tantric *siddhi*. As a crystal palace that could revolve like a wheel, Caer Sidi obviously represented one of the "crystalline spheres" of the turning heavens; it may have been portrayed in a circular underground chamber by a circling procession of zodiacal figures. Priestesses, or "witches," took charge of Peredur's initiation, which covered a period of twenty-one days, recalling both the twenty-one Taras of both Hindu and Druid tradition, and the twenty-one Tarot trumps.

Myths plainly show many connections between Celtic and Hindu prehistory. Peredur's fairy ladylove (or Shakti) told him in so many words that he must seek her in India.[34] That the rites were still carried on in Christian times is suggested by a later translation of the story, wherein Peredur was laid under an oath not to speak a single word to any Christian during the period of his trials.[35] It is not unlikely that such initiations took place often during the Christian era, with the injunction to secrecy reflecting fear of ecclesiastical persecution.

Orphism was known in medieval England, where the bards referred to the old Thracian god as "Sir Orfeo," a son of King Pluto and the Goddess Juno. His bride Eurydice—whose name meant "Universal Dike," or Fate—became the Lady Heurodis. He descended into her underworld and found a fairyland of eternal spring, with a crystal palace inhabited by "people supposed to be dead, but they were not so." He returned to the daylight world and became a divine king, ruling from his royal shrine at Winchester, which, the bards claimed, "used to be called Thrace."[36]

Unlike the orthodox Christian savior, the Gnostic savior was not always the son of a mortal mother and a divine father. Like Sir Orfeo, he came of the reverse combination: a mortal father and a divine mother, after the pattern of the *hieros gamos* ("sacred marriage") of ancient kings, who had to mate with the Goddess before they could rule. According to Gnostic texts, the Judeo-Christian God misrepresented the original female divinity, out of a desire to inflate his own importance. He was able to administer the universe only because his Great Mother, Sophia (Wisdom), gave him some of her own ideas and creative powers. "It was because he was foolish and ignorant of his Mother that he said, 'I am God; there is none beside me.' " In many Gnostic writings he was punished for his arrogance by the superior female power who preceded him and gave him his being. Early Christian monks collected these scriptures and burned them, or rewrote them for centuries, until nothing was left except the few scanty remnants now enshrined in the canonical Bible, with all formerly luxuriant feminine imagery of the divine either diabolized, degraded, or completely eliminated.[37]

This policy was clearly set forth in the canonical Gospels, which directed that the Great Goddess "should be despised, and her magnificence should be destroyed, whom Asia and all the world worshippeth" (Acts 19:27).

When Christians, under Bishop Theophilius, wrecked the great library at Alexandria, in 389, they eradicated the last significant collections of pagan sacred literature—including scriptures devoted to the Goddess.[38] St. John Chrysostom boasted that "Every trace of the old philosophy and literature of the ancient world has vanished from the face of the earth," thanks to Christian zeal.[39] Modern scholars have often deplored this wholesale destruction of precious material that would have shed much light on the history of Western thought; art historians have deplored the demolition of hundreds of beautiful shrines and temples, whose like will never be seen again on this earth.[40]

There is no doubt that Christian fanaticism directly contributed to the onset of the Dark Age, when the intellectual and moral progress of the classical world was wiped out, and all of Western civilization regressed to a state of crude barbarism.[41] Education was forbidden by the church, which taught that the end of the world would be hastened by "the spread of knowledge," which could only bring on more heresy.[42] As a result, the fairly high rate of literacy attained by the Roman Empire declined to almost nothing, while science gave way to superstition, and the sophisticated engineering techniques of antiquity were forgotten. Art, crafts, manufacturing, and construction all reverted to earlier, cruder levels.[43]

The church has claimed that Christian suppression of paganism destroyed little of real value, but historians disagree. It has been pointed out that the eclipse of the ancient deities affected much more than theology alone; it caused the decline of art, philosophy, secular literature, mathematics, astronomy, medicine, architecture, and the whole psychology of the West.[44] It was accomplished not by kindness, but by unremitting violence. An old chronicler said: "The bishops bless the waters and convert the heathen. If any man protests, he is burned or put to the sword."[45]

With so unsympathetic an orthodoxy, it was only natural that some groups would try to perpetuate the pagan Mysteries underground, following priests and priestesses who did not wage holy wars on fellow humans. Their traditions were remembered by country people who thought their living literally depended on performing the right ceremonies at the right times and seasons. The narrow view of history fostered by a dating system that *begins* only a mere 2,000 years ago tends to mislead modern minds into imagining a void where earlier religions ruled. Modern bias finds it particularly hard to envision the earlier thousands of years when the primary divinities were Mothers, not Fathers. Isis was adored as the Lady of Life since Neolithic times in Egypt, for eight centuries in the Greek world, and for at least five centuries in the Roman. Great Mother Cybele came from prehistoric times in Phrygia to be passionately revered in Italy for more than half a millenium. Mother Demeter supported the hopes of Aegean civilization since at least 1300 B.C. at Mycenae and for more than eleven centuries at Eleusis until her shrine was destroyed by Arian Christian monks in the fourth century A.D.[46]

It was Christian Rome, not pagan Rome, that introduced the element of murderous intolerance. The Roman Empire tolerated all faiths, demanding only that the deities of the state receive lip service on official holy days. The Roman church, however, insisted on persecuting all rival faiths as well as its own sectaries who happened to deviate from the orthodox party line. There was no room in the world for any god but the Christian one, according to his spokesmen.[47]

Nevertheless, the common people doggedly retained their old deities, especially the Mother who used to rule the Wheels of Becoming and the whole cyclic system of time and space. The system never really disappeared. Even today there are people who call themselves Christian, yet earnestly believe in the theory of reincarnation that Christianity anathematized. The Oriental doctrine of karma may be more widely credited among Western laymen than the doctrines of transubstantiation or the virgin birth. And a thousand years earlier, when even the pious were growing tired of a church that damned them for someone else's sin, the Tarot may have shown the common people a diagram of salvation that they could understand. Therefore, like the Old Religions themselves, the cards persisted no matter how loudly they were denounced from the pulpit. They persisted because they were wanted.

The Yoni
Yantra

What medieval churchmen most disliked—officially at least—was sexuality. In particular they disliked female sexuality, which they said must be suppressed even within the legal framework of marriage. Sex was for procreation only, and they claimed a woman couldn't conceive if she experienced "joy" in sex.[1] Some churchmen insisted that a man who loved a woman and tried to please her was, in effect, loving Satan.[2] Clergymen generally preached against all aspects of love, pouring scorn on the very idea that men should love any creature other than God.[3]

St. Augustine had established church policy with his opinion that "concupiscence" (sexual passion) was inherently evil, because it transmitted original sin to all generations.[4] By Augustinian reasoning, sex was never sinless, even within marriage.[5] Church fathers bitterly condemned the ancient temples of love, where sacred hierodules taught young men how to be successful lovers of women. Eusebius called them schools of wickedness, "dedicated to that foul devil who goes by the name of Venus."[6]

Opinions were different in the East. To the Tantric *sadhaka* as to the pagan worshiper of Venus, sex was a supreme sacrament. Female sexuality was revered as the elemental power of creation and bonding. Thousands of years before Freud, the sages recognized "infant sexuality" in the reciprocally sensual relationship between mother and child, and realized that ramified adult manifestations of interpersonal feeling

45

THE YONI YANTRA

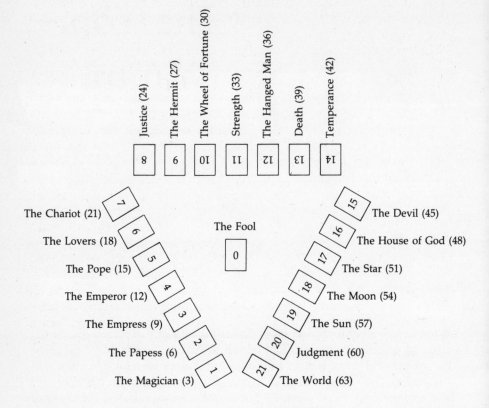

evolved from this primary one. They called the power behind loving patterns of behavior *karuna,* which combined the meanings of tenderness, desire, enjoyment, affection, passion and compassion, sharing and caring, all based on the concept of mother-love. As women give birth, nurture, and love, so *karuna* meant all kinds of voluntary giving, including mutual giving of erotic pleasures.

The symbol of *karuna* was the Yoni Yantra: a downward-pointing triangle, representing both the female genital *(yoni)* and the triune nature of the Goddess. Also known as the Kali Yantra, this was described as "the meditation-sign of the vulva," the Triangle of Life, or the Primordial Image.[7] Pious meditation on the Yoni Yantra was the duty of an enlightened sage: "The object of the worship of the Yantra is to attain unity with the Mother of the Universe in Her forms as Mind, Life, and Matter . . . preparatory to Yoga union with Her as She is in herself as Pure Consciousness."[8]

The same Yoni Yantra appeared everywhere in the ancient world as a symbol of "woman" or "motherhood" or "Goddess." It was a hiero-glyph of Men-Nefer, the Virgin Moon Goddess who gave her name to Egypt's oldest capital city, Memphis.[9] Egypt's version of the Triple Goddess was a Kali-like Mother of Time, the three sides of her triangle standing for past, present, and future. The inscription on her temple at Sais said: "I am all that has been, that is, and that will be."[10] The Christian writer of the Book of Revelation borrowed the phrase for his own God, who accordingly claimed to be that "which is, and which was, and which is to come" (Revelation 1:8); but the original phrase was the Mother's.

The many images of the three Fates in pagan religions were founded on the older concept of the Goddess's Holy Trinity. In Greece, where the Fates governed every life, even the lives of gods, the sacred triangle was the *delta,* symbol of Demeter whose name was literally "Delta-Mother." According to the Suda Lexicon (A.D. 1000), the *delta* was "the letter of the vulva." The Hebrew alphabet made it *daleth,* the Door (of life). It figured prominently in the sigils of Greco-Roman Goddesses. Gnostics said it represented "creative intellect," and the basic triangle was always a symbol of "woman."[11] Among gypsies, the oldest hiero-glyphic sign for "woman" was a triangle.[12]

Since the triangle was as sacred to worshipers of the Goddess as the cross was to Christians, and gypsies were worshipers of the Goddess, it is hardly surprising to find the triangle embedded in gypsies' Tarot symbolism. Chief among the gypsies' formal full-deck divinatory lay-outs was the Yoni Yantra:

> The first card drawn from the pack is placed in the center and then eleven cards are used to form the right side of the triangle going from the top down. A second series of eleven cards forms the left side of the triangle going from the bottom to the top. A third series of eleven cards forms the top of the upside-down triangle and are laid out from the right to the left. The top side of the triangle represents the present, the right side represents the future, and the left side represents the past of the client whose fortune is being told. Next, thirty-three cards, or three more sets of eleven cards are laid out counterclockwise to form a full circle around the triangle. The remaining set of eleven cards are then placed under the first card drawn in the center of the triangle.[13]

This divinatory layout incorporates not only the Goddess's triangular symbol, counterclockwise circle, and three categories of past, present, and future; it also has several repetitions and multiplications of her sacred number three, as well as the "seven elevens" so significant in dice games.

There was also a short form of the Yoni Yantra utilizing only the Major Arcana, whose numbers 1–21 fell naturally into three divisions of seven cards each. Twenty-one was long regarded as a magical number because its only multiplicands were the sacred numbers 3 and 7, associated with the Triple Goddess and her Pleiadic priestesses, the Seven Sisters, known in Syria as the Seven Pillars of Wisdom. By ancient tradition, each human life was normally divided into three trimesters of twenty-one years apiece, foreshadowed by the three prenatal trimesters. Tarot cards clearly associated the first third of life with the "past" leg of the triangle, the second third with the "present" leg, and the last third with the "future" leg.

The end of the first trimester of life was said to be attained at 21 years of age, which is why we still consider this the age of maturity. The end of the second trimester, or "middle age," came at 42. The end of the third trimester was 63, which European peasants still call "the grand climacteric," or death year, an age supposed to be especially dangerous for men.[14] Apparently, women were supposed to live longer—an additional seven years—giving them the "threescore and ten" that the biblical God later promised to men, in order to outbid the Goddess for men's devotion.

The Yoni Yantra formed by the Major Arcana assigned three years of life to each card. As every student of the cards knows, the traditional meanings of the cards do indeed correspond very well to the likely events and attitudes of a lifetime so numbered. The "grand climacteric" matching the card of the Naked Goddess, or cosmic Shakti (the World), recalls the Oriental belief that, at the moment of death, a sage would be sexually and spiritually united with his Goddess in divine bliss. This was the ultimate orgasm implied by the word "climacteric," from Greek *klimax*. Classical authors mentioned a similar belief in the approach to spiritual grace *(venia)* through sexual exercises taught by priestesses of the Goddess.[15] Having been initiated into her mysteries, Ovid prayed that he would be able to die "in the act of coming to Venus."[16]

Slavic paganism presented the same belief. Kali-Shakti and her *dakinis* (death nymphs) became the Slavs' Samovila, "Mother Death," and her priestesses the Vilas, or Wilis. They provided a sweet, painless passage into the otherworld when they held a dying man in their arms.[17] Such ideas may be traced back to Tantric priestesses whose special function was to comfort the dying with sensual pleasure, as mothers comforted their infants to soothe away the birth trauma.

It was everywhere typical of savior-gods that they returned to the same matrix that gave them birth, to be "born again" in their endless cycles. This was usually mythologized as divine incest in the Oedipal style. The Son, a reincarnation of his Father, mated with his Mother and was reincarnated yet again after his sacrifice. Hence Osiris, for example, was hailed at his rebirth as "husband of thy Mother."[18] The Christian deity was no exception. Christian theologians held that God and Jesus were identical. Therefore, the Mother of God and the Bride of

God were also the same person—Mary. If God was both Father and Son, he begot himself upon his own mother in the classic pagan manner.

A god's return to his mother's womb was graphically shown in a series of symbols based on the Yoni Yantra. Within the maternal triangle appeared a dot, the *bindu*, "spark of existence." It grew like a fetus, and eventually emerged, to become an upward-pointing triangle representing the male principle. The two triangles then moved closer to each other until they touched, and finally interpenetrated. Their full union made two interlocked triangles, the hexagram known to the Hindus as the Sri Yantra or Great Yantra.[19] This stood for the "Great Rite" of sexual intercourse and complete merging of God and Goddess.[20]

This same hexagram is now considered the symbol of Judaism in the Western world. It has been called Solomon's seal, the Star of David, or Magen David (Shield of David). In reality it had nothing to do with either Solomon or David. It was not mentioned in Jewish literature until the twelfth century A.D., and it was not adopted as the official emblem of Jewry until the seventeenth century.[21]

The Magen David came into Judaism by way of the medieval Cabala, a mystical system showing strong Tantric influences. The Tantric Shakti was translated into the Cabalistic Shekina, "Female Soul of God," and the *bindu* became the Cabalistic *bina*, spirit of the womb of creation. Cabalists said God had lost his Shekina; universal harmony could be restored only by making God and Goddess once more "one." The Shekina alone has the power to "put God back together," as Kali-Shakti put Shiva back together through his cyclic deaths and rebirths. Sex magic was the key. The Cabalists certainly understood that, as in the East, the hexagram stood for sex magic. Cabalistic-rabbinical tradition developed the story that "a picture is supposed to be placed in the ark of the covenant alongside of the tables of the laws, which shows a man and a woman in intimate embrace, in the form of a hexagram."[22]

Inevitably, images of God and Shekina were found in earthly sex partners. The Cabalistic Rabbi Eliahu di Vidas said no man can attain the love of God unless he experiences "the force of passionate love for a woman." Shekina as the Supernal Mother was manifested in a wife, to whom her husband should make love on the Sabbath (as opposed to the Christian custom of forbidding marital relations on the Sabbath). From this union, "all the six days of the week derive their blessing."

> The obvious piety of these passages from the Zohar re-institutes sexual intercourse as a sacramental act in the service of a God and his consort (or perhaps vice versa: a Goddess and her consort), and to this extent is highly reminiscent of the concepts which led to temple prostitution in the various cults of the Goddess. The efflorescence of such beliefs into orgiastic rites suggests itself too readily not to be attempted, and indeed, in the further development of Cabalistic doctrine, such attempts were made.[23]

49

Tarot interpreter Eliphas Lévi drew many parallels between the Cabala and the Tarot, even going so far as to claim the cards were of Jewish origin. He insisted that the twenty-first trump card showed the same Bride of God as the Cabalistic Shekina, in the form of the Naked Goddess. "The supreme purpose of human existence" was to re-unite her with her divine bridegroom.[24]

God needed his Shekina, according to the old Tantric theory that any male, divine or human, lacked spiritual potency if he lacked a female partner. Hindu gods and priests needed their wives or Shaktis, who embodied their power, and "without whom they avail nothing."[25] Thus there was ample precedent for the Cabalistic belief that God is unable to cope with the world's evil because he lacks the female principle.

Like Hindus, the Jews used to bar unmarried men from the priesthood, because the invocations and spells of a womanless man were thought ineffectual.[26] Only a woman could provide *ruach*, "spirit," a Hebrew derivative from the Arabic *ruh*, meaning both "spirit" and "blood-red color." The Arabs said *ruh* was the female counterpart of male *sirr*, "whiteness," referring to semen.[27] *Sirr* and *ruh* in turn were based on the two essences of the Great Rite in the secret language of the Tantras: *sukra* or "seed" (semen) and *rakta*, "menstrual blood," always simultaneously feared and revered as the taboo essence of life itself, mysteriously empowered to form the child in the womb.

For the Great Rite, it was specified that the priestess impersonating the Goddess must be menstruating, so her lunar energy should be at its peak. The conjunction of her red and her partner's white fluids was "a profoundly important symbolic conjunction throughout Tantra."[28]

> When the semen, made molten by the fire of great passion, falls into the lotus of the "mother" and mixes with her red element, he achieves "the conventional mandala of the thought of enlightenment." The resultant mixture is tasted by the united "father-mother" (Yab-Yum), and when it reaches the throat they can generate concretely a special bliss . . . the *bodhicitta*—the drop resulting from union of semen and menstrual blood . . . empowers his corresponding mystic veins and centers to accomplish the Buddha's function of speech. The term "secret initiation" comes from the tasting of the secret substance.[29]

This was not an exclusively Oriental idea. It was long known and practiced in western Europe, even by some early Christian sects. Aristotle and Pliny taught that every human life begins with the mysterious magic of menstrual blood, somehow stimulated by the semen to solidify, to be retained in the womb and form a "curd," which developed into a child.[30] It was widely believed that eating the white/male and red/female essences of life at the moment of their union was even more beneficial, spiritually and physically, than eating the bread and wine symbolizing white flesh and red blood of a Savior.

Nineteenth-century theologians chose to interpret the early Christian *agape*, "Love Feast," as a synonym for the Eucharist. But it seems the *agape* was actually an imitation of the Tantric Great Rite. Even though the Eucharist continued through the centuries, the word *agape* was dropped like a hot potato early in the Middle Ages, after suppression of the Gnostic sects, and this "Love Feast" was never referred to again. Another obsolete word for the ceremony was even more suggestive: it was called *synesaktism*, literally, the Way of Shaktism.[31]

With obvious disapproval, Epiphanius described at some length the *agape* practiced by Ophite Christians. It was a Tantric rite in almost pure form. "After they have consorted together in a passionate debauch . . . the woman and the man take the man's ejaculation into their hands, stand up . . . offering to the Father, the Primal Being of All Nature, what is on their hands. . . . And when the woman is in her period, they do likewise with her menstruation. The unclean flow of blood, which they garner, they take up in the same way and eat together."[32]

Gnostic writings revealed a Kali-like Christian Goddess who was carefully concealed by later editors of the canon, when they eradicated as many descriptions of her as they could find.[33] The Clementine Homilies called her the All-Maternal Being, the Queen, and Wisdom (Greek Sophia, Latin Sapientia). "She was with the first God at the creation of the world."[34] More precisely, she was "with child," and he was the child. The *Trattato Gnostico* said she was "the great revered Virgin in whom the Father was concealed from the beginning before He had created anything."[35]

Even as the Son, he was intimately dependent on her: "The Son of Man agreed with Sophia, his consort, and revealed himself in a great light as bisexual. His male nature is called 'the Savior,' the begetter of all things, but his female 'Sophia, Mother of All.' "[36] This image strongly suggests the bisexual figures representing union of male and female principles in Kali and Shiva, which may still be seen in the Ellora caves in anthropomorphic form, as well as in symbolic form like the hexagram.[37]

Some of the Gnostic sects who practiced Tantric-style *coitus reservatus* may have been responsible for the curious Christian legend of the "test of faith." It was claimed that certain Christian men and women slept naked in one another's arms, without indulging any lustful desires, as proof that their faith was strong enough to withstand extreme temptation. It may well have been that, like Tantric saints, they controlled not sexuality per se, but male orgasm, according to the principle of *maithuna*.

51

There are hints that some Europeans remembered more sophisticated sexual techniques as taught by Eastern sages, rather than obeying the church's simplistic sex-for-procreation directive. Just as the gypsies practiced "occult" sexual rites, so did Christian heretics like the Brothers and Sisters of the Free Spirit, the Antinomian heretics, and the Adamites. The latter revered a cult hero said to have prolonged sexual intercourse with a "prophetess" for twenty days, and reached unprecedented heights of spiritual grace. A sect that worshiped St. Nicholas preached that "the only way to salvation lay through frequent intercourse between the sexes."[38]

Medieval bards, much disliked by the clergy, promulgated a sexual-philosophical system in which the ladylove played essentially the same role as the Tantric *shakti* and the Sufic *fravashi* or "Spirit of the Way." Tales of the famous lover/bard Tristan concealed some sly puns that may have been deliberate signals. On meeting his ladylove, Tristan reversed the syllables of his name and introduced himself as Tantris—a suspiciously Tantric title.[39]

Witches may have practiced *maithuna*, for it was claimed that even though the witches' Sabbat included sexual orgies, no woman was ever impregnated as a result.[40] If male witches played the role of "demon lovers" skilled in pleasing their partners, it could explain the churchmen's insistence that women enjoyed the lovemaking of their "demons" more than that of Christian men. After consorting with "demons," women found their husbands' sexual performance "paltry and unable to arouse them to any degree."[41] The women of India made the same complaint about European men: "Eighteenth-century Indian harlots mocked European men for their miserable sexual performance, calling them 'dunghill cocks' for whom the act was over in a few seconds."[42]

Christianity may have taken the fun out of sex, but to the pagans who spoke archaic German, the word *Lust* meant "religious joy."[43] German witches were *Hexen*, "those who make the Six"; a traditional "hex sign" still has six points like the Tantric hexagram. Six was a sacred number of Aphrodite as Love-goddess (in German, *Minne*); therefore, Christian authorities called six "the number of sin."[44] Many such hints together seem to form a shadow of the Yoni Yantra over Europe as well as the Eastern "heathen."

As Christianity eventually conquered Europe, so another patriarchal religion that excluded women eventually conquered the Goddess's former territories in the Middle East. Before Arabia fell under the yoke of Islam, its population worshiped the same trinitarian Mother under the names of Al-Ilat, Al-Uzza, and Manat. Ironically, the famous Black Stone now enshrined in the Kaaba, in Mecca, once embodied the Goddess and was marked with her genital symbol.[45] Here, where no woman is now permitted, men gather in their pilgrimages to render homage to what was once the aniconic image of the Great Goddess. Her priestesses are gone, having been replaced by a male priesthood whose official title was "Sons of the Old Woman." The Old Woman was simply the trinitarian Mother, whose three names meant The Goddess, The Powerful One, and Fate. Thus, the earlier female Allah was the same trinity as the Greek Moerae, Norse Norns, triple Kali, or the three aspects of Roman Fortuna. Even now one of her names is used by the Arabs to mean Lady Luck.[46]

Even within intensely patriarchal Islam there were some sects that remembered the Goddess, more or less, and insisted on introducing a feminine element into their faith. The Sufis occupied a position in the Moslem world like that of the Tantric yogis in India, worshiping the female principle as the world's true unifying power. Sufi troubadours contributed many secret writings and ideas to the underground culture of Europe, in an age when most Europeans looked to the East for everything exotic, marvelous, and interesting. It was the land of fairy tales, which merged with the fairy realm still existing in the imaginations and the spiritual yearnings of nominally Christian Europe.

As in Europe the qualities of the Goddess were largely assimilated by the cult of Mary, so in Arabia the Goddess was transformed into Fatima, a mythical "daughter" of Mohammed, nevertheless described as "Mother of her father." Her name meant "the Creatress." She was also called Fate, the Moon, the Tree of Paradise, and Mother of the Sun.[47] Her cult attracted the same kind of devotion in Arabia as Mary's cult in Europe.

The first headquarters of the Christian Order of the Knights Templar in Jerusalem stood next to the al-Aqsa mosque, revered by Shi'ites as the central shrine of the Goddess Fatima.[48] The Knights Templar were sometimes credited with the invention of Tarot cards, though it is more probable that they adopted cards from the Saracen warrior fraternities, on which their order was modeled.[49] The inexplicable disappearance of the four knights from the Tarot court cards—leaving the now standard thirteen cards per suit instead of fourteen—has been linked with the church's extermination of the Knights Templar in the fourteenth century, after they were accused of adopting "some of the mysterious tenets of the Eastern Gnostics."[50]

Among these tenets were remnants of Goddess worship that contributed to the cult of Fatima, as to those of Mary and Minne by way of bardic romance and courtly love, promulgated by European troubadours inspired by their Moorish counterparts. The al-Aqsa mosque provided a foundation for legends of the Temple of the Holy Grail, before the Grail was Christianized and proclaimed the chalice of the first Eucharist. The older Grail was the same womb-symbol as the Celts' Cauldron of Regeneration, represented by the temple itself, whose "door" was a yoni. In India to this day, the word for a temple means "womb."[51]

Legend said the Grail temple was guarded by heroic knights called Templars, servants of the Goddess, sworn to defend women from patriarchal injustices, and to uphold the feminine divinity invested in the Grail. According to the Grail cycle of legends, these knights were such as Galahad, Perceval, Lohengrin: invincible warriors, the flower of chivalry. But in real life, the Knights Templar were victims of the Inquisition.

Like other Christian orders initially dedicated to poverty, the real Templars became very rich. Over two centuries, through bequests, gifts, and contracts of protection, they acquired estates and treasure houses in France, Spain, Portugal, and the Levant. They became the leading bankers and moneylenders of the thirteenth century. Their original charter, signed by Pope Innocent II, declared them exempt from church taxes and from papal claims on their property. This financial independence was to prove their downfall.

The campaign to confiscate the Templars' wealth began early in the fourteenth century with accusations of heresy, blasphemy, and devil worship. The Grand Master and other dignitaries of the order were arrested, and tortured until they confessed having denied Christ, trampled the cross, kissed the devil's private parts, and forced novices into homosexual acts: these and similar charges were to become all too familiar in subsequent witch trials. The crimes were largely invented by the judges. Each Templar confessed to one set of sins when tortured by one judge, and a different set when tortured by a different judge.[52] The trials were blatantly rigged. During a trial of Templars at Paris, the court repeatedly refused to hear depositions from 573 witnesses for the defense.[53] When leaders of the order publicly renounced their confessions, proclaiming their innocence before a large crowd of people, they were declared relapsed heretics and were burned at the stake the same afternoon.[54]

Some Templars escaped to England, where torture was illegal. The notably inclement Pope Clement V, however, wrote to the English king, demanding arrest and torture of the fugitive knights, on pain of immediate excommunication of the king and all his court. King Edward was also offered the bribe of a Plenary Indulgence for forgiveness of all his past sins. So, "out of reverence for the Holy See," as he put it, Edward changed the English law to allow papal judges to torture the Templars.[55] Naturally they were convicted, and the usefulness of torture was legally established. Techniques for the later persecution and torture of witches were established by the church's success in exterminating the Templars.[56]

If the Knights Templar really were heretics, their heresy might well have been the one that the church fought hardest: the idea of a female divinity, which kept arising again and again, and had to be constantly put down. Templars were said to have worshiped a bisexual idol named Baphomet, "a symbol of the Absolute," whose influence made them rich, made flowers grow, and the earth germinate. A bisexual idol with such clear-cut connotations of fertility and abundance could only have been of the Kali/Shiva type. The name Baphomet was regarded as an ignorant mispronunciation of Mohammed. But the Templars, living among Mohammedans, would certainly have known how to pronounce Mohammed's name. An alternative theory derived Baphomet from Greek *Baphe Metis*, "Baptism of Metis," another name for the Lady Wisdom—the same Gnostic Goddess called Sophia in eastern Europe, Sapientia in Rome, Shekina by Spanish-Jewish Cabalists, and Fatima by Sufi and Shi'ite "poets of love."[57]

Since the Yoni Yantra was widely recognized as a symbol of this Goddess, representing the "door" of her Holy of Holies, consequently it would have implied a mystical process of initiation into her central mysteries. The Tarot layout of the Yoni Yantra preserved by gypsies clearly imitated the maternal triangle with its indwelling *bindu*, often represented by the numberless Fool in the center of the design. Like knights of the Holy Grail before their secret initiation, the Fool was a clown, a know-nothing, a newborn child, ignorant of the revelations to come during the trimesters of his life, and ignorant of their prophetic enactment during initiation. Thus, from the card of the Fool to the card of the World was obviously a journey of enlightenment.

Part II

The Greater Secrets

'Tis mute, the word they went to hear on high Dodona Mountain
When winds were in the oakenshaws and all the cauldrons tolled,
And mute's the midland navel-stone beside the singing fountain,
And echoes list to silence now where gods told lies of old.

I took my question to the shrine that has not ceased from speaking,
The heart within, that tells the truth and tells it twice as plain;
And from the cave of oracles I heard the priestess shrieking
That she and I should surely die and never live again.

—A. E. Housman, *The Oracles*

0. The Fool

0

The Fool

Of all the Major Arcana, only one card was allowed to remain in the new standard deck: the Fool, or Jester, or Joker. Among his other names were: The Foolish Man, Folly, Le Mat, and El Loco—the madman.[1] Such names suggest a pre-Christian lunar religion, in that all aspects of lunar religion were later vilified as "madness." The word lunatic used to mean a devotee of the Moon-goddess under her classical name of Luna. One of her older names, Mania, likewise became a synonym for madness.

Originally, Mania the Moon-mother gave birth to the ancestors of humanity, whom the Romans called *manes* (moon-children), or Di Parentes, "ancestral deities" whose souls still dwelt in the earth.[2] Northern European tribes knew the same Moon-mother as Mana; Arabs knew her as Manat. Her chosen prophets and sybils were "moon-struck" or "touched by the moon," which led to the colloquial English "tetched" (touched). Mana's special children were "moon-calves" (offspring of the Moon-cow), a term later applied to lovers and idiots. When the Moon's sacred games or *ludi* became "ludicrous," her ceremonial kings became clowns who performed the *antic* (ancient) dances. They were called "silly," which used to mean a person particularly blessed.[3]

The Tarot Fool seems to have been "silly" in the older, pagan sense. His typical dunce cap was derived from the *apex*, a conical miter worn by Rome's ceremonial high priest, the Flamen Dialis.[4] Celtiberian medals showed the Lord of Death in the same conical cap, calling him Helman—a man belonging to the underworld Goddess Hel, who was often equated with the moon between her setting and rising.[5] The Norse Lord of Death, Frey, also wore the *apex*.[6]

Even earlier, in Egypt, the Fool's Cap was a diadem of the Two Lands, placed on the heads of symbolic Carnival Kings who once functioned as doomed surrogates for the pharaoh. They were still annually burned to death in effigy, as late as the nineteenth century A.D., emerging from their own ashes like the pharaonic Phoenix.[7] In symbolism like that of the obelisk, the *apex* represented the phallus of the Earth-god (or, the god on earth) standing up to reach the Queen of Heaven, variously named Nut, Hathor, or Isis. "In the symbolism of dreams and of myths the hat is usually the phallus."[8] Tantric sorcerers in Tibet still

58

wear the same conical cap to demonstrate their union with the Goddess.[9] Another name for the dunce-capped Carnival King in medieval Europe was a Tantric one: "Prince of Love."[10]

Egyptian tradition probably contributed the "ass ears" of the Fool's conical cap. *Asinine* became a pejorative term and the ass an animal of ill repute, for the very reason that in pre-Christian times it was holy, especially in Egypt. The ass-god Set was crucified as a surrogate for the divine king, Osiris-Ra, as his seasonal alter ego. Even Jesus rode a young ass, in his role of sacred king, amid other traditional trappings of the sacrificial "triumph" (John 12:14). His reed scepter may well have carried a pair of ass ears like the reed scepter of the crucified Set, which became a token of royalty for all the dynastic gods.[11] The same ass-eared scepter was inherited by medieval jesters and Carnival Kings.

The Fool's costume and acts both suggested ancient Oriental origin. "Jester" came from Spanish *chistu,* in turn derived from Chisti, a school of apostolic mystics from Afghanistan. Members of this sect appeared in Europe during the thirteenth century. Attracting crowds with their music, drumming, antics, and horseplay, they presented mystery plays that held a religious message. Similar Sufi dervishes performed mystery plays throughout the East, often feigning idiocy and calling themselves Fools of God.[12]

Some Tarot decks showed the Fool dressed in leaves, like the Green Man, or Green George, who led springtime processions in European folk festivals.[13] Green George's Day was Easter Monday, the Moon-day of the lunar hero. It was later Christianized as St. George's Day, on the rather specious ground that George symbolized the newly risen Christ embodied in the spring foliage.[14] Tradition thus identified Christ with the fertility god sacrificed in spring. Some said Christ was crucified on the first of April, the Fool's Day, which came at the end of the pagans' regular Holy Week and once celebrated the resurrection of Attis with jokes, horseplay, and pageants at the festival of "foolishness," the Hilaria.[15]

If the Fool was identified with a pagan Christ figure such as Attis, it could have been at the early, unenlightened, infantile stage of the hero's life. The Tarot Fool carried a bag slung on a staff over his shoulder. It was generally understood that the bag contained symbols of the elements (suits), which appeared in plain sight on the Magician's table, on the following card. As the suits themselves were thought to reveal the fate of a querent—who, in the Yoni Yantra layout, was actually represented by the Fool—so the suit symbols in the Fool's bag were thought to reveal his fate, though he couldn't see it. Christian iconography similarly depicted the Christ child descending from heaven to enter his mother's womb, all ignorant of his ultimate fate, shown by the miniature cross that he carried behind his back, on a staff over his shoulder.[16]

Ignorance was prominent in the concept of the blessed or "silly" Fool, whose number zero was "the age of the child before the first birthday."[17] The oval zero itself began as a symbol of the World Egg, consequently of all fetal beginnings. Gnostic doctrines of metempsychosis taught that before each rebirth, the soul must drink the waters of Lethe (Forgetfulness) to blank out memories of previous lives, and make the mind a zero. Such infantile ignorance in Tantric tradition was *Avidya*, "want of knowledge," or unconscious will, animating the newborn before any reasons for living can be understood.[18]

On the Tantric wheel of karma, this ignorance at life's beginning was represented by a blind man stepping toward a precipice.[19] Some early Tarot decks showed the Fool likewise heading for a fall. Another of his names, Adam-Kadmon, was a Gnostic image of the innocent newborn— or reborn—soul at the start of a new aeon, on either an individual or a cosmic scale.[20]

It may have been this element of ignorance that saved the Fool's card from determined attack by churchmen, so it survived to become the modern Joker. The Fool could be likened to Adam before the Fall, sinless by his very ignorance. As pagan Mysteries found refuge in carnival clownishness, so the Fool was preserved by his know-nothing character, like that of pagan heroes before their enlightenment. The Desired Knight of the Grail myth cycle similarly began as a rustic clown, both ignorant and innocent, before his awakening to the mystic meanings of his quest—which was, under a thin Christian overlay, the quest for paganism's unforgotten symbol of the holy womb of all rebirths, the Cauldron of Regeneration.[21]

It could be argued that the Fool symbolized the unenlightened man, who knew nothing as yet about the pagan Mysteries unfolded by the following pageant of Tarot trumps: as the sacred king who led the *paginae* was not necessarily aware of what followed him. So the Fool was permitted to stay *with*, if not exactly *in*, the deck of cards, because he had no heresies to teach.

Since the other Major Arcana certainly had something to teach, the Fool would have suggested a novice at the start of his journey toward the enlightenment waiting at the end of the sequence (the World). He was always walking forth, beginning a journey, facing pitfalls of which he seemed unaware.

His relationship to the corresponding card in the spiritual realm, Judgment (Trump #20), could be understood on several levels. Judgment was the very quality a Fool would lack, until initiation and experience provided it. The card of Judgment was also interpreted as a conventional image of doomsday, with the dead rising from their graves and the usual angel blowing the Last Trump—actually, the next-to-last trump card. Christians and pagans shared the same notion of end-of-the-world events. On a deep psychological level, doomsday predictions simply formalized and projected every man's fear of death. Though Christians rejected the doctrine, pagans and Gnostics believed rebirth waited beyond each person's day of doom.[22] Accordingly, with the turning of Fate's "wheels of becoming," the Fool was born again from the ranks of the dead (or, unenlightened), to begin a new life of learning.

Commonly found on the Fool's card was a doglike animal, snapping at his heels. According to many ancient beliefs, including those of Egypt, the dog symbolized death and guarded the gates of the after-world—as shown on the Tarot card of the Moon. Hence, the Fool's card may have hinted at a later escape from death, as promised by pagan as well as Christian Mysteries.

Sometimes the Fool followed a butterfly, which the Greeks called Psyche, a symbol of the soul. At one time it was widely believed that human souls, after death, occupied the forms of flying creatures like birds and insects. Sometimes the Fool carried a flower, the mystic Alchemical Rose, another image of the female World Soul that was the object of many spiritual quests.

Like many other examples of folkloric "foolishness," the Fool meant much more than was apparent.

The Magician

1. The Magician

The first of the numbered Major Arcana figures was a manipulator of the elements. The suit-symbols of the elements lay before him on a small table, like the stands used by carnival mountebanks and jugglers. His titles suggested a similar profession: Juggler, Wizard, Gypsy Master, Magus, Thimblerigger, Bateleur, Magician.[1]

The Tarot Magician was also consistently identified with Renaissance Europe's most popular transmutation of a pagan god: that inimitable manipulator of the elements, Hermes Trismegistus (Thrice-Great Hermes). The Mantegna Tarot showed the Magician as Hermes the god, complete with his caduceus, flute, winged helmet, and winged

61

boots.[2] In other decks the Magician's pose was the same as that of Hermes in Botticelli's *Primavera*, his arms forming the alchemical glyph for Mercury—which was Hermes's Latin name as well as his sacred metal of elemental transformations.[3] Both European and Arabian alchemists claimed Hermes as the founder of their craft.[4] Alchemists often tried to "marry Hermes and Athene," by coloring mercury yellow with sulfur, then trying to solidify it into synthetic gold.

All agreed that Thrice-Great Hermes could easily change base metal into gold, since he had the Philosophers' Stone that could control the elements, and change any matter into any other. Mystics, *philosophes*, and occult fraternities pored over the *Corpus Hermeticum*, a collection of magical texts that became an alchemical Bible after a Greek version of it was presented to Cosimo de' Medici. These texts were supposed to have been written by Hermes himself. Renaissance scholars were sure he had been a real person. Siena Cathedral displayed his portrait in mosaics, with the inscription, "Hermes Mercury Trismegistus, Contemporary of Moses." Lazzarelli's *Calix Christi et Crater Hermetis* (Chalice of Christ and Cup of Hermes) stated that all learning was invented by Hermes and given by him to Moses in Egypt. Agrippa von Nettesheim cited Hermes as a grandson of Abraham. Sir Thomas Browne wrote that Hermetic magic was "the mystical method of Moses bred up in the Hieroglyphical Schools of the Egyptians," and that the Egyptians called Hermes either Mercurius or Anubis, "the Scribe of Saturn, and counsellor of Osyrus, the great inventor of their religious rites, and Promoter of good unto Egypt." He was deified, and ascended to heaven in the form of the star Sirius.[5]

There was a long-standing confusion of Hermes Trismegistus with the corresponding Egyptian god of magic, Thoth. This carried through into the Tarot deck, which was sometimes known as the Book of Thoth. According to Egyptian legend, the original Book of Thoth contained magic formulas so powerful that they could make a person understand the language of birds and reptiles, bring himself back to life out of the tomb, and associate as an equal with the divinities of sun and moon. He could command the waters, the earth, the airs of heaven, and the fire of the stars (that is, the elements).[6]

Coptic Christians further identified Thoth with Christ. They created Christian Scriptures from parts of the Book of the Dead, substituting Christ's name for Thoth and Mary's name for his feminine counterpart Maat, or Isis.[7]

Early Roman Christians similarly identified Hermes-Mercury with Christ. The Gospels' description of Christ as the Logos, or personified Word of God, was copied from the pagans' description of Hermes as the Logos of Zeus or Apollo-Helios. Old hymns to Hermes prefigured Christian hymns, with similar sentiments:

I will hymn the Lord of Creation, the All and One. . . . He is the light of my spirit. . . . Hymn, O Truth, the Truth, O Goodness, the Good, Life, and Light. . . . Thine own Word through me hymns thee: through me receive the all by thy Word, my reasonable sacrifice. . . . Thou pleroma in us, O Life, save us; O Light, enlighten us; O God, make us spiritual. The Spirit guards my Word . . . from the Eternal I received blessing and what I seek. By thy will have I found rest.

We give thee thanks, O Most High, for by thy grace we obtained this light of knowledge, Name (Logos) ineffable. . . . Saved by thee, we rejoice that thou didst show thyself to us completely; we rejoice that even in our mortal bodies thou didst deify us by the vision of thyself. . . . We have come to know thee, O thou Light perceptible alone to our feeling; we have come to know thee, thou Light of the life of man.[8]

Popular identification of Hermes the Magician with the Light of the World may underlie the Tarot's numerical identification of the Magician with the card of the Sun (Trump #19). Initiates into ancient Hermetic and Mithraic Mysteries said they were filled with sunlight, the spirit of the god himself. So they became immortal like him. Their scriptures promised: "This is the good end for those who have attained knowledge, namely, Deification." The initiate spoke the formula: "I know thee, Hermes, and thou knowest me; I am thou, and thou art I . . . thy name is mine, for I am thy image *(eidolon)*." [9]

Christian Scriptures attributed the same promise to Jesus, who told his followers they would become immortal through becoming his *eidolon:* "Because I live, ye shall live also. . . . I am in my Father, and ye in me, and I in you" (John 14:19–20). There were durable links between Christian and Hermetic ideas of salvation. As late as the sixteenth century A.D., German coins showed the crucified Christ on one side, the crucified Hermetic serpent on the other, suggesting that they were two faces of the same deity.[10]

Also significant in the Tarot system was the ancient concept of Hermes as a "Good Shepherd" who guided the souls of the dead—a title he shared with Osiris, Mithra, Tammuz, the Hindu Yama, the Persian Yima, and other versions of the same savior figure. Greeks called him Hermes Psychopomp, "Conductor of Souls." The Cabiri said he was the most accessible third of the Holy Trinity formed by Mother Demeter along with her consort Hades; thus Hermes could come and go freely in their nether realm.[11] Because he had once been androgynous—the original Hermaphrodite united in the same body with Triple Goddess Aphrodite—he had deep, chracteristically feminine wisdom, and knowledge of the uterine underworld, from which all men were periodically born again.

This may explain why the Hermetic Magician is the first trump card to be encountered by the unenlightened Fool. As guide to the realms of mystery, the Magician must have played the same role that deified Aeneas played for Virgil, conducting him on a sacred journey through the underworld. Aeneas too was once a part of the body of Aphrodite, though his separation from her was described as a birth. In his turn, Virgil conducted Dante on the same kind of symbolic journey of enlightenment through the underworld, purgatory, and paradise.

Hermes was always a god of journeys, which is why his *herms* or phallic pillars stood at main crossroads throughout the Greco-Roman world, often in conjunction with images of the triple underground Goddess known to the Romans as Hecate Trevia.[12] During the Christian era, roadside *herms* were replaced by crucifixes. However, Christians still thought crossroads were haunted by Hermes and Hecate. Invocation of these supposedly all-wise deities made crossroads the preferred places for oracular ceremonies. Hermes and Hecate became the still small voices that foretold the future in one's ear at the crossroads on Christmas Eve.[13]

The Magician identified with Hermes as Conductor of Souls, god of spiritual journeys, and guide to the mysteries of the afterlife, was an obvious choice for the beginning of an initiatory progress through the stations of the Major Arcana, which would include sacrifice, death, and descent into hell. The Magician revealed elemental mysteries hidden from the Fool. He wore the lemniscate hat that symbolized infinity and an entrée into both worlds. He introduced the first half of the pageant of enlightenment. And his first encounter was with a personage almost entirely unknown outside of the Tarot—for the reason that the origins of her legends and symbols were deliberately obscured.

2. *The Papess*

.2

The Papess

The Papess was perhaps the least acceptable Tarot figure to the Christian establishment, since the latter was dedicated to the idea that ecclesiastical authority was for men only. Clerical pressure forced French card painters to change the Papess to the Goddess Juno in eighteenth-century packs. A Belgian pack even changed her into a man, called the Spaniard.[1] Modern packs euphemize her title as "the High Priestess." Christian orthodoxy insisted that there never was, and never could be, a female pope. But other traditions suggested a different opinion.

Gnostics preserved some Gospels that were eliminated from the orthodox canon early in the Christian era. These texts said the first "pope" was not St. Peter, but St. Mary Magdalene, who received spiritual authority directly from Jesus after the Oriental custom of cross-sexual transmission—male to female, or vice versa. Jesus loved Mary Magdalene above all his other followers; he called her Apostle to the Apostles, and the Woman Who Knew the All.[2] He said she would rule all other disciples in his future Kingdom of Light.[3] "There was no grace that He refused her, nor any mark of affection that He withheld from her."[4] He gave to her, not to Peter, the power of the keys of heaven. Peter angrily tried to force the secret from her. The *Gospel of Mary* said Levi had to rebuke Peter for his violent attack on Mary. In the *Pistis Sophia*, Mary said, "Peter makes me hesitate; I am afraid of him, because he hates the female race."[5]

Some early Christian fathers recognized a spiritual authority vested in Mary Magdalene, which was erased by later church historians, who decided she was a simple harlot. Origen said she was, on the contrary, "the mother of all of us," as a male pope was supposed to be a spiritual father to the whole flock. Origen gave Mary Magdalene the title of Ecclesia, "the Church," which was applied to the Virgin Mary as well. He identified Mary Magdalene with the Great Goddess, by saying she had lived since the beginning of time, and was immortal.[6]

Many believed him. Mary's fame waxed. During the seventh century, an old Roman temple of the Goddess was renamed Santa Maria Maggiore, and dedicated to Mary Magdalene as the foundress of women's ecclesiastical orders, especially teaching orders, and the combined male-and-female "double monasteries" that flourished before the tenth century.[7]

In a way, Magdalenian teaching nuns continued the Roman tradition of the *collegia*, a temple of teaching priestesses with the title of *alma mater*, "soul-mother." The derivation was from Al-Mah, oldest Indo-Iranian name of Mother Moon.[8] A Hebrew cognate, *almah*, meant moon-soul embodied in a young woman. This was the term for the Virgin Mary in Hebrew versions of the Gospels. Christians translated *almah* as "virgin," but that was not its meaning.[9] As with the Roman "female soul," *alma*, there was an implication of a holy woman linked with the moon, as a spiritual leader. Plutarch said the moon was the source of all "reason and wisdom."[10]

On Gnostic gems, Luna Regia (Queen Moon) appeared in the same dress and pose as the Tarot Papess, sitting before the same temple veil, wearing a papal tiara decorated with a crescent moon.[11] A fourteenth-century manuscript showed the same Goddess as a papess, abbess, or nun.[12] Significantly, the Tarot Papess was numerically linked with the card of the Moon (Trump #18), and also with the concept of teaching, symbolized by the book in her hand.

Official church histories tried to hide the fact that even within Christianity the pagan tradition of feminine spiritual authority remained strong up to the thirteenth century, when monks began to encroach on the educational convents ruled by supreme abbesses, who were formerly ordained like bishops. Abbesses' older titles included *Matris Spirituale* (Spiritual Mother), *Sacerdos Maxima* (High Priestess), and Matriarch. They had political and economic autonomy, ruling male as well as female clergy.[13]

Certain orders of nuns were famed as educators, until the Council of Trent ruled that women's orders must relinquish their property to men's orders, and no more teaching convents were allowed.[14] Theological studies of the Beguines, for example, were forbidden. The women were forced to give up their houses and lands, which were taken over by the Inquisition. Nuns were obliged to integrate into orders approved by the pope, where they would remain secluded, and uneducated.[15]

Church histories were often edited to eliminate references to women in the higher ecclesiastical ranks. Yet, up to the sixteenth century, even church historians were firmly convinced that there had been at least one real papess, popularly known as Pope Joan, whose profound learning earned her the rank of cardinal, then of pope. The Tarot Papess was sometimes called Joan also; she wore the same tiara shown on Pope Joan's head in old engravings.[16] Pope Joan's likeness appeared in the row of papal busts in Siena Cathedral, labeled *Johannes VIII, femina ex Anglia*: Pope John VIII, an Englishwoman.[17]

The first recorder of Pope Joan's pontificate was her contemporary,

Anastasius the Librarian (d. 886). Scotus's chronicle of the popes said: "A.D. 854, Lotharii 14, Joanna, a woman, succeeded Leo, and reigned two years, five months, and four days." De Gemblours's tenth-century chronicle said, "It is reported that this John was a female, and that she conceived by one of her servants. The Pope, becoming pregnant, gave birth to a child, wherefor some do not number her among the Pontiffs." The reason given for striking her from the record was not that she was nonhistorical, but that she was a mother. Thomas de Elmham's official list of the popes in 1422 gave a similar reason: "A.D. 855, Joannes. This one doesn't count; she was a woman."[18]

The papal historian and Vatican librarian Platina wrote in *The Lives of the Popes* that Joan was English, and more learned in the Scriptures than any man. She disguised herself in men's clothes. Her deception was revealed when her labor pains came on her. She died in a certain street between the Lateran Palace and St. Clement's Church.[19] Martin Polonus said she was buried in the same street, which papal processions ever afterward avoided by a detour, "out of detestation for what happened there. Nor on that account is she placed in the catalogue of Holy Pontiffs, not only on account of her sex, but also because of the horribleness of the circumstances."[20] The "horribleness" was that when her sex was discovered, she was dragged into the street and stoned to death, and buried on the spot in an unmarked grave.[21] The real reason for subsequent popes' avoidance of the street seems to have been superstitious fear of Joan's vengeful ghost.

The period of Joan's pontificate was the only one ever stricken from the record, though it was better documented than many of the early popes, some of whom were only names, invented and inserted centuries after their alleged reigns. The church now claims that Pope Joan was entirely legendary. The most it will admit is that there was an "antipope" named John (Joannes) about this time, enthroned by popular demand against the will of the Curia.[22]

In 1886 a Greek writer, Emmanuel Royidis, published the biography of *Papissa Joanna*, saying "Every sentence in my book and almost every phrase is based on the testimony of contemporary authors." The church immediately banned his book and excommunicated him.[23]

Whether Pope Joan was legendary or not, a strange Vatican custom appeared after what the church insisted was not her reign. Candidates for the papacy seated themselves naked on an open stool, like a toilet seat, to be viewed through a hole in the floor by cardinals in a room below. The committee then had to render a formal verdict: *Testiculos habet, et bene pendentes*—"He has testicles, and they hang all right."[24]

The notion of a female pope persisted despite every precaution. Some of the Gnostic sects, who admitted women to ecclesiastical rank on an equal basis with men, held that only a female pope could counteract the abuses of the cynical, greedy Renaissance papacy. One such sect, the Guglielmites of Lombardy, elected their own papess to serve as the successor of their own saint, Guglielma of Bohemia, who died in Milan in 1281. The sectaries believed that Guglielma was the incarnation of the Holy Ghost, and would return to earth in a Second Coming at the Feast of Pentecost in the year 1300, whereupon the male-dominated church would wither away, and a better Christianity would rise under a line of female popes. The first of these, Manfreda, was placed in office by the sectaries. Wealthy Lombard families provided costly sacred vessels for her first Mass, supposed to take place in Rome at the Church of Santa Maria Maggiore. Because the followers of Papess Manfreda began to grow to really threatening numbers, and to demonstrate an enthusiasm that the incumbent papacy thought dangerous, the sect was exterminated by the Inquisition and the unlucky female pope was burned at the stake.[25]

More than these footnotes to history helped create the Tarot Papess, a fixture of the Major Arcana from its beginning. The Papess was also known as the Wise Woman, or *Sophia*—Greek for "female wisdom".[26] This was the former name of the Holy Spirit in its (her) original female form, as the spouse or Shakti (Power) of God. One of her emanations was the alchemical Mother of Wisdom—Sophia in Greek, Sapientia in Latin. Identified with the moon in alchemical texts, she bluntly told the male deity: "Thou dost nothing alone if I am not present with my strength, as a cock is helpless without a hen."[27]

Some medieval mystics presented her as a wholly female trinity: *Sapientia creans*, the creatress; *Sapientia disponans*, who unified all things in harmony; and *Sapientia gubernans*, the Governess, "otherwise known as Divine Providence." She was called "the basic and primordial foundation of all things . . . the being, life, and light of intelligible things," equal and commensurate with the Divine Essence. Spenser defined her as Queen of Heaven, "sovereign darling of the Deity," and Spouse of God, who sat enthroned in his bosom "clad like a Queen in royal robes."[28]

To the Gnostics, Hagia Sophia (Holy Sophia) was the Great Mother. She gave birth to Jehovah, who became the jealous God of Eden, forbidding humans to obtain the knowledge they needed. To undo this harm, Sophia gave birth to the spirit of Christ, and sent him to earth in the human body of Jesus. After Jesus's death, Sophia and Christ made him a Hermes-like Conductor of Souls in heaven. Some of the Gnostics said Jesus married a Virgin of Light, Sophia's emanation, much as the pagan savior Heracles married the Virgin Hebe, an emanation of the Mother Goddess, Hera.[29] The early Christian father Irenaeus declared that Sophia also gave birth to all the angels.[30]

In honor of this Gnostic Goddess, the great church of Hagia Sophia was built in Constantinople during the sixth century. Christian authorities now deny that this church was ever dedicated to any form of the Great Mother. They pretend the name Hagia Sophia really meant "Christ, the Word of God."[31] It is difficult to see how "Christ, the Word of God" can be made out of a name that means, in plain Greek, "Holy Female Wisdom."

Another emanation of Sophia was Christianized as a fictitious virgin martyr, who, despite her virginity, had produced three daughters: St. Faith, St. Hope, and St. Charity. Credulous hagiographers took these legends seriously, though they obviously were no more than an allegorical statement that Wisdom gives birth to Faith, Hope, and Charity. The physical beauty of St. Faith was much praised, and a crypt was dedicated to her in St. Paul's Cathedral in London.[32] There was also a pagan "St. Faith," one of Aphrodite's three lawgiving Charites. She was an ancient Roman Goddess named Bona Fides, "Good Faith." She was served by three senior *flamines*, the oldest core of Rome's official clergy.[33]

Thus it seems the Tarot's first teacher, to whose presence the Magician conducted the know-nothing Fool, was the very spirit of Female Wisdom, without whom not even God could act. It was typical of Gnostic reasoning that her spirit should be embodied in a Papess.

The position of the Papess corresponded to the third figure on the Tantric Wheel of Life, called Vijnana, the stage of development of conscious experience through teaching.[34] One of the first lessons taught the *sadhaka* was that no god could wield any power without his female "Wisdom," an emanation of the Great Shakti (Kali). The same lesson apparently belonged to the secret Gnostic tradition.

3. The Empress

3

The Empress

When an Orphic initiate entered the inner sanctum, he encountered images of the All-Mother Demeter and her daughter Kore, seated side by side, just as the Empress and the Papess appeared side by side in the Tarot.[1] Kore represented "Virgin Wisdom" and the Sacred Heart (or core) of Mother Earth. She was the apple of her Mother's eye, which is why the ancients discovered her pentacle in the "core" of the apple. She was a spirit of springtime and creation; but she was also confused with Persephone the Destroyer, the crone aspect of the same Goddess. Among many widespread variations of her name were Car, Kari, Q're, Kauri, Carna, and Car-Dia. Romans called her Ceres Legifera, the Lawgiver. Her *ius naturale* or "natural law" governed matriarchal societies in ancient Latium.[2] She was attended by avenging death-dogs, emanations of herself known as Keres or Furies, who pursued offenders against the Mother's law. The Tarot Papess, another Wise Virgin, was similarly attended by the lunar dogs of her corresponding card, the Moon.

If the Papess occupied the position of the Wise Virgin, the Empress occupied that of the All-Mother herself. The Empress's corresponding card was the Star (Trump #17), a common epithet of the Great Goddess. Several of her old names meant simply "Star," such as Ishtar, Astarte, Esther, Astraea, Stella Maris, or Ostara, who was the same Goddess Eostre that gave her name to Easter. The star-shaped Easter lily was once her yonic symbol, probably named from Assyrian *lilu*, "lotus," an adaptation of the *padma*-lotus that was the Goddess's genital sign in the East.[3] Another of the Goddess's old names, Lilith, also derived from this flower, was an alternate name for the Tarot Empress.[4]

In Egypt the same flower represented Isis or Hathor, "the great world lotus flower out of which rose the sun for the first time at the creation."[5] With the same flower, Blessed Virgin Juno miraculously conceived her savior-son Mars.[6] She was, of course, a pagan prototype of the Christian Goddess who inherited her lily, her crown of stars, and her title Stella Maris. The same crown of stars appeared on the head of the Empress in many Tarot decks, and the same lily is often displayed by the queens of standard card suits.

As Mistress of Earth and Sea, Demeter held up an ear of grain and a dolphin in her iconic promise to multiply loaves and fishes: the Eleusinian miracle that was copied into the New Testament. The Tarot version conveyed the same meaning of earth-and-sea fertility through the Gnostic symbol adopted by Freemasons: an ear of grain near a waterfall.[7] Hence, the Empress sometimes sat enthroned in a wheat field, next to a waterfall, holding a wheat ear in her hand. Some Tarot interpreters further emphasized her power of fertility by insisting that she was supposed to be pregnant.

In Demeter's principal temple, called *Eleusis*, "Advent," important rites celebrated the advent of her Divine Child, the grain reborn from the earth's womb. Represented by her savior-son, this vegetation-god was variously named Dionysus, Triptolemus, Iasion, or Elenthereos, "the Liberator."[8] Like the grain, he was laid in a manger or winnowing basket.[9] He was killed (reaped), buried (planted), and resurrected (sprouted). His flesh was eaten as bread, his blood was drunk as wine. He was deified at the Haloa, Festival of the Threshing-Floor (Greek *halos*). From this Eleusinian apotheosis came a Christian symbol of deification, the halo—and, of course, the concept of a savior sacramentally cannibalized.[10]

The final revelation of the Eleusinian Mysteries was an ear of grain "reaped in silence," showing simultaneously the Savior's death for the sake of humanity, and the seed of his future life.[11] The same symbol represented other vegetation-gods such as Syrian Adonis, Tammuz, Osiris, the early agrarian Mars, and the Middle-Eastern Baal, "the Lord," a consort of Astarte. At Astarte's temple in Byblos, the ear of grain had a special name, *shibboleth*, adopted by the Jews as a magical password (Judges 12:6). Because it was associated with pagan ceremonies, *shibboleth* later came to mean a false deity.

Eleusinian initiations involved certain secret "things seen, things heard, and things tasted," which suggests that the famous Three Monkeys covering eyes, ears, and mouth may have originated as a warning against pagan Mysteries. Christians specifically objected to the Eleusinian sex rites, an integral part of the Mysteries since time immemorial. Tertullian denounced "the whoredoms of Eleusis," and Asterius wrote:

> Is not Eleusis the scene of descent into the darkness, and of the solemn acts of intercourse between the hierophant and the priestess, alone together? Are not the torches extinguished, and does not the large, the numberless assembly of common people believe that their salvation lies in that which is being done by the two in the darkness?[12]

Certainly the people did so believe. The belief comforted them with a conviction of having been saved from final dissolution after death. The solemn acts of intercourse were said to bring about "regeneration and forgiveness of sins."[13] Pindar wrote, "Happy he that hath seen those rites ere he go beneath the earth; he knoweth life's consummation, he knoweth its divine source."[14]

Later Christian Gnostic sects practiced sexual sacraments for the same reasons. The Valentinians performed a "rite of spiritual marriage with angels in a nuptial chamber," the manifestations of which were as much physical as spiritual.[15] Members of this sect adopted the old god as a mythical St. Valentine, patron of lovers. His feast day developed from pagan orgies of the Lupercalia, in the month sacred to Juno February, the Goddess in her divine "fever" (*febris*) of sexual passion. After the ceremony she became a virgin once more, to reconceive her Divine Child. This pagan festival was appropriated by the Christian church in the late fifth century, and renamed the Festival of the Purification of the Virgin.[16]

The message conveyed by side-by-side virgin and sexual-maternal aspects of the Goddess was a message that patriarchal societies particularly rejected: that is, that the archetypal feminine spirit is never all one nor all the other, but like real women a cyclic combination of both. Patriarchal civilizations, especially Christian civilizations, insisted that females—mortal or supernatural—could only be "good' or "evil." The former was typified by the asexual divine Virgin, martyr, or nun; the latter by the lascivious she-devil, temptress, pagan "Love Goddess," as well as by the majority of ordinary women with normal sexual desires. Thus, most women were made to feel disgraced by their own physicality, in a way that most men were not. The pagan view was more realistic: the Goddess herself, and all women who embody her spirit, are both virginal/spiritual and sexual/maternal according to their own inner cycles, or at different periods in the same lifetime. The idea was that no aspect of the feminine archetype should be neglected, or favored at the expense of another. Most important (and most un-Christian), the Goddess was to be worshiped as much for her overwhelming sexuality as for any other facet of her complex being.

Despite the hostility of Christian authorities, people continued to worship the Eleusinian Goddess through the Christian era. Demeter was actively adored for a much longer time than the Judeo-Christian God. Her cult was already well established on a Mycenaean-Egyptian foundation before the thirteenth century B.C.[17] Greek peasants worshiped their Mistress of Earth and Sea, at Eleusis, all the way up to the nineteenth century A.D., when two Englishmen named Clarke and Cripps caused a riot by taking the Goddess's image for a museum in Cambridge.[18]

Though it was never made official, Demeter was informally canonized during the Middle Ages as St. Demetra, who had the power to give life to the dead—an echo of her old doctrine of reincarnation, which the new religion had pronounced heretical. The white dove of rebirth and the apples of eternal life belonged to her, as much as to her Syrian and pre-Hellenic twins, Aphrodite and Hera. Like her Phrygian counterpart Cybele, and her Hindu counterpart Kurukulla (Kali), Arcadian Demeter was also associated with caves and tombs. As queen of the underworld she was surnamed Melaina, the Black One, or Chthonia, the Subterranean One.[19] Sometimes she was called simply Daeira, "the Goddess."[20]

The many names of this archetypal Mother figure were only masks for the same monotheistic female deity, whose essential unity was revealed in the overlapping and interchangeability of her functions, no matter how the later scholars tried to classify her into a multitude of "goddesses." She made more than one appearance in the Tarot. Some interpreters have equated her with the *anima*, the female part of the soul, to which Jung assigned the function of creativity, directly evolved from the first formative experience of the mother. The *anima* was identified as timelessly wise, and symbolically connected with both female elements, earth and water.[21]

Like her virgin aspect the Papess, the Tarot Empress sometimes underwent revisions as a result of pressure from religious or political sources. During the post-revolutionary period in France, when imperial titles were in bad odor, she was renamed the Grandmother.[22] However, this was not as new as the French cardmakers believed. Grandmother had been another common title of the Great Goddess since the dawn of history.

4

The Emperor

4. *The Emperor*

Among the significant symbols of the Emperor were the following: (1) He showed only his left profile; (2) He crossed one leg over the other; (3) His shield bore an eagle, like that of the Empress; (4) He held a scepter in his right hand, an orb in his left.

The scepter and orb were male and female sexual symbols of great antiquity. Ancient kings displayed these symbols to demonstrate a union of male and female sacred principles in their own persons, imitating the manner in which Oriental gods united with various aspects of the Great Goddess to form a cosmic androgyne, male on the right half of the body, female on the left.[1] Therefore, the scepter was always in a king's right hand to show his own phallic power; the orb was always in his left hand as an emblem of his divine consort, Mother Earth.

The Brhadaranyaka Upanishad said the cosmic androgyne was "of the same size and kind as a man and a woman closely embracing," but other scriptures and icons described one bisexual body.[2] The Greeks' Eros, Phanes, and Hermaphroditus were similar bisexual entities, whose real power lay in their feminine attributes.[3] According to the Mithraic Mysteries—whose tenets deeply influenced the Gnostics—an emperor's right to rule was embodied in his Goddess under her name of Glory. Antiochus of Commagene accordingly declared himself ruler on the ground that his Goddess was part of him.[4] Perhaps for a similar reason, the Tarot Emperor displayed his left, "feminine" profile as he looked toward his Empress.

The ubiquitous left/female, right/male symbolism evolved very long ago, probably in southeastern Asia. Worshipers of Shiva said their god followed the Left-Hand Path, known as the Way of the Goddess.[5] In Egypt also, the left hand was the female hand, representing the Goddess Maat. The right hand represented her consort Thoth. Babylonians prayed that the Goddess might stand at one's left hand, the God at one's right.[6] Greek Pelopids tattooed a female sign on the left shoulder, a male sign on the right. Even Jewish tradition claimed that the left hand of God was female. The universal gesture of prayer was—and still is—to place the two hands together, originally a sign of the sexual sacrament, uniting male and female powers as male and female bodies unite face to face. However, Christian fathers maintained that one should not let the feminine hand know what the masculine hand was doing (Matthew 6:3).

Only recently has it been discovered that these ancient concepts may have had some basis in reality. The left side of the body seems to be controlled mostly by the brain's right hemisphere, to which are attributed traditionally feminine qualities of intuition, imagination, emotional understanding, perception, and response. Conversely, the right side of the body seems to be controlled by the hemisphere of reasoning and abstract thought, traditionally called conscious, or masculine. Of course, no individual, male or female, can be characterized as all one way or all the other; both halves of the brain always work together, so the modern notion of left and right sides of the personality may be as simplistic as the ancient one.

However, certainly during the Christian era everything connected with the left hand was anathematized, as shown by the very words for "left"—Latin *sinister*, French *gauche*, German *Linke*, meaning bad, wrong, or backward. Witches danced widdershins, to the left; made magical gestures with the left hand; and trod on the cross with the left foot, according to their inquisitors. Witches ignored the masculine Right-Hand Path of the sun, and followed the moon's leftward retrograde motion through the heavens.

The scepter in a ruler's right hand was based on Shiva's lightning-phallus, which also gave rise to the Tarot wand, rod, or club. Originally, the scepter held erect by Shiva had three prongs: it was a triple phallus to unite with the Triple Goddess. Shiva as a sexual god became known, therefore, as "the trident-bearer."[7]

The same trident was borne by western phallic gods like Jupiter, Neptune, Hades, Poseidon, Pluto, and Lucifer, the lightning-god of the New Testament. The Tarot Emperor similarly displayed his potency with a three-pronged scepter or a fleur-de-lis, sometimes called *fleur de luce*, "flower of light," said to represent a royal marriage, lightning, and the male fire element.[8] Mantegna Tarot cards showed the Emperor as Jupiter himself, with his whole figure set within a *mandorla*, that is, a double-pointed oval sign of the yoni, which yielded the earliest name of Jupiter's consort Juno, or Uni, Mother of the Uni-verse.[9]

In Christian times the trident was inherited by the devil. Lucifer was supposed to control lightning in his role of "Prince of the Power of the Air." Lucifer's lightning figured prominently on the Emperor's corresponding card in the spiritual sphere: the House of God, or Lightning-Struck Tower (Trump #16). If this card implied a prophecy of the Emperor's ultimate fate, traceable to the fourteenth-century prediction of the fall of the Holy Roman Empire, then it may have warned against excessive pride over a high position in the mundane world.[10] This was a common theme throughout the Tarot, and throughout Gnosticism generally.

The eagle on the Emperor's shield signified both his life and his death, according to the tradition of Roman emperors (Caesars), whose totem and title both were inherited by Germanic Holy Roman emperors (Kaisers). When a dead Caesar was cremated, an eagle was released above the pyre. This was supposed to be his imperial soul, flying to heaven to join his celestial brothers the gods.[11] Such an imperial apotheosis was the model for the Christian ceremony of canonization, at which a white dove was released to carry the beatified soul to heaven to join the angels.[12]

As a totemic form of masculine spirit, the eagle was associated with fire, lightning, and the sun. It was the bird of Jupiter, who was "made flesh" in the emperors. The corresponding imperial bird in Egypt was the Horus-hawk, a reincarnated spirit of Osiris. Some old Tarot decks showed this hawk on the Emperor's card, and one of his alternate names was Osiris.[13] The lightning and bird symbols appearing with the Emperor clearly attached him to the traditionally masculine elements, fire and air; whereas the Empress's fertile soil and waterfall equally clearly attached her to the traditionally feminine elements, earth and water. Here, and at many other points, Stoic doctrines of the paired elements permeated the Tarot.

The Emperor's crossed legs formed another sign of Jupiter, the older Heavenly Father wedded to the Earth Mother. Jupiter's sign was similar to the Hermetic 4: the number of the Emperor's card. This figure was traced as a Sign of the Cross on the heads and breasts of Hermes's worshipers, before it was adopted by Christians, who pretended it referred to Christ's cross. For many centuries previously, however, it had referred to the Hermetic cross, and in northern Europe to the Cross of Wotan.

The Emperor's crossed legs also recalled the Mithraic torchbearers of the sun: the Son of Morning with his legs crossed in one direction, the Son of Evening with his legs crossed in the other direction.[14] Formation of a cross with the legs was a crucial (cross-like) piece of Tarot symbolism, repeated on the card of the Hanged Man encountering his death, and again on the card of the World who appeared as the Lady of Life, or reincarnation.

Connection of the Emperor with cards of cyclic destruction and rebirth hinted at a recurrent Gnostic message: that material success and pride brought karmic retribution in the form of a fall. The Emperor enthroned was a god in his glory, securely wedded to the Empress who embraced his eagle shield, making him the husband of his land. Yet there were the usual indications that his potency would fail and his day of glory would end. Like the Hanged Man, he would face obliteration. Some Tarot decks showed the Emperor sitting before a vista of barren mountains. A flight of carrion crows suggested his inevitable end. So did his corresponding card, the lightning-struck phallic tower called

House of God (Trump #16). Sometimes "the Proud Tower" was taken as a description of the Holy Roman Empire.

An alternate title of the Emperor was Guardian of the Holy Grail.[15] This meant the lame Fisher King of the Grail cycle, to whom Wolfram von Eschenbach gave the name of Anfortas. At first the king's battle cry was *Amor* (Love). In the conflict between Christianity and paganism he was emasculated, and *Amor* ceased to guide him. Like the rest of the world he was left waiting for the Desired Knight to bring him salvation. And who was the desired Knight? According to the earliest versions of Grail mythology, it would be the initiate himself: Peredur/Perceval, who began his mystic journey as the Fool, and after many trials and dangers won the World.

Like the Empress, the Emperor was divested of his imperial title in post-revolutionary France and renamed the Grandfather. But he soon reverted to his original title, as Tarot interpreters continued to view him as a symbol of secular power.

5

The Pope

5. The Pope

The Tarot Pope is an especially enigmatic figure. He was surely not intended to suggest Christian orthodoxy. Those few scholars who equated him with the Roman pope did so with many reservations. "Writers interpreting the Pope as the card of established religion usually imply that the seeker after truth must look much deeper."[1] Symbolic significance has been seen in classical Tarot designs where the "pillars of the church" behind the Pope's throne support nothing at all.[2]

Numerically, the Pope was equated with the Devil (Trump #15), recalling the thirteenth-century Gnostic belief that the Jehovah of the Roman church was a demon, who made the material world only to trap souls in it. Some alternate designs for the Pope's card depicted various "gods of the heathen" which the church automatically defined as devils. French packs transformed the Pope into Jupiter, to match the Papess's Juno.[3] In other packs the Pope appeared as Bacchus, clothed in vine leaves, straddling a wine barrel, drinking from a bottle.[4] Bacchus was widely remembered and often worshiped in medieval Europe. Italian peasants still swear by him, saying the equivalent of "God's body" as "Corpo di Bacco." As late as the nineteenth century, German wine-growers still took omens for their harvest from Bacchus's ruined altar on an islet in the Rhine.[5]

Other names for the Tarot Pope, such as Grand Master or Gypsy Prince, suggest an association with magic.[6] Several real popes were known to occultists as masters of the black art, notably Leo III of *The Enchiridion*, and Honorius III, purported author of another grimoire, *The Constitution of Honorius*. Among its many magic charms, the *Constitution* gave the seventy-two secret names of God, whereby a practitioner of magic could work all sorts of miracles.[7] There was a general belief that the real popes' power rested on a carefully guarded knowledge of these secret names: a belief based on the ancient tradition of name magic, which evolved into the Christian dogma of the Logos (Divine Word).

From the earliest times, priests of India and Egypt pretended to control their gods by spoken mantras containing the gods' secret names. Mohammedans likewise thought Allah would be forced to answer any prayer if his ninety-nine secret names were pronounced.[8] In the same way, Christians thought a priest could compel God to do whatever was asked, by using his secret names in a special Mass of the Holy Spirit.[9]

Such notions about the verbal powers of ecclesiastics were natural developments of the church's own doctrine of the keys. It was claimed that each pope inherited the keys to heaven and hell, perhaps in the form of secret words or symbols, given to Peter by Jesus. The keys guaranteed God's response to anything the popes wanted: blessings or curses, absolution or anathema.[10] "Whatsoever thou shalt bind on earth shall be bound in heaven: and whatsoever thou shalt loose on earth shall be loosed in heaven" (Matthew 16:19).

Actually, the doctrine of the keys existed long before Christianity. It was common to most pagan mystery religions. A high priest often impersonated the celestial key-holder at the gates of heaven. Roman Mithraists had a supreme pontiff called Pater Patri (Father of Fathers), who held the keys to heaven and hell.[11] Christian popes took over both his keys and his title, which was gradually corrupted into *papa*, then *pope*.[12] The name Peter was another variant of the priestly title.

"Jesus did not institute Peter the head of his Church, he did not 'found the papacy.' "[13] The so-called Petrine passage of Matthew 16 was a forgery, inserted at a late date to uphold the primacy of the Roman See against the rival claims of Constantinople. Byzantine patriarchs had adopted their own apostle, Andrew (from Greek *andros*, "man"), claiming that he was the first of Christ's followers, the elder brother of Peter, and the first apostle to be martyred.[14] For these reasons, they said, the Byzantine church must be considered the true papacy. The legend that Andrew was crucified on an X-shaped cross was not of Byzantine origin. It didn't appear until the late Middle Ages, apparently from northern Europe, perhaps as a confused re-interpretation of the Cross of Wotan.[15]

Deeper investigation of the Roman legend of Peter finds the curious tradition of a Peter, Petra, or Pater acting as keeper of the keys of the afterworld, centuries before the Christian era. The etymological relationship of the words for "father" and "rock" *(petra)* had a common source in the phallic pillar of stone, planted in the Vatican mount, where Christian mythology later located the upside-down cross of St. Peter.[16] Even before there was a Rome, an Etruscan high priest called *vatis* guarded the gate of this sacred mount. The "peter" or *petra* seems to have been the phallus of Ju-piter (Ju-pater), "Holy Begetter," derived from the ancient Aryan god Dyaus Pitar.

There were other manifestations of this "rock of ages." Egyptians knew an obelisk spirit called Petra, perhaps the same rock pillar worshiped by Edomites at the holy city of Petra. In the Bible, this deity was "the Rock that begat thee" (Deuteronomy 32:18).[17]

St. Peter's upside-down cross may have been derived from a symbol of the heaven-father's *petra* coming down to fertilize the womb of Mother Earth. The pointed crown of an obelisk or phallic pillar was inverted as the god descended. An inverted *petra* formed the bridge between heaven and earth, which pagan Rome identified with its sacred Palladium, sometimes called the Scepter of Priam, "in the likeness of a male sex organ."[18] The priest called Pontifex Maximus (Great Bridge-Builder) was charged with sexual rituals uniting the male spirit of the Palladium with the female spirit of the Vestal altar.[19] Such priests wore the conical hat called *apex,* which evolved into the pope's pointed tiara; thus, scholars now say "the Pope's tiara is phallic."[20] There is reason to suspect that Vatican authorities even preserved a more graphic representation of the phallic *petra*-god through the centuries. A Victorian visitor in the nineteenth century said the Vatican priests "kept in secret a large stone emblem of the creative power, of a very peculiar shape."[21]

Thus, it seems likely that the Christian legend of St. Peter's foundation of the Roman church had no basis in historical fact, but was grafted onto an older tradition of the masculine spirit of Rome. It may be that the Tarot Pope represented at least a part of that older tradition, however inaccurately remembered. In pagan terminology the pope was the *eidolon,* "image of the god," like high priests of old. It is interesting that some modern Tarot packs changed the Pope's title to High Priest or Hierophant—the same title that distinguished the man chosen to mate with Demeter in the Eleusinian Mysteries, or to impersonate Osiris in the Mysteries of Isis.[22] Common folk usually saw a high priest as an embodiment of the deity.

The link between the Pope and the Devil in Tarot symbolism could have descended from the legends of several Roman popes said to have attained their office by making a pact with the devil.[23] Medieval folk seemed to see no incongruity in assuming that the papal throne was at the devil's disposal. Perhaps the devil's most famous papal protégé was Gerbert de Aurillac, who became Pope Silvester II. Gerbert grew up in a tenth-century France still saturated with Dianic fairy-religion, and may have belonged once to a group who worshiped Diana Silvia. Even as pope, it was said, he had a fairy mistress named Meridiana (Mary-Diana), who taught him the secrets of magic.[24] The name he chose as pope used to be a title of consorts of Diana Silvia.

The truth about Pope Silvester was that he was more intelligent and learned than most of his ecclesiastical contemporaries, whose custom it was to attribute diabolical influence to anything that was beyond their ken. "The list of great men in those centuries charged with magic . . . is astounding; it includes every man of real mark, and in the midst of them stands one of the most thoughtful popes, Silvester II (Gerbert). . . . It came to be the accepted idea that, as soon as a man conceived a wish to study the works of God, his first step must be a league with the devil."[25]

Out of all these possibilities, who really contributed most to the Tarot image of the Pope? Was it Silvester? Honorius? Leo? Jupiter? Bacchus? Osiris? The pagan *petra?* The Mithraic Pater? The Pontifex who became a "pontiff"? The devil? Interpretations are largely a matter of choice. One can only guess at the lessons learned in the thirteenth century from this strange portrait of a holy man.

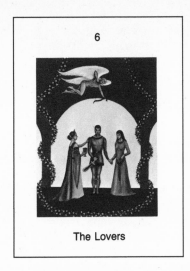

6

The Lovers

6. *The Lovers*

On a Tantric Wheel of Life, the sixth picture showed two lovers kissing. The meaning of the picture was *Sparsa*, "contact," a first encounter of self and other. The next picture was *Vedana*, "feeling," awakening awareness through the senses, symbolized by an arrow entering a man's eye.[1]

The sixth picture of the Major Arcana also showed a pair of lovers, with the love-god aiming his arrow at them. Early Gringonneur cards showed a man and woman kissing, while divine *amoretti* aimed arrows of love at other couples in a pageant or procession.[2]

These pictures gave a message typical of Tantric philosophy: only through physical union with a female can either a man or a god achieve true "contact" with reality, and the power to deal with it. "Women are Devas" (Goddesses), said the Tantric sages; "women are life itself."[3] The Goddess represented the real world under her title of Bhavani, "Existence." A man or god remained incomplete until he united himself with her spirit in his life-stage of Bhavanan, "husbandship."[4] For the enlightened man, life meant a search for the Goddess, who could be apprehended only through *Vedana*. The poet Ramaprasada said, "By feeling is She known. How then can lack of feeling find Her?"[5]

Mystics throughout the world held similar opinions of the importance of female influence in a sage's life. The Sufis maintained that every man needed a female *fravashi* or "Spirit of the Way," equivalent of a Tantric sage's *Shakti*. She was each man's Qis-Mah, a ladylove sent by the Moon (Mah). Her title was corrupted by the Turks to *kismet*, or "Fate."

Orphics said each man must embrace his Dike or "Fate" as a beloved woman, like Orpheus's own Eurydike, whose name meant "Universal Fate" like the Tantric spirit of karma. The novice on the Orphic bowl met his Dike in a form like that of a fairy queen, who touched him with her magic wand to open his eyes to the reality of life.[6]

It was a general rule in the East that shamans, priests, sages, and other holy men required a spiritual/sexual marriage before they could come into full possession of their powers. "An important division of the 'mythology of woman' is devoted to showing that it is always a feminine being who helps the hero to conquer immortality or to emerge victorious from his initiatory ordeals." Like medicine men of the American Indians, the Brahman, Israelite, and Roman priests also had to attain their spiritual authority through marriage. Rome's high priest, the Flamen Dialis, kept office only as long as he was married to the Flaminica, high priestess of Juno. If she should die, he immediately lost his position and status.[8]

Such customs could be traced to the old idea of sacred marriage, whereby a man, king, or god developed his powers through sexual union. King Solomon thus united himself to Ishtar-Astarte through her priestess, who was called the Shulamite in the wedding songs still preserved in the Bible. Through powers thus acquired, Solomon received 666 talents of gold in a year (1 Kings 10:14). This was not a real number but a magic number, listed elsewhere in the Bible as the famous "number of the Beast" (Revelation 13:18).

The 666-Beast was originally the beast with two backs, or Primal Androgyne, said to resemble a man and woman in sexual union.[9] Like the hexagram it described, 666 was a sexual charm sacred to triple Aphrodite (Astarte). Pythagorean mystics called her number 6 the perfect number, or The Mother. In Latin, six was *sex*, in Egyptian *sexen*, meaning to embrace, to copulate. A derivative Egyptian word *seshemu*, "sexual intercourse," had as its hieroglyph a phallus inserted into an arched yoni-gate.[10] The word was repeated in Sufi love rituals and became the magic charm that opened the gate of the secret uterine cavern in Arabic fairy tales—that is, Open, Sesame. Hence the number 6, *sex*, which Christian authorities called the number of sin, was especially appropriate to the sixth Tarot trump with its message of love.[11]

In the Middle Ages, the church poured scorn on the religion of love, though it was practiced by half-pagan *minne*singers and *min*strels who worshiped the Goddess as Minne, or "Love." One wrote of her: "She resembles nothing imaginable. Her name is known; her self, ungrasped. . . . She comes never to a false heart."[12] For each man, she was incarnate in his ladylove. But the priests and monks protested against "the vile condition of lovers who, forgetting God, make a divinity of the woman they love." Instead of loving God, they said, the bards "sinfully love women, whom they make into deities . . . whosoever adores them, doth certainly adore Satan, and make a god of the most disloyal devil."[13] Grunewald's ugly painting, *The Damnation of Lovers*, graphically demonstrated the horrible fate of couples guilty of the crime of love, which celibate monks chose to describe as an offense in the eyes of God.[14]

It was not just adulterous love that churchmen disliked, but marriage too. Believing in the need for universal celibacy to bring about salvation, early Christian fathers opposed marriage as "a polluted and foul way of life."[15] Tertullian called marriage a moral crime, "more dreadful than any punishment or any death."[16] Origen said, "Matrimony is impure and unholy, a means of sexual passion." St. Jerome declared that the chief purpose of a man of God should be to destroy the institution of marriage.[17]

For the first half of the Christian era, marriage was not a Christian sacrament. Scholars say the wedding ceremony was "imposed on" a reluctant church, and "nothing is more remarkable than the tardiness with which liturgical forms for the marriage ceremony were evolved."[18] Only in the thirteenth century A.D. did it become possible for Catholic priests to bless a newly married couple. Even then, the "pollution" of marriage had to be kept outside the church. The blessing was allowed only *in facie ecclesiae*—on the steps of the church, outside the door.[19]

Churchmen objected to the ceremony of marriage because by a centuries-old tradition, that ceremony was handled by priestesses of the Goddess who governed every phase of human love: sexual union, conception and gestation, birth, nursing, and maternal care. The trappings of a wedding are still largely pagan to this day, even though Christian churches have adopted them. "The religious service of the church is intrusive, no real part of the ceremony of marriage, but an elaborate way of calling down a blessing on the ceremonial, or what is left of it, which constitutes the real wedding."[20]

In pre-Christian times, the real wedding was the one performed by a priestess or tribal wise-woman. Minnesingers' romances told of lovers united by an elder woman—sometimes a nurse or a healing sorceress, typical bardic transformations of the priestess. The famous lovers Tristan and Iseult were brought together by the sorceress Brangwain, actually none other than the Goddess Branwen, who kept the Cauldron of Regeneration.[21] Female jurisdiction over marriage was usual among the gypsies, whose weddings included exchanges of blood, and witch ceremonies like jumping over the broomstick. Couples were instructed in their marital duties by an elder priestess dedicated to the moon.[22]

Though the Tarot card showed a young couple facing an older woman, who appeared to be speaking to them, or blessing them with an upraised hand, and though the card was often plainly entitled "Marriage," male interpreters usually refused to perceive the scene as a wedding, because the officiating elder was female.[23] Some strained interpretations have been drawn from this card to avoid the obvious one. It has been claimed that the card of the Lovers shows a man making a difficult choice between wife and mother, or between virtue and vice, or between passion and conscience.[24]

Yet, as symbols of an initiation, the Tarot trumps would have to include a marriage. Romance literature and Oriental beliefs showed that a sacred marriage was necessary to the initiate at the sixth stage of *Vedana*. The system was recognizable in Europe as well as in the East. Perceval spent his early years as a rustic Fool, then he began to learn the secrets of chivalry under the tutelage of his ladylove, Blanchefleur (White Flower). She was so greatly disliked by Christian monks that they claimed she was the devil's bride, and the mother of Antichrist.[25]

There is little doubt that Blanchefleur was a western version of the *Shakti*, a concept once known as well in the northwestern corner of the Eurasian continent as in the southeastern one. The older version of Perceval, Peredur of the Welsh folk epic, was instructed by his fairy ladylove whose home was India and whose colors were the sacred *gunas* of the Great Shakti: white, red, black. The oldest known Saxon folk epic, *Beowulf*, said India was the home of the Saxon Easter-goddess, Eostre, who was also Astarte, and strongly resembled triple Kali.[26]

Another correspondence between the Tarot and Tantric symbolism, too exact to be merely coincidental, is shown by numerical connection between the card of the Lovers and that of the angel Temperance (Trump #14), pouring her waters from one jar into another. Tantric sages said an ideal sexual union, blessed by the deity of love, merged the lovers as completely as "the pouring of water into water."[27] The angel Temperance therefore represented a spiritual ideal of earthly lovers.

Some Tarot interpreters have taken the name of Temperance in the modern sense of "moderation." But that was not its meaning seven centuries ago. It came from the Latin *temperare*, "to mix or combine elements." Another derivative was *temperament*, the particular mixture of the four elements that created any given personality, and guided knowledgable lovers to merge themselves with those of compatible temperament.[28] As an earthly representative of the element-mingling angel, the wise-woman would have helped lovers to find one another.

7. The Chariot

7

The Chariot

The seventh trump was alternatively named The Charioteer, or The Triumphal Car, or The King in Triumph.[1] In traditional designs it showed a young hero riding high, apparently successful in both love and battle, raised to the seventh degree of initiation—or, newly arrived at the peak of full, early manhood at the age of twenty-one, according to the Yoni Yantra layout. With its four pillars and its blue canopy spangled with stars, the Chariot clearly represented the world.[2] The hero seemed to be in command of it. Paralleling the experience of life itself, the Tarot made a place for young-adult arrogance, in a brief moment of conviction that some sort of paradise had been attained, following the card of marriage.

In consequence of his marriage, Kali's consort Shiva attained the character of Jagannatha, "Lord of the World." His world was envisioned as a gigantic chariot, rolling along the track of time. Great Tantric temples were built at Khajuraho and Konarak to represent this world chariot, wheels and all.[3] During the god's annual triumphal procession, his image was enthroned on another enormous chariot drawn by his worshipers, some of whom sought a martyr's death by throwing themselves under its ponderous wheels. From this Hindu practice of self-sacrifice came the English word Juggernaut, a corrupted form of the chariot-god's title.[4]

The Lord of the World stood for a transitory earthly glory. Like every Oriental god-king, he was doomed to the inevitable fall after his day of pride. Another cycle of death and resurrection would follow his triumph. This could be the reason for numerical correspondence between the Tarot Chariot and the card of Death (Trump #13). It was thought necessary that a hero should be mindful of his karmic debt even at the pinnacle of his glory. Death lurked in the background.

Though Oriental courtiers piously greeted their rulers with the formula, "O King, live for ever," everyone knew the king must die. The practical Romans never tried to disguise even a ruler's mortality. When a Roman hero was honored in his triumphal parade, a masked figure of Death stood at his shoulder in the chariot, whispering in his ear, "Man, remember you are mortal."[5]

The prototypical Roman hero-charioteer was the god Mars, son of the Blessed Virgin Juno. The twelfth-century *Liber Imaginum Deorum* said Mars in his chariot symbolized leadership, glory, war, and death.[6] Rome's Mars was a late development of a much older Sabine fertility god, born of the famous Capitoline trinity of Juventas-Juno-Minerva, killed each year to be resurrected like all other vegetation gods. He in turn might be traced back to the pre-Vedic "red god" Rudra, entitled Tryambaka, "He Who Belongs to Three Mother Goddesses." In his native land, Rudra merged with both Shiva and Krishna, who expounded the secrets of Fate to Prince Arjuna in the guise of a divine charioteer.[7] That the secrets of Fate involved a consciousness of death was already documented as early as the third millenium B.C. in Akkad, halfway between India and Europe. There, the road to death was called either "the road of no-return" or "the road of the chariot."[8]

Red chariot-riding heroes who passed from high glory to a martyr's death frequently personified the sun, as in Greek myths of Hippolytus, Phaethon, and Helios. People of northern Europe called the rider of the Sun Chariot Njord, "the first god of the Swedes, before Odin brought other deities from Asia."[9] Njord represented the declining sun in the latter half of the year, while his alter ego Frey signified the waxing sun of the first half. Together, Njord and Frey were the *blotgodar*, "blood-gods," alternately sacrificing each other, like Horus and Set in Egypt. Each year at Yuletide, when Frey was reborn during the twelve days of the winter solstice, it was taboo for any person to allow chariot wheels to roll for any reason.[10] Aryan sacred kings from India to Ireland were assimilated to the divine chariot rider. Even their titles showed a common source: Vedic *raj*, "king," was the same as Latin *reg* or *rex*, Celtic *rig*, Frankish *roi*.[11]

Pagan riders of the Sun Chariot merged with the sacred King of the Wood in the Breton cult of Diana Nemetona, and entered the realm of romance in Chretien de Troyes's famous poem, *Le Chevalier de la Charrette* (The Knight of the Chariot). As in all romances, the drama allegorized religious beliefs that had been forbidden, and grafted them onto a tale of courtly love.

According to the Platonic idea set forth in the *Phaedrus* and disseminated by medieval scholars, the charioteer represented the human soul. Heavenly charioteers rode the celestial airs until they lost their winged vehicles and fell to earth to be born as human beings. Then "comes the imprisonment in the body until Eros gives the souls strength enough to make a new ascent."[12] Oriental philosophers often referred to the soul (or mind) as the body's charioteer, and to sensual desires as its horses.[13] On a macrocosmic scale, the Great God Jagannatha is the Oversoul riding the chariot of the world-body. According to the Katha Upanishad, the horses of desire must be firmly reined in by the inner charioteer.[14] The true sage is one "who has controlled the senses, is a truth-seeker, ever engaged in worship, and who has sacrificed lust and all other passions."[15] Carl Jung also pointed out that in the symbolism of dreams and fantasy, horses usually represent uncontrollable emotional drives.[16]

The horses of the Tarot Chariot merit some close study. Always of two contrasting colors, like day and night, they were sometimes recognizable horses, sometimes doglike animals like the lunar death-dogs, sometimes sphinxes with female breasts, sometimes a strange two-headed creature with four forelegs and no hind legs, facing opposite directions like a pushme-pullyou. This may have been a copy of the Egyptian hieroglyph for *xerefu* and *akeru*, "the Lions of Yesterday and Today."[17] The secret meaning of this was that Mother Hathor, the Sphinx, governed the passage of Time, and in this guise always devoured heroes no matter how glorious or "timeless" their earthly deeds seemed to make them.

Oddly enough, the Tarot charioteer seldom drove his chariot. Most packs showed him without reins. He simply stood erect in his vehicle while his beasts went their own ways, heading in opposite directions as if they would eventually tear the chariot apart. The message may have been a corollary to the message of the Death card: man is not in control of his Fate, even when he thinks he is.

Oriental sages continually emphasized the futility of pride in earthly glories, which were only a hand dealt by Fate (karma), soon to be replaced. A proud hero had yet to attain the wisdom of the "true self," which could realize the inexorable turning of the karmic wheel, as unstoppable as a Juggernaut chariot. "He who has seen his true self looks down upon transmigrating existence as upon a rolling chariot-wheel."[18]

During the Renaissance in Europe, pageants and parades were staged in the same manner as the ancient Roman triumph, to display celebrities riding in chariots along with allegorical figures of mythological origin. Sometimes, instead of promenading through public streets for the admiration of the masses, a chariot procession was organized as private entertainment for the inhabitants of a castle. Decorated chariots moved around and around a central courtyard, to be viewed from inner windows. This was known as a *carrousel*, "a round of chariots."[19]

Like many other pagan symbols, the carrousel passed into carnival customs and became a plaything for children. Today its chariots are stationary on a turntable; its horses are mechanical. It is also called a merry-go-round. But its deeper meaning was not so merry when derived from visions of the turning wheels of Fate.

To occupy the Chariot is no longer a Siege Perilous, yet the Tarot message is not inappropriate for modern heroes. As the subsequent trump cards made clearer and clearer, the newly married aspirant to worldly success must take care that the "road of the chariot" does not lead to hell.

8

Justice

8. Justice

After the transitory glory of the Chariot ride, the Major Arcana presented a rather grim figure: the Goddess Justice, balancing pleasures against pains in her scale, apparently demanding payment of a karmic debt.

Oriental sages said life's pleasures usually come before its pains; but the greater the glory, the deeper must be the corresponding atonement. From this notion of karmic balance arose the Gnostic precept traditionally associated with Lucifer, that pride must precede a fall. Though men might feel themselves to be gods, yet the Goddess of Fate, under her varying names, exacted just compensation for her gifts. It was precisely those who rode highest in the world-chariot who must eventually endure the most painful sacrifice; "for every action an equal and opposite reaction."[1] Such was the karmic law.

The Gnostic view of Justice with her balances was essentially the same as the Oriental view of the Fate-goddess who worked out the karmic laws. She appeared in classic Greek philosophies under various names, such as Dike (Justice), Ananke (Necessity), Nemesis (Retribution) and Heimarmene (Allotted Fate). These were not abstract principles but a firmly personified Goddess figure in each case, worshiped as a Mother of both generation and destruction—that ubiquitous birth-and-death Goddess whose character has been so thoroughly eradicated from Western imagery. Stoic philosophers regarded her as the ruler of the entire universe, a creator and destroyer of the very gods themselves. Orphics accepted this opinion of her and also declared that her spouse was Chronos (Time), in whose realm the principles of justice inevitably acted, sooner or later. The whole creation was subject to the manipulations of the Goddess from whom nothing could be concealed.[2]

The inexorable lady of Fate or Justice was older than Stoic philosophy. She appeared early in the cultures of Egypt, Babylon, and Phoenicia. To the Egyptians she was Maat, the Mother, whose name was synonymous with Truth or Justice.[3] In her balances, a man's heart-soul *(ab)* was weighed against her symbol, the Feather of Truth. A man who was "weighed in the balances and found wanting," as the Bible translated the Egyptian phrase (Daniel 5:27), would be consumed in the underworld by the Goddess's Destroyer aspect, a monster called *Am-Mut*, the "devourer of hearts."[4]

West of Egypt, Phoenician/Carthaginian worshipers of Astarte established societies having the same concept of the Goddess's retributive duality. As Astraea the Starry One, she was the Virgin Queen of Heaven associated with the constellation Erigone (Virgo), accompanied by the black bitch Maera, her Fury-like "dog of the law."[5] In Homeric myth, Maera was the spirit of retribution embodied in the Trojan queen Hecuba or Hecabe, who was Hecate as Moon-goddess "made flesh." After Hecuba's death, her soul appeared as Maera and terrified her Greek murderers, who greatly feared their victim's curse of vengeance.[6]

Romans knew the Carthaginian Queen of Heaven as the Mother of Libya, or Libera, presiding deity of the Liberalia festival. Her consort was Bacchus, titled Father Liber.[7] Her name was sometimes rendered Libra. She became the astrological Lady of the Scales, holding her balance and sword, as she was shown by the Tarot. The astrological version of Libra was always associated with Venus, another Latin title of the same Goddess.[8]

An ancient stele from the site of Carthage showed the Goddess in conjunction with her figure-eight symbol of "perfect equilibrium," which became the infinity sign, as well as the numeral given to Justice's Tarot card.[9] Perhaps the appearance of the same symbol on Trump #11, Strength, contributed to the confusion between the two cards, which led the Golden Dawn Society to transpose them in certain Tarot packs. From a Gnostic viewpoint, Justice made more sense in her original #8 position, between the brash hero of the Chariot (#7) and the lonely Hermit (#9) starting his solitary pilgrimage. In sequence, the three cards strongly suggested the typical Oriental idea that, after the period of *bhavanan*—husbandship and worldly success—karmic law demanded that a man should renounce his material possessions before any fatal retribution could fall on his family. He should go alone into the wilderness to fast and meditate. Thus he might pass into a more spiritual stage of life and acquire the enlightenment of deeper maturity—which seemed to be the basis for the Hermit's card.

The card of Justice was also known as the Judge, Ma (Maat), or Mary Magdalene.[10] The appearance of Mary Magdalene in Tarot tradition may have been a result of the Gnostic opinion that she, not St. Peter, was the true pope who received spiritual power directly from Jesus, and transmitted it to her Gnostic disciples. *The Dialogue of the Savior* called her "the woman who knew the All," and said her wisdom, vision, and insight surpassed all the male apostles.[11] *The Gospel of Mary* equated her with the Virgin Queen of Heaven as a trinitarian Goddess figure, saying all three Marys of the Gospels were one and the same. In Jesus's words, she was "Mariham the Happy, heiress of the Kingdom of Light."[12] Other Gnostic writings called her the "primal feminine power," the first and the last, the whore and the holy one, the wife and the virgin, the mother and daughter.[13] Medieval Christians, honoring her as a saint, made her yet another transformation of the pagan Great Mother by claiming that she governed all wisdom, love, birth, and death. She ruled the earth's production of food, and could restore life to the dead.[14] Therefore, the scales she held meant the same as the similar scales in the hand of many earlier Goddess figures: she controlled the balances of Fate and meted out Justice.

According to more recent representations of Justice in Western iconography, she wore a blindfold. The origin of this is obscure. It may have been an ecclesiastical addition, implying that the Goddess's judgments were blindly arbitrary or unenlightened. However, the Tarot agreed with earlier images. Her card showed Justice with the straight, piercing, All-Seeing Eye that used to be attributed to Maat.

That a female should be the natural judge of men's activities was a profoundly ancient idea, dating back to the matriarchal Neolithic, or perhaps even earlier—to a time when women chose their mates, like other female animals, by critically assessing men's performance in tasks or contests. The oldest mythologies show the original Tablets of Law given on mountaintops by the Goddess, not by the God as depicted in the Bible. Sumerians said Mother Tiamat, the Creatress, gave the Tablets of Law to her firstborn son Kingu, the first Lord of the World, whose sacrificial blood nourished future generations.[15] The Aegean Great Mother Demeter, under her older name of Rhea Dictynna (Rhea the Lawgiver), dictated her edicts to Minoan kings from Mt. Dicte, her holy mountain of the Word.[16] She long remained the supreme arbiter of law under the title of Nemesis or "Due Enactment."[17]

Tribal matriarchs were the judges in pre-patriarchal Israel (Judges 4:4), and also in pre-Christian Europe until the church usurped their authority and began to call them witches. Yet, they retained their judicial function for a long time. The Magna Carta of Chester mentioned *iudices de Wich*—justices or judges who were also witches.[18] That is, they were the "wise-women" descended from the tribal matriarch. Up to the Renaissance, the figure of Justice was still synonymous with Astraea-Erigone. The poet Filelfo called her "that royal and great Goddess by whom cities and empires are preserved in pride; without her no kingdom can long endure."[19]

9. The Hermit

9

The Hermit

Tantric tradition taught that the secular life of marriage and worldly affairs *(grihastha)* should be followed by a compensatory life of seclusion and meditation *(vanaprastha)*.[1] During this latter period, a wise man must confront the concept of oncoming death, and meet the spirits who would eventually take his soul on its fatal journey.

Greek Orphics taught the same doctrine. From their "little Hermes" came the word *hermit*, for Hermes was the spirit who conducted men's souls to their proper resting places. Those who were properly taught, and meditated on the right Mysteries, would become like the god himself, and would be welcomed by Persephone to "the seats of the Hallowed."[2] Christians had much the same notion of a holy hermit's shortcut to heaven, though they substituted "a seat at the right hand of God" for the one offered by Persephone.

The Tarot Hermit always seemed to be starting a journey, in the opposite direction to that of the Fool. Like Hermes he carried a staff, sometimes in the form of a Hermetic caduceus. Often he was led by the Hermetic serpent.[3] Numbered ninth in the Major Arcana—the crucial number of the Muses who gave inspiration—and poised to enter the second, lunar sphere, the Hermit seemed to be starting a journey into the inner world of the unconscious and the mystical. His numerological counterpart, the Goddess of Strength (Trump #11), stood for the inner strength of the solitary seeker after his own *I-dea*, literally the Inner Goddess, a classical term for the Shakti.

It has always been the custom of seers, sages, shamans, saviors, mages, prophets, and other holy men to spend some time in solitude, preferably in a wilderness, often in a pit or cave symbolizing the womb of spiritual rebirth. "Religious and mythical symbolism has countless images for introversion: e.g., dying, going down, subterranean crypts, vaults, dark temples, into the underworld, hell, the sea, etc.; being swallowed by a monster or fish (as Jonah), stay in the wilderness, etc."[4] Jung noted that there may be sound psychological reasons for such isolation and inversion. It "results as a rule in the animation of the psychic atmosphere, as a substitute for loss of contact with other people. It causes an activation of the unconscious."[5]

Even Christian Gospels recorded a period of ascetic isolation for both John the Baptist and Jesus—both of whom, scholars believe, belonged to an Essenic cult. Extended meditation in the wilderness was an initiatory rule among the Essenes, who also had in each of their groups a functionary called "Christ" or "Teacher of Righteousness," trained to bear painful punishments in the role of scapegoat for the sins of others.[6]

Eastern yogis also trained themselves to bear physical trials such as hunger, thirst, and bodily immobility or even mutilation, to overcome physical desires and heighten inner awareness. They often used techniques of controlled breathing, as is still suggested by the word *inspiration*—literally, "breathing-in a spirit." Having the spirit within was known to the Greeks as *enthousiasmos*, "divinity-within," a kind of possession. Of course, when the Christian church ruled that all the old gods who used to cause *enthousiasmos* were demons, then the same *inspiration* was viewed as demonic possession. Group *enthousiasmos* was still common in the present century among such groups as the Shakers or Holy Rollers, camp-meeting frenzies, or the ceremonies of voodoo.

The Tarot Hermit was often identified with Diogenes, a famous yogi type of sage who lived in a large earthen pot at the door of the Great Mother's temple. With his lantern, it was said, Diogenes constantly searched for one honest man. The real reason for his search was seldom included in the Greek legend. His sectaries, the Cynics, taught that the end of the world would come when there was not one honest man left among the living. As long as one honest man yet remained, doomsday might be postponed. There are indications that the Essenes taught the same doctrine.

In Greece, the "hermits" of Hermes were said to practice ritual masturbation, which Hermes invented, as another technique of self-contemplation in search of the god within the self. Similarly in India, many autoerotic practices were attributed to Krishna as the god of self-love. Pagans and Orientals often believed that masturbation purified the body, as opposed to the Christian view that it was a sin and a "pollution."[7] Some scholars accordingly interpreted the Hermetic caduceus as a phallic symbol of masturbation—the almost inevitable practice of any solitary man—and also to link this meaning with the Tarot Hermit.[8]

At times, the sage's autoeroticism was supposed to represent sacred marriage with his spirit-wife or Shakti: a sexual union with his own soul or with his Goddess. The reason most commonly advanced for a sage's celibate life was that, having tasted the love of a Goddess, he was forever unable to enjoy the lesser charms of ordinary women.[9]

This notion too was repeated in Christian tradition. Monks claimed to make themselves bridegrooms of the Virgin Mary, by giving a wedding ring to her image.[10] Just as the Cyprian priest Pygmalion married the statue of Aphrodite-Galatea, so Breton Black Friars continued to marry the Queen of Heaven up to the late fifteenth century. Brother Alain de la Roche described his own wedding with Mary. Before a crowd of "angels," she presented him with a ring made of her own hair.[11]

Christian female ascetics were styled "brides of Christ," because the nuns copied the Roman Vestal Virgins who were *amatae*, "loved ones," of the masculine spirit of Rome, embodied in the priapic Palladium.[12] In a number of ways, sexuality and spirituality have always been more closely related than patriarchal religions like to admit. On hearing the confessions of nuns who claimed to have copulated with Christ, priests sometimes inconsistently declared such women demon-possessed. But in view of the church's own teaching, the premise was logical enough.

Spirit-wives of Tantric sages were supposed to come from the ranks of the Dakinis of the Intermediate State. These death angels could be beautiful fairies who gently carried their lovers into heavenly bliss; or, they could be fearsome, devouring succubae. The Tantric *Bardo Thodol* displayed a remarkable flash of insight by saying all the spirits of the death world are one's own mental projections:

> May I recognize whatever appeareth as being mine own thought-forms,
> May I know them to be apparitions in the Intermediate State. . . .
> Fear not the bands of the Peaceful and Wrathful, Who are thine own thought-forms.[13]

If the Hermit seemed about to plunge into the nether world of the unconscious, he was certain to encounter many of his own thought-forms, even if they hid behind conventionalized symbolism. The freedom of interpretation allowed by Tarot symbols left plenty of room for the pre-verbal, mythographic language of any individual to make its own statement. Some have claimed that this is the whole secret of the Tarot. Like contemplation in the wilderness hermitage, solitary contemplation of the Tarot could lead to new kinds of insight.

10

The Wheel of Fortune

10. The Wheel of Fortune

Fortune's Wheel came from a Latin title of the Triple Goddess as ruler of Fate, derived from an earlier Etruscan Great Mother, Vortumna, "She Who Turns the Year."[1] Like Kali, Fortuna-Vortumna personified all the cycles of Time and Being. Her virgin form was Fortuna Primigeneia, "who bestows on her worshippers every grace of body and every beauty of soul." Her mother form was Bona Fortuna or Bona Dea, "the Good Goddess." Her crone form was Mala Fortuna, the Destroyer, who took every man sooner or later.[2] At her Esquiline temple, the Goddess was represented by an all-seeing eye in the shape of a wheel.[3]

As in other ancient societies, the Goddess was the foundation of ruling power in Rome, in this capacity known as Fortuna Augusti or Fortuna Regia, the "Fate of kingship"—a translation of Greek *Tyche Basileos*. Every Caesar had a golden image of the Goddess with him at all times, even sleeping or traveling. The people swore oaths by the emperor's Fortuna.[4] Romans believed odd numbers were sacred to Fortuna, so they scheduled religious ceremonies only on odd-numbered days, because these were more propitious.[5]

A worldwide symbol of the Goddess Fortuna was the wheel of time, originally derived from the heavenly star-wheel that marked earth's seasons and cycles: the Milky Way. Most mythologies said this heavenly wheel was made of milk from the breasts of the universal birth-giver. Greeks claimed the Milky Way spurted from the breasts of Hera; the very word "galaxy" came from the Greek *gala*, "mother's milk."[6] Italian *latte*, "milk," came from Lat, or Latona, the Mother Goddess of ancient Latium. Arabs called her Al-Lat, the Moon, and later masculinized her name to Allah. One of Egypt's oldest shrines, Latopolis, was dedicated to her as "an archaic queen."[7] Egyptians called her shrine Menhet, "House of the Moon."[8] About 3000 B.C. the Two Kingdoms of Egypt were combined under a ruler named Mena, whom scholars chose to call the first pharaoh. But "his" name meant Moon, having the hieroglyphic sign of a female breast.[9]

In other words, it was found everywhere that the Goddess of the heavenly star wheel ruled Time and Fate, whether she was called Lat,

Fortuna, Vortumna, Hera, Isis, Mena, Tyche, Artemis, Bona Dea, Kali, or anything else; and her primary symbol was the moon, sometimes envisioned as a world-sustaining breast whose starry milk created the galaxy.

There was a classic descriptive palindrome in Tarot lore: ROTA TARO ORAT (TORA) ATOR: the Wheel of the Tarot expresses (the law of) Hathor.[10] Like Isis or Neith, Hathor was another virtually interchangeable name for the same milk-giving Goddess, who often took the form of the white, horned Moon-cow revered everywhere and still representing divinity in India.[11] In her grimmer mood, she was the Sphinx who devoured men: Mother Time, cyclically eating up all that she brings forth—which may be why the Sphinx presided over the Wheel of Fortune.

The Tarot showed the female Sphinx at the peak of the Wheel, with two other personifications of time cycles. Hawk-headed Horus, the rising half of the year, climbed the ascending half of the Wheel. Ass-headed Set, his perpetual rival in the declining half of the year, slid down the Wheel's descending half. The two gods' never-ending alternation under the Law of Hathor was mythologized as a perpetual battle. Set seems to have been the same Vedic ass-god slain by Krishna.[12] This god was shown with one central ass head and ten human heads, indicating that he was incarnate in at least ten different kings.

Ass-eared or ass-headed Set was a basic symbol in the famous Visconti-Sforza Tarot, which showed the Wheel of Fortune ridden by a rising figure just beginning to sprout ass ears, holding a banner with the word *Regnabo*, "I shall rule." The descending figure sported an ass's tail, and the word *Regnavi*, "I have ruled." Between them, at the top, rode a man with full-grown ass ears, saying *Regno*, "I rule." Underneath the Wheel, holding it on his shoulders, a man with only human characteristics crawled on all fours, his banner reading: *Sum sine regno*, "I am without rule."[13] Clearly, the ass ears constituted a badge of kingship in this Tarot deck just as they did in ancient Egypt when the pharaoh adopted the emblems of both Set and Horus to show his divine right to rule.

The same messages given on this Tarot card appeared also in a fourteenth-century Italian manuscript, where four male figures rode the Wheel of Fortune.[14] In England a century later, the Wheel was shown with six riders, ranging from a king enthroned above, to a peasant crawling below. The hub was centered in the giant body of the Goddess, who turned and supported the entire Wheel.[15] There was also a satirical woodcut showing a Wheel of Fortune ridden by an ass-headed man ascending, an ass-haunched man descending, and a bestialized ass-king at the top.[16]

The kingly ass-god Set was the biblical Seth, whom the Romans called Pales, once the eponymous deity of Palestine. The ass was sacred to the cult of the Bridegroom of Zion, impersonated by Jesus when he rode the divine animal during his triumphal procession (Matthew 21:5; John 12:15). The traditional association between the ass and the "King of the Jews" was not forgotten. Medieval cathedrals perpetuated the Roman festivals of Pales with a midwinter Feast of the Ass, when a costumed Madonna and Child entered the sanctuary on an ass, and "hee-haws" were chanted in response to the litany.[17]

Though its origins were pagan or heretical, the Rota Fortuna was among the most popular medieval symbols. A twelfth-century *Hortus deliciarum* (Garden of Delights) showed the Wheel of Time turned by the Goddess Fortuna rather than by God. The western wheel windows of many cathedrals were styled as a Rota Fortuna, with human figures climbing up one side and falling down the other. Medieval writers said "cathedral churches and royal abbeys" gave space to the pagan Dame Fortune, possibly because the Gnostic Masons' guilds built secret symbols of heresy into the churches. Hugo said, "Sometimes a porch, a facade, or a whole church represents a symbolic meaning entirely foreign to worship, even inimical to the Church." According to Honorius of Autun, Fortune's Wheel shown in churches and elsewhere represented "the glory of the world." Its riders rose and fell "because those who have been raised by their power and riches are often precipitated into poverty and misery."[18]

Medieval German horoscope designs laid out Major Arcana pictures in wheel formation, very like Buddhist "life-wheels," with symbols of power and impotence placed on opposite sides like the enthroned ass-king and the human slave. On one side sat the Emperor with his orb and scepter. On the other side, he was a wretched criminal imprisoned in the stocks.[19] Doubtless, common folk found this Oriental-Gnostic idea of the ruler's transient glory more appealing than the church's teachings about the divine right of kings. In Dante's time, the Wheel of Fortune had eight opposing spokes that copied Buddhist doctrines about the virtues of the enlightened man: Peace, Patience, Humility, and Poverty were placed diametrically opposite their antonyms on the Wheel: War, Passion, Glory, and Riches.[20]

It seems clear that Tarot symbolism was based on the Oriental-Gnostic concept of cyclic duality, death followed by rebirth, all things rising and falling on the Wheel. Joining material and spiritual planes at the center of the two spheres, the Wheel formed a transition between the Hermit (#9) and Strength (#11). Like Egypt's evening sun god Ra-Harakhti, the Hermit approached his Fate as a feeble old man leaning on a staff. Just so was the third trimester of life described in the famous Riddle of the Sphinx. After the Wheel's turn, Strength appeared in his place, suggesting the burgeoning vitality of new birth in the spiritual realm. Egyptians, Persians, and Essenes used to believe the same sun god was literally born anew every morning as Ra-Horus, the rising sun. He was hailed as King of Glory, Sun of Righteousness, and Helios (biblical Elias). His advent was announced with the phrase now familiar in the New Testament: "He is risen."[21]

Celtic pagans said all dead heroes and sacred kings rode to a new birth on the Milky Way, which they called the Silver Wheel of Arianrhod (Goddess-mother of Aryans), or sometimes the Oar Wheel, a starship created by the Triple Goddess in the guise of "three druidesses."[22] Christian authorities disliked this pagan imagery and insisted on calling the Druids' heavenly Oar Wheel "the Ship of Fools." Still, like the carrousel and other paganisms, it was retained in folk custom, Carnival, and the Feast of Fools. It became the Fairy's Wheel, later Ferris Wheel. A description of the Fairy's Wheel in the dream of King Arthur matches the Ferris Wheel of today's carnivals.[23]

The Goddess Fortuna was secularized as Lady Luck, who governed the turning of the big Fairy's Wheel as well as the turning of the *roulette* or "little wheel" at carnival games. The name of Luck may have come from Sanskrit Loka, an incarnation of the Goddess as a Heavenly Midwife ruling the planetary spheres, or "ascending light-planes of experience."[24] During Midsummer Eve festivals up the nineteenth century, models of the Lady's wheel were set afire and rolled down hillsides. "The Pagan rites of this festival at the summer solstice, may be considered as a counterpart of those used at the winter solstice at Yule-tide . . . the people imagine that all their ill-luck rolls away from them together with this wheel."[25]

Associated with the Wheel were the symbols of the four seasons, marked off by the solstices and equinoxes with their festivals: bull, lion, eagle, and serpent, the last sometimes changed into a man or angel. These totems were adopted by Christians on behalf of the four evangelists, to explain their presence in sacred art.[26] Originally they represented the four "pillars" of the year, like the Four Sons of Horus in Egypt, or the Four Sons of Margawse in Celtic Britain. This may explain why the Tarot Wheel of Fortune often supported four male figures at its quarters. When there were only three figures on the Wheel, symbols of the seasons appeared in the corners of the card. The same symbols, or modifications of them, appeared in the same positions on the card of the World (#21), which rounded off the second decade of trumps as the Wheel rounded off the first decade.

The Wheel of Fortune marked a turning point in the initiatory process. Indeed, it may have been the very source of the term *turning point*. Situated at the point in space/time where the clockwise solar sphere reversed its turning, to lead into the counterclockwise lunar sphere, at the center of the infinity sign, the Wheel indicated the "still point of the turning worlds."[27] This was the very point that ancient civilizations indentified with any mystical center: the temple's Holy of Holies, the hub of the galaxy, the *omphalos*, the navel or genital center of the Goddess's body.

Like ancient mystics approaching such a center in the depth of meditation, the Hermit approached the Wheel as if to descend its other side into a reversal of direction. Such a reversal has been perceived in the normal development of life, not only by ancient mystics but by modern psychologists also. "At the stroke of noon," said Jung, "the descent begins."[28] The first half of life expands outward, learning, adapting, manipulating the material world; yet nearly every intelligent individual turns inward at the midpoint of life, asking what it all means, facing the inevitability of death, and striving for new insights.

According to Tarot symbolism, the descent was the important part of the psychic journey. Beyond the gateway represented by the Wheel of Fortune lay the real meanings of life and death, locked in the graphic language of the lunar sphere (or, the unconscious). Certainly the second group of trump cards were more mysteriously allusive than the first group; more subtle, more demanding of sophisticated interpretation. They had a universality that could only be related to genuinely religious concepts. In the second circle of "infinity," the Tarot trumps grew up.

11

Strength

11. Strength

Since Christian society officially designated woman the weaker sex, the Tarot's representation of Strength as a woman persuasively suggests pagan and Tantric influences. Most of the classical gods and all the Tantric ones were helpless without their female Shaktis who embodied their strength—or, as it was sometimes called, their power. The implication was that the power of *mana*, or magical efficacy, belonged only to the Eternal Feminine.

Aryan gods of northern Europe were also made strong by female connections. One of the strongest of them, Thor, was married to the Goddess Thrud, whose name meant Strength. She owned the land he lived on, which was called Thrudvangar, "Thrud's Field."[1] She seems to have represented the irresistible strength of the earth. A hero who tried to steal her from Thor was defeated when he was prevented from making contact with the earth, like the similar giant Antaeus in Greek myth.[2]

Many other versions of the Goddess Earth were associated with the idea of strength and with the symbol of a lion, like the Tarot's Lady of Strength. In Egypt, Phrygia, Canaan, Babylon, Phoenicia, and Libya, the Great Mother tamed lions, rode lions, or transformed herself into a lion during her Destroyer phase. One of her numerous incarnations was the Amazon queen Cyrene, foundress of the city of the same name. She appeared in Greek myth as a nymph who could wrestle lions, and win. Of course she was not really a nymph, but an earthly incarnation of the Goddess; her name meant "Sovereign Queen."[3] The Greek story probably was deduced from an icon showing the Goddess taming a lion. Both Greeks and Phoenicians knew her as the Goddess Athene, Ath-enna, Anatha, Anat, or Neith, called Strength of Life. In the time of Rameses II, the Egyptians styled her "Queen of Heaven and mistress of all the gods."[4]

The Tarot card of Strength sometimes bore one of the Goddess's Egyptian names: Neith.[5] This name may have come from a very old Sanskrit title of the Goddess as Primordial Abyss, Kala-Nath, the guise in which she devoured the offspring she brought forth.[6] The Ras Shamra texts depicted her as a grim Anath or Anat, slaying hecatombs of human sacrifices in her temples: "Violently she smites and gloats, Anat cuts them down and gazes; her liver exults in mirth . . . for she plunges her knees in the blood of the soldiers, her loins in the gore of the warriors, till she has had her fill of slaughtering in the house, of cleaving among the tables."[7] Yet this grim Destroyer was the Mother of Nations, "mother of all the gods, whom she bore before childbirth existed"; in Egypt, "the Cow, who gave birth to Ra."[8] Semitic texts called her Virgin Daughter of Palestine, and Virgin Wisdom Dwelling in Zion.[9] Her temple Beth-Anath is mentioned in the nineteenth chapter of Joshua.

She also appeared in the Bible as the mother of Shamgar (Judges 3:31), and as Asenath (Isis-Neith) of the city of Aun, which the Hebrews called On and the Greeks called Heliopolis.[10] Later Jewish writers humanized her into a mere "priest's daughter," to conceal her historical appearance as the Queen of Heaven mated to Yahweh himself in the fifth century B.C.[11] Her Semitic names were invoked as a death curse in the Gospels (1 Corinthians 16:22), Anathema Mar-Anatha, or the Curse of Mari-Anath.

The same Goddess represented the death curse under the Libyan title of Athene Gorgo, the Grim One.[12] The inscription on her temple at Sais said, "No mortal has yet been able to lift the veil that covers me," because her veil concealed the dread Gorgon face that turned men to stone. This probably referred to funerary images, since the World Mother in her

Crone phase became Mother Death. Throughout the ancient world it was the custom, also, to pronounce the Crone's solemn death curse on any sacrificial victim, prior to the ceremonial killing.[13]

The Gorgon's other name, Medusa, was a cognate of Athene's Greek "mother" Metis. Actually, they were the same Goddess. Both Medusa and Metis meant "female wisdom," related to Sanskrit Medha, the Wisdom of Kali. Athene carried the Gorgon face on her aegis; and though classical writers pretended she was born from the head of Zeus the Father, older myths admitted that she came from Libyan Tritonis (Three Queens), a shrine of the Triple Goddess.[14] Egyptians regarded Athene as an alternate name for Neith, and said the name indicated one who gave birth to herself.[15]

Considering the subsequent cards, it seems natural that the second decade of Tarot trumps should be introduced by a grim Goddess representing both Strength and Death in the #11 slot. A symbolic sacrifice occurred next (the Hanged Man), followed by the card of Death and a sojourn in the underworld; later came cards of resurrection and immortality. This death-and-transfiguration theme was common to all Mysteries, pagan and Christian alike. But in the Tarot, its motivating power was female. The number of Strength was also the traditional number of martyrdom—the "eleventh hour" before the death and resurrection of the sun hero on the stroke of twelve.[16]

The Golden Dawn Society seems to have been unjustified in exchanging Strength and Justice to make the Major Arcana conform to a cabalistic arrangement of the Hebrew alphabet.[17] Strength wore the same lemniscate hat or halo as the Magician, who began the presentation of the lesser mysteries of life. At the eleventh stage of the Fool's enlightenment, Strength began the presentation of the deeper mysteries in the lunar sphere. She opened the lion's mouth—recalling the symbol of the Hell-mouth as that of a lion-like creature. Such a dread image would have to be faced by one determined to plumb the secrets of the underworld— or of the underground religion that the church stigmatized as mysteries of hell.

The twelfth-century Winchester Bible showed King David in the same pose as the Goddess Strength, opening a lion's mouth, from which issued a newborn lamb.[18] The lamb was a traditional sacrificial victim standing for spiritual rebirth, often viewed as a totemic form of Jesus. But centuries before Christianity, the lamb was a totemic form of the Middle Eastern savior Mot, sacrificed by Anat, or Anatha, or Neith.[19] He called himself the lamb to be sacrificed "in expiation." He was one of many pagan or Gnostic "saviors" credited with teachings of salvation for his worshipers.

A few Tarot packs featured a different form of Strength. Rather than a woman opening the lion's mouth, she became herself a lion-woman in the Charles VI or Mantegna cards, wearing Neith's lion mask and breaking a marble pillar in her hands.[20] Apparently influenced by the patriarchal claim that Strength must be a masculine quality, some modern packs transformed her into a male Hercules or Samson. On the whole, however, the symbolism of Strength remained fairly consistent even when her interpreters didn't understand what they were dealing with. Sacred traditions have often been preserved in this way, simply because copyists fear to change them.

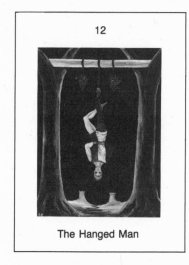

12

The Hanged Man

12. *The Hanged Man*

The Hanged Man has been identified as one of the Tarot's clearest indications of a non-Christian belief system, drawn from a symbolism of unequivocally pagan origin.[1] His door-shaped gallows was typical of the old sacrifices to Odin, God of the Hanged. Such a gallows was sometimes known as the Wooden Horse, or the Horse of Yggr—Odin himself was called Yggr, the Terrible One, which became *ogre* in later Christian terminology.[2]

Odin's own myth showed men that they must win mystical enlightenment by a self-sacrifice leading to death and subsequent resurrection. Odin learned the secrets of Fate, magic, the runes, verbal charms, and poetic inspiration by giving himself up to death on the gallows. He said, "Nine nights I hung on the windy tree, wounded with the spear, sacrificed to Odin, I myself to myself."[3]

Real sacrifices to Odin were still performed at his sanctuary of Uppsala, up to the tenth century A.D.[4] Symbolic versions of his worship persisted for centuries afterward. Perhaps related to Tarot imagery of the twelfth trump was Odin's mention, in the Edda, of the magical twelfth rune, which could make a Hanged Man speak from the gallows, and answer all questions that could be asked.[5]

This particular version of the universal dying-god myth was based like all the others on the belief that a man crossing the threshold between life and death could see into both worlds, and could reveal the secrets of eternity. Because of this belief, relics of hanged men became popular ingredients for witch charms and other recipes for gaining "words of power," as Odin did. The famous Hand of Glory, or Devil's Candle, was supposed to be a hanged man's hand impregnated with wax; its light would reveal "hidden things." Gallows earth, gallows wood, the bones, flesh, or clothing of hanged persons were easy to find, in an age when it was the custom to leave such corpses to rot on the gallows, as a warning to other malefactors.

But the Hanged Man of the Tarot was no ordinary executed criminal. He might be better described as a "hanging man" rather than a Hanged Man. He never died. He was hanged in a nonlethal way, by one foot instead of by the neck. He was shown with open eyes, and an expression of untroubled serenity on his face. Sometimes he wore a halo. He seemed to be undergoing a trial, which was not expected to kill him despite his uncomfortable situation.

Hanging from a gallows by one foot was a medieval custom known as "baffling." Like a sojourn in the stocks, baffling was inflicted as a public humiliation on debtors, and sometimes on those convicted of treason, before their execution.[6] The Hanged Man's "baffled" position links him with ancient traditions of ritual humiliation of the sacred king before his sacrificial death—as Jesus was scourged, mocked, and spat upon (Matthew 26:67, 27:30). Ritual humiliation is very much a part of most initiatory ceremonies, as in men's fraternities from primitive jungles to modern college campuses. Yet, there was more than mere humiliation involved in the Hanged Man's inverted pose.

The female World figure on the last trump showed the same pose right side up as the Hanged Man upside down: one foot bent behind the other knee, so the legs form a triangle. Here may be a distant echo of the Tantric hexagram: a male triangle pointing one way, with a female triangle pointing the other way. Even more suggestive is the Egyptian hieroglyph of a stick figure with legs arranged in this same design. As a verb, this hieroglyph meant "to dance." As a noun, it meant the *ab* or "heart-soul," the most important of an Egyptian's seven souls: the one given by the mother's blood, the one that would be weighed in the balances in the underworld of Maat.[7] Surely it was no coincidence that the Hanged Man's numerological counterpart was Maat, the Lady Justice with her balances.

Egyptians as well as other ancient peoples viewed the heart as the seat of one's true essence. The heartbeat was the "dance of life" within the body. When Osiris lay dead, in his mummy phase, he was called the Still-Heart.[8] When Isis brought him back to life, his inner "dance" began again.

These concepts were older than Egypt. India's oldest god, Shiva, perpetually danced the dance of life in Chidambaram, the Center of the Universe, a mystic place located in the Cave of the Heart, "where the true self resides."[9] His dancing spirit could be felt within the breast of every worshiper, and his universal soul dwelt in the heart of the World Mother. He too was a sacrificed god who periodically died and rose again. In his inactive phase he was Shava, the Corpse, or the Lord of Death, like Osiris the Still-Heart.

Other gods aspired to the title of dancer in the universal heart. What Sylvia Plath with true poetic insight called the brag of the heart—"I am, I am, I am"—was the brag of Brahma and other Oriental gods who later claimed heavenly supremacy. Brahma announced himself in the Vedas with the phrase, "I Am."[10] Similarly, the God of Abraham announced himself in the Bible with the phrase, "I Am" (Exodus 3:14). A Vedic source may be adduced for many biblical stories, including this one, as Abraham probably meant "Father Brahm." In any case, "I Am" was what the dancing deity in the heart said to Oriental sages. Heard by every human being even in the womb before birth—for it has been established that a fetus listens constantly to the maternal heartbeat—it was called the basis for every subsequent form of dance, song, and music.

Even Jesus presented himself as the dancer in the heart, according to the *Acts of John.* Jesus said to his disciples, "To the Universe belongs the dancer. He who does not dance does not know what happens. Now if you follow my dance, see yourself in Me who am speaking. . . . You who dance, consider what I do, for yours is this passion of Man which I am to suffer."[11] Christian mystics gave Jesus's own divinity such curiously female-symbolic titles as "the moon dwelling in the heart," or "the temple in which dwells the life of the world," or "the bridal chamber."[12]

Like other savior figures, the Hanged Man obviously underwent a kind of martyrdom calculated to apotheosize him, or put him in touch with the Lord of Death (Trump #13). That is, he "died" to discover the divinity in his own heart. This could well have been done through the process of baffling. Normally a disgraceful punishment (like crucifixion), baffling seems to have been used by secret sects as a step toward mystic initiation. A person hanging upside down for any extended time becomes acutely conscious of his own heartbeat, for it throbs its ceaseless "I am, I am, I am" through the pulse beating in his head.

This was the very sound much prized by Eastern mystics in their progress toward revelation. They said: "Sound (*nada*) represents the State of Power. It is experienced by the yogi when he plunges deep into himself. It is made manifest in the heartbeat. And since the microcosm is finally identical with the macrocosm, when the yogi hears the Nada, this Sound of Power, he is listening to the heartbeat of the Absolute."[13]

Implicit in the symbol of the dancing god in the heart was a crucial difference between Eastern/Gnostic/pagan religions, and Christianity. The latter insisted that God and man were not to be confused with each other. The Creator and his creation were seen as separate entities, the one filled with power and goodness, the other weak and sinful. In

103

contrast to this Judeo-Christian view, more subtle theologies of the East tacitly admitted that man was the creator and God the creation; for the essence of the divine could be found only within the self. There was, then, no external deity, but only a mythic projection of human wishes, credible only as long as humans maintained its image among themselves.

This may have been the heretical secret discovered by the Hanged Man during his mock martyrdom, as he listened to his own heart, earned his halo, and waited for the next image: Death.

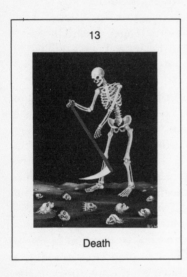

13

Death

13. Death

Tarot interpreters often ignore the obvious connotations of the Death card, preferring to view it as a card of "change" or "transformation."[1] Something comes to an end, and something else begins—as the angel Temperance subsequently implies, with her two vessels of pouring-out and pouring-in. Yet, the card certainly showed the typical Grim Reaper of the medieval mystery play. In France, he was called Macabre, which became an alternate name for the Tarot's thirteenth trump.[2] Wearing his skull-mask and skeleton-suit, waving his scythe, this familiar figure performed the *danse macabre* before thousands of holiday audiences annually. Perhaps some in those audiences knew the secret meaning of his dance, like that of Dancing Shiva as the Lord of Death.

The "Grim" part of the Grim Reaper originally meant a mask. Death's skull-mask was sometimes identified with the Helkappe or Hildegrim, "Hel's Mask," a magic helmet whose wearer could come and go at will through the gates of Mother Hel's underworld. A Teutonic shaman with such a helmet was on intimate terms with the underground Crone-goddess Hilde or Hel, who allowed him to visit her jeweled Palace of Death and return to life again.[3] Sometimes the magic helmet was called Tarnkappe, the Cap of Darkness, which made its wearer invisible. Death, of course, had the same power. As a rule, the ghosts of the dead were thought to be invisible.

The Reaper's scythe was a long-handled version of the Goddess's lunar sickle, representing the waning crescent—the harvesting phase anciently sacred to the Crone. First users of the scythe may have been the Scythians, a matriarchal "Amazonian" people living in the Black Sea area from the eighth to the first centuries B.C. Their Great Goddess —whom the Greeks called Rhea or Gaea or Hestia or Artemis—was served by priestesses, and by eunuch priests in women's clothing.[4]

She whom Europeans called Hel or Mother Death had several other names that might be traced to the Scythians. The Irish called her Scatha, the Vikings called her Skadi, or Skathi. As the "dark Venus" Scotia, she was the eponymous mother of Scotland—otherwise known to the Scots as the Caillech, or Crone.[5] To be reaped or cut down by her, was to be "scathed." In Celtic legend she was the Queen of the Isle of Skye. Cu Chulainn and other heroes went there to learn battlefield skills and the kinds of magic suitable for warriors. Skye was also considered an Isle of the Dead. After an honorable demise in battle, heroes could spend eternity there. Such heroes were Helleder, "man belonging to Mother Hel."[6]

Mystery plays in honor of Mother Death were still performed in Tibet up to the present century, featuring the same figure in skull-mask and skeleton-suit that medieval Europeans saw at their festivals.[7] Similar mystery plays of the Sufis associated the lunar number 13 with the magic circle, or *halka*, a cognate of the Tantric *chakra*. Thirteen participants called *maskhara* stood for the thirteen annual lunations. It has been suggested that the so-called witches' sabbat was derived from the Sufi *zabat*, "an occasion of power," when the thirteen *maskhara* might enact the descent into the underworld and raise the spirits of the dead for divinatory purposes.[8]

As in the Tarot system, the number 13 was usually associated with death, because the thirteenth month was the time of death and renewal by the old lunar reckoning. Often, the thirteenth Major Arcana card was given only a number without a name, though it still bore the figure of Death. This was the result of a superstitious belief that writing a spirit's name was equivalent to invoking the spirit—and no one wanted to invoke Death. Evidently, the taboo didn't extend to the making of a picture, nor yet to the impersonation of Death with a mask and costume.

Mystery cults and secret societies used the mask and costume of Death to represent the initiate's descent into the underworld, following his mock sacrifice—as Death followed the Hanged Man. There were extremely old precedents for this. A dramatized meeting with the Lord of Death figured prominently in Apuleius's initiation into the Isaic Mysteries. Afterward, he was "born again" in the guise of a sun-child— perhaps the same sort of sun-child depicted later in the Tarot sequence on the card of the Sun.[9] Early Christian-Gnostic mystery cults, which seemed to advocate ritual suicide, may have been recommending instead a symbolic initiatory encounter with Death to overcome the fear of it. In the *Secret Book of James*, Jesus said, "Truly I say to you, none of those who fear death will be saved; for the kingdom of death belongs to those who put themselves to death."[10]

Martyrs, of course, took this advice literally, in order to achieve what they called "the crown"—a privileged place in heaven. Other early Christians tried to deny death by insisting that deathlessness was man's natural state. The church officially taught that man was created immortal, and death came into the world only because of the sin of Eve; thus woman could be blamed for the very existence of death. Enochian literature said God intended man to live forever like an angel, but after Eve caused Adam to sin, God appointed death as the fate of humanity (and of all other creatures as well) on account of that sin.[11] Ben Sirach said, "From a woman was the beginning of sin; and because of her we all die." Following such precedents, by the fifth century the church declared it heresy to view death as a natural necessity, not the result of sin.[12]

Many Gnostics and pagans deliberately taught this "heretical" doctrine, seeing death and birth alike as intrinsic parts of the natural cycle. Paganism professed no infantile evasion of the fact of death. It was to be accepted, with belief in rebirth and renewal in the fullness of time and season.[13] The philosopher Lucretius said the fear of death was more to be feared than death itself, because it could poison one's life: "Sometimes the fear of death will bring a man to hate the sunlight fostering his life, till, tortured, he will toss his life away, forgetting that his pangs are fear of death, the fear that weakens decency. . . . This fear, this darkness of the mind, we break, not by the sun, the glittering shafts of day, but by perception of the natural truth."[14]

Perception of the natural truth was what the pagan Mysteries purported to convey through their symbolic dramas. "Man in general," said the Oriental sages, "must rise through and by means of Nature, not by an ascetic rejection of Her."[15] This was the lesson of the Death figure seen in initiatory tableaux. The implication was that Death must be confronted, not denied. A similar message must have been conveyed by the appearance of Death in the Major Arcana. The skeletal Grim Reaper, whose meaning was well known everywhere, would have been an odd choice of symbol to represent mere "change."

A Renaissance mystical drawing showed Death accompanied by a figure of Time carrying an hourglass, and wearing wings to show that Time flies. Skeletal Macabre bore an arrow, and a large snuffer to put out the light of each life when Time so directed.[16] Just as in this picture Death was followed by winged Time (*tempus*), so in the Tarot, Death was followed by winged Temperance—whose pouring of fluid from one vessel to another might be likened to the pouring of sands in an hourglass. Temperance could be understood on several levels at once, as the "mixer" *(temperare)* of the elements, and as the "times and seasons" *(tempor)*. It was said that Death and Time wait for no man. The Tarot placed them together in the spiritual realm.

Death was numerologically linked with the Chariot, or King in Triumph (Trump #7), symbol of royal glory. Classic Tarot packs showed a crowned head among those gruesomely reaped by Macabre.[17] The Death card seemed to be giving to the world's eminent ones the same message given by the psalmist: "When he dieth he shall carry nothing away; his glory shall not descend after him" (Psalms 49:17).

14. Temperance

14

Temperance

Many interpreters of the Tarot have puzzled over the position of the benevolent looking angel Temperance, between such dire cards as Death and the Devil. It was another indication of the Tarot's non-Christian sources. Christian tradition populated the underworld with devils brandishing fire, not angels pouring water.

The true key to this angel's appearance lay in her relationship to the card of the Lovers. Gnostic alchemical texts placed Love in a central position between Death and the Devil: "What is stronger than Hell and Death? Yet Love is the triumphant conqueror of both. . . . Love is of a transmuting and transforming nature. The great effect of Love is to turn all things into its own nature, which is all goodness, sweetness, and perfection."[1]

Why should transforming Love be represented by an angel pouring water from one vessel to another?

The answer is found far back in the antiquity of Southeast Asia, Mesopotamia, and Egypt, where the mingling of male and female waters symbolized universal sexual union. Sumero-Babylonian myths attributed the cosmic fertilization of creation itself—the birth of the world—to the pouring of seminal waters from Apsu, Father Heaven, into the uterine waters of Tiamat, Mother Sea, from whose "deeps" all things were born.[2]

It became standard mythological imagery to view father gods as rainmakers, and mother goddesses as personifications of the sea. According to Hindu scriptures, the merging of God and Goddess (Shiva and Kali) in perfect bliss was "like the pouring of water into water," and all human sexual union was a brief, imperfect echo of this cosmic union.[3]

In India a vessel of water is still used as a sacred image, representing the god in his character of cosmic lover. "The water is regarded, for the period of the worship, as a residence or seat *(pitha)* of the god."[4] The word was comparable to the Greek *pithos*, a vessel or vase representing the womb of rebirth in the cult of Demeter as "Mistress of Earth and Sea."[5] The Tarot's figure of Temperance governed the same two female elements, for she stood with one foot on the earth and the other foot in water. So did Isis in medieval magic texts.

As a human incarnation of the primordial rain-father, the Babylonian savior Nebo was preceded in triumphal procession to his annual love-death by his own symbol, a vessel of water, carried by a special functionary called a jar-bearer.[6] The appearance of this same functionary in the Gospel story of Jesus's triumph, as a man walking ahead of Jesus with a vessel of water (Luke 22:10), is one of the hitherto inexplicable details indicating a Christian copy of the pagan sacred marriage.

The Egyptian savior Osiris was another such "male vessel," carried to his love-death in the form of water in a vase.[7] Like Shiva's bride-mother-sister-shakti-devourer Kali, Osiris's bride-mother-sister-shakti-devourer Isis stood for the female waters in another vase. Together, the two vases made the ubiquitous *menat* displayed throughout Egyptian sacred art by gods, goddesses, pharaohs, priestesses, priests, and human souls in the underworld. This holy amulet consisted of a narrow male vessel pouring its fluid into a broader female vessel.[8] In hieroglyphics, the *menat* meant sexual intercourse and expressed the mystery of impregnation.[9] It was supposed to enhance the virility of Osiris when he was resurrected as the ithyphallic god Min, or Love, hailed as "he who impregnates his Mother."[10] Several names and titles of his Mother—Isis, Nut, Queen of Heaven, Great Mother—were also alternate titles for the Tarot card of Temperance.[11]

The *menat* was as popular an amulet in ancient Egypt as the crucifix was in Christian Europe. Its chief purpose was to insure sexual capacity in the afterlife: an important consideration for Egyptians, who could not envision a paradise without family ties and sexual love. They would have disliked the Christian heaven which had "no marrying or giving in marriage," as Jesus put it (Matthew 22:30).

Like Egyptians, the Greek sect of Cabiri worshiped God and Goddess as two water-filled vessels. Cabirian Mysteries were second only to the Eleusinian Mysteries in popularity, to which their sexual orgies doubtless contributed. The young god called Cabirius, Ganymede, or Hermes was shown pouring his "waters" into a broad vessel representing the

Mother: Demeter Cabiria, Mistress of Earth and Sea. The broad vessel, an archetypal womb symbol, was what Northern pagans called the Cauldron of Regeneration, later confused with the Holy Grail. The confusion may have arisen from a Gnostic notion that the vessel of Christ's blood was really two vessels, like the sexual *menat*. Raphael's *Crucifixion* showed a winged female angel, similar to Temperance, catching the blood of the dying Christ in two vessels.[12]

Temperance's appearance as the #14 Trump probably referred to the mystery of love beyond death. Fourteen was the number of Osiris's days in the underworld. His entire round-trip from the deepest Pit to the crest of Heaven occupied one lunar cycle. His body was divided into fourteen pieces, one for each night of the waning moon. In many similar myths, it was the sustaining power of feminine love that brought a hero or savior back from the underworld. Osiris needed Isis, Tammuz needed Ishtar, Adonis needed Aphrodite; even Dante needed his Beatrice to bring about his passage from the nether regions to the heavenly mount.

Temperance's name seems not to have been taken from the common meaning of the English word: moderation, or abstinence from alcoholic drink. Rather, it has been derived from the Latin *tempor*, a time period, like the biblical "season" for all things under heaven. The angel of the two vessels may have represented "a time to love."[13] Again, *temperare* meant to mix, blend, combine, or regulate the elements in their fitting seasons. In astrological terms, the angel's mixing produced "temperament"—the blend of elemental humors that gave rise to each individual personality. As far back as Babylon, sacred writings spoke of the Wise Goddess (or Crone) who mixed the elements to produce all things in their seasons; the heavens themselves were her lapis-lazuli mixing bowl or cauldron.

Another occult meaning attributed to Temperance was the "tempering" of the male sword (phallus) in the sacred fire of passion, according to the sexual mysticism of sects like the Cabiri and others. Temperance's relationship to the card of the Lovers suggests a sexual interpretation. On several old Tarot packs, the bridegroom of the Lovers card held his sword hilt suggestively, directly in front of his genitals.[14]

Temperance was also a word of good advice for lovers, which might have been spoken by the older woman to the young couple on Trump #6. Compatible "temperament" in marriage was to be developed by "tempering" one's behavior with courtesy and kindness. Medieval men would have learned such lessons only in the "underworld" of heresy, when the established church taught that wives should be slaves.

15. The Devil

15

The Devil

The Devil surely needs no introduction, but his presence in the Tarot needs explanation. He was the nearest medieval approximation of the ancient Lord of the Underworld, long worshiped as a true god under such names as Pluto, Hades, Nergal, Saturn, Zeus Cthonios, Apollyon, Ahriman—various versions of the Black Sun, a shadow-twin of the celestial light-god.

According to the Persian concept of the dualistic universe, God and the Devil were twins, born simultaneously from the womb of the first and oldest of deities, the androgynous being known as Infinite Time.[1] This being resembled Kali as Mother of Time, who gave birth to all gods and demons.

Close fraternal relationships between gods and demons in mythology arose from the fact that they were not differentiated from each other, until late patriarchal religions set up certain deities as "gods" and declared all others "devils." The Devil's title came from the same Aryan root as "divinity" or God—Sanskrit *deva*, Persian *daeva* or *div*, Latin *diva*, *divus*, *deus*, and so on.[2] Similarly, to the Greeks a demon was not an evil spirit but a sort of interior soul or guardian angel, like the Roman *genius*.

An Orphic name for the Lord of the Underworld was Agathodemon, Spirit of Good Fortune, consort of the Goddess Fortuna.[3] In the sequence of initiatory figures he appeared "halfway around the circle, at the point of midnight . . . holding in his right hand the poppy stalk of the sleep of death, turned downward."[4] Some Tarot packs showed the Devil's torch turned the same way, hinting that he occupied the underworld throne at its central, lowest level, as his twin the light-god occupied the throne at the center of the Empyrean.

The Devil's old identification with the underworld god of good fortune, or Lord of Riches (Pluto), developed a belief that the Devil controlled all the mineral wealth that could be dug from the earth, including buried treasure. Christians persuaded themselves that the Devil could make them rich, if only they could discover the right charms to strike a bargain with him. Hence the popularity of the so-called Faustian books, which were full of such charms, and many folktales of the devilish pact. The ancients told the same tales of any god who either occupied or visited the underworld. Heracles was one favorite guide to buried treasure.[5] Hermes was another, because, as psychopomp and chthonian serpent, he was eminently familiar with the mysterious land below the earth's surface.

Many Christians gave more overt respect to the Devil than to God, on the theory that the Devil had more influence in the immediate affairs of this world. The theory led to such customs as that of the Slavic Easter, to sacrifice one sheep to Christ, and thirty sheep to the Devil, because he was thirty times more effective.[6]

The medieval Devil was often surprisingly similar to God—as if to repeat the Persian dualistic concept of the twins, dark Ahriman and bright Ahura Mazda. In Scotland, every village set aside a plot of woodland for the Devil, calling it "the goodman's croft." The Devil was summoned by such identical "secret names of God" as Messias, Soter, Emmanuel, Saboth, Adonai (Messiah, Savior, Immanuel, Lord of Hosts, My Lord). Some Gnostics worshiped him as Lucifer, ill-treated brother of Jehovah, with a better moral character.[7] Meister Eckhart wrote: "Lucifer, the angel, who is in hell, had perfectly pure intellect and to this day knows much."[8] The Devil or his minion could appear as a helpful spirit, who "talketh of divine virtue, he giveth true answers of things present, past, and to come; and of the divinity, and of the creation; he deceiveth none, nor suffereth any to be tempted; he giveth dignities and prelacies."[9]

One reason for the Devil's appearance among the Major Arcana was the idea that any sort of divination needed his help, because he "giveth true answers" if properly addressed. Under the biblical name of Beelzebub, he was once a famous oracular god of Philistia. Kings of Israel sent emissaries to Beelzebub's shrine to hear his prophecies and seek his aid (2 Kings 1:2). As the Canaanites' Baal-Zebub, "Lord of Flies," he was another psychopomp or Conductor of Souls like all-wise Hermes. His title came from the common belief that human souls took the form of flies when passing from one incarnation to the next; hence the European peasant's conviction that a woman could become pregnant by swallowing a fly.[10] Beelzebub was declared an emanation of the Devil not because the biblical writers accused him of any evil, but only because he was one of Yahweh's more popular rivals.

Another reason for the Devil's appearance in the Tarot may have been the mandatory meeting with the Lord of the Underworld in most pagan versions of the sacred Mysteries. The usual belief was that the secret of immortality could be had only by penetrating to the innermost chamber of that immemorial Womb of Rebirth, where every savior figure went before he could be resurrected. It seemed necessary to consult with the Devil in person, rather than relying on the word of another. Prerequisite to spiritual rebirth in the Mysteries of Isis and Osiris was a face-to-face meeting with the king of the abyss, who often appeared in serpent form because the ancient world believed serpents immortal. Instead of dying, snakes shed their old wrinkled skins, and emerged "born again." This is why the Greeks gave a snake's cast skin the name of *geras*, or "old age." The Sumerian Goddess Ninhursag, "She Who Gives Life to the Dead," was called a mistress of great serpents.[11]

The very name of Satan may have originated with an Egyptian name for the underground serpent-king, Sata, a variation of Set who was the dark twin of the savior Osiris. According to the Book of the Dead, a man could obtain long life by identifying himself with Sata in the underworld as well as with his celestial form, the risen Osiris. He must say: "I am the serpent Sata, whose years are infinite. I lie down dead. I am born daily. I am the serpent Sata, the dweller in the uttermost parts of the earth. I lie down in death. I am born. I become new, I renew my youth every day."[12]

This Satan-serpent came of the same symbol complex as the Hindus' Supreme Snake, who dwelt in the abyss of Kali's womb.[13] The Vedas called him the Goddess's firstborn, dwelling forever at the bottom of the ocean that encompassed the world.[14] Egyptians also placed him on the Mount of Sunrise as Ami-Hemf, "Dweller in His Flame," another version of Lucifer the Star of Morning.[15] On descending into the abyss, he usually took the form of lightning, which is why Jesus claimed to have seen Satan descending as lightning (Luke 10:18).

Some thought Jehovah was only another incarnation of the underworld serpent god. It was said the Levites used to worship him under the ancestral name of Leviathan; and as Nehushtan, he was the god of Moses (2 Kings 18:4). This latter name, related to Hebrew *nahash*, "serpent," might be traced to the Vedic serpent-king Nahusha, once a supreme ruler of heaven, until a rival cast him down to the underworld.[16] A similar story was told by Jewish Gnostics who called Jehovah a devil who usurped the original Kingdom of the Wise Serpent.[17] In the second century B.C., Jewish medallions represented Jehovah as a part reptilian god identified with Zeus Sabazius or Ophion, a snake ancestor worshiped in Phrygia where he was supposed to have lived in the Tree of Life in a primal Garden of Paradise.[18]

The familiar Garden of Eden story, where the Devil appeared as the snake in the tree, was only one of many versions of this myth. Some versions were much more sympathetic toward Eve and the snake than the version copied into the Book of Genesis. Gnostics claimed the Devil in this snake form was really the helper of humanity. He supplied Eve and Adam with essential knowledge that God had intended to withhold.

Anxious to maintain belief in only one God, translators of the Bible wrote "God" where original manuscripts said "the gods" *(elohim).*

Gnostic scriptures shed more light on these plural beings, called *archons:* they were selfish beast-gods who created the world, but wanted to keep humanity enslaved in ignorance. The one "who is wiser than all of them," who came to be called the Devil, told Eve and Adam to eat the fruit of knowledge *(gnosis)*. Eve and Adam then "understood very much," and when they saw the deities who had made them, they loathed these deities.[19]

The biblical God says, "Behold, the man is become as one of us (plural), to know good and evil; and now, lest he put forth his hand, and take also of the tree of life, and eat, and live for ever," he must be cast out of the Garden (Genesis 3:22). This was a deliberately abbreviated fragment. Gnostic scriptures told more of the story: the archons decided to dispose of Adam "lest perhaps . . . he also comes to the tree of life and eats from it and becomes immortal and rules and condemns us and regards us and all our glory as folly—afterward he will pass judgment on us and the world—come, let us cast him out of Paradise down upon the earth, the place from whence he was taken, so that he will no longer be able to know anything more about us." God's curses on Eve and the serpent were interpreted as evidence of a malignant archon nature. The serpent blinded the archons' eyes so they couldn't injure him badly; but, "they merely cursed him since they were impotent. Afterward they came to the woman, and they cursed her and her sons. After the woman they cursed Adam, and they cursed the earth and the fruit because of him. And everything which they created they cursed. There is no blessing from them. It is impossible that good be produced from evil."[20]

Obviously, the Gnostic concept of humanity's creator(s) was quite different from the canonical concept that was dissected out and passed on to Western civilization. The Gnostic view was closer to that of the ancient Babylonian scriptures, in which power-greedy gods made humans to be their slaves, denying them both enlightenment and immortality. It was only through the compassion of the Mother, who sent a savior to earth to help them, that humans began to learn.

In both orthodox and heretical Christian traditions, then, though for different reasons, the Devil was the revealer of knowledge. This may account for his presence at the vital midpoint of the underworld circle of Tarot trumps. Here, having become acquainted with the deepest secret, the initiate could begin the return journey toward a new life of the spirit. If a proper Gnostic, he would be fortified now with the secret knowledge that the established church adored a wicked spirit, who imprisoned the world in folly.

Actually it was no secret that the Gnostic thought the orthodox church mistaken, in that it had chosen the wrong twin for its God and consigned the true helper of humanity to hell. This was the real meaning of Gnostics' so-called Devil worship. They refused to worship Jehovah, because they thought him the creator of evil—as even he plainly admitted in the Bible (Isaiah 45:7).

Whether the Devil was believed helpful to humans or not, to Christian theologians he was absolutely necessary. Christianity's basic dualism demanded a principle of evil to oppose the principle of good. Despite Isaiah's allegedly authoritative word, the church dared not make God responsible for evil. Even with the Devil to shoulder the blame, there arose a nasty paradox, not resolved to this day: if God wants evil to exist, he can't be good. If he doesn't want evil to exist but can't prevent it, he can't be God.

Orthodoxy needed the Devil to account for the doctrine of original sin, to which the church was irrevocably committed. If there were no tempter in Eden, hence no temptation, no fall, no sin, there would be no need for salvation. The church would become irrelevant. As de Givry rightly said: "If the Satanic concept is tampered with, the whole edifice laboriously erected by the Fathers of the Church crumbles to the ground."[21]

Moreover, since the Devil and his minions were officially charged with the job of punishing sinners as well as tempting them, without their underworld prison there would be nothing for the saved to be saved from. Churchmen had to admit that the Devil must be a faithful servant of God, because he faithfully carried out the tasks God assigned. A true enemy of God would have released the sinners.

Thus, for many reasons the Devil remained unassailable. He was the necessary shadow, without which God's light couldn't shine. As the nighttime, lunar religions continued along with cults of the new solar gods, so the old religion of the underworld sovereign continued along with that of his erstwhile twin, the deity in heaven. This may help explain the Tarot Devil's close relationship with the Pope (Trump #5), graphically emphasized by his customary pose, his hieratic gesture, and his two worshipers.

Laymen often regarded the Devil with a kind of affection, as if he were more like a charming scamp than the epitome of evil. He represented the sexual libido that a puritanical religion commanded men to deny in themselves, so they were forced to project it elsewhere. Theologians said the Devil was cast out of heaven for the crime of *hubris*, translated "pride"; but the meaning of *hubris* in the original Greek was "lechery."[22] Like many of the elder gods, the Devil frequently appeared with both male and female characteristics, symbolizing sexual union. Traditional Tarot Devil figures were drawn in this way.[23] The Devil also wore horns, because he was "horny" like ancient fertility deities, such as Pan, Dionysus, Cernunnos, El, Apis, and all the divine bulls, rams, stags, he-goats, and satyrs. Throughout the world, horns have been associated with sexuality for thousands of years, ever since early Tantric sages postulated the mystic ascent of sexual energy to the head and its outgrowths in various formations.[24]

On the Devil's Tarot card, as on the five-pointed diagrams of Macrocosmic Man in Renaissance art, his genitals occupied the exact center of the design. His focus on sexuality led Christian authorities to declare that all devil worship arose from the "carnal lust" of women, who were supposed to be insatiable.[25] It may well have been that, in an era when patriarchal authorities deliberately denied women sexual satisfactions, if the Devil had not been already invented, women would have had to invent him.

16

The House of God

16. The House of God

The House of God, also known as the Lightning-Struck Tower, presented a uniquely medieval symbolism. If the crumbling structure represented the Holy Roman Empire, which was sometimes called "the proud tower," the card could be seen as a graphic version of the popular underground prophecy of this Empire's downfall.[1] It was said that as long as the Empire stood intact, Antichrist could not come to the world. Therefore, destruction of the Empire would be an early symptom of the oncoming doomsday.[2] If the card was intended to prophesy this, then the two figures falling from the tower would have been emperor and pope, the combination of church and state.

The same picture carved in the stonework of Rheims Cathedral may have come from the hand of a heretical Freemason.[3] Like adolescent boys today, members of Renaissance fraternities dearly loved hidden signals and occult messages "concealed in plain sight." Often, they had good reason to hide their beliefs in a jungle of esoteric symbolism, in an age when the wrong beliefs could so easily bring their owner to the torture chamber and the stake.

But there was more than this behind the sixteenth trump card. Both the lightning and the tower were age-old symbols of the phallic god— the heavenly Father of the ancient world, the Devil of the Christian one. Lightning was once the phallic trident wielded by Shiva as "tri-dent-bearer," representing his sexual union with triple Kali.[4] It also meant the male "jewel" enclosed by female "lotus."

The trident was inherited by Zeus, Neptune, Pluto, Jupiter, Hades, Poseidon, and other classic gods—also by their medieval amalgam, Christianity's Devil. Another name for the Tarot trump, "Fire from Heaven," suggested the ancient belief that the heavenly Father descended as lightning to fertilize the abyssal Womb, and the blood of all living creatures was made of female waters warmed and reddened by his fire.[5] As the god's "blazing lingam" was quenched in the Mother's watery yoni, so lightning striking the sea was supposed to die and beget itself anew, like every dying and resurrected god.[6]

It is clear the Gnostic sects calling themselves Luciferans looked forward to the second coming of the same Light-bringer who brought the light of knowledge to humanity's first parents. Like the early Manichean groups, medieval Luciferans thought their world was ruled by an evil deity whose church held the masses of people in slavery and oppression. Scriptures written by Mani, the founder of the sect, said, "It is the Prince of Darkness who spoke with Moses, the Jews, and their priests. . . . Christians are involved in the same error when they worship this God, for he led them astray . . . he was not the God of Truth."[7]

According to Asiatic philosophers, the sudden en-light-enment of Truth could come like a "bolt from the blue," destroying all falsehood in an instant.[8] The symbol of a god (or devil) flashing down from heaven in an abrupt fall, like the descent of lightning, often meant fertilization of the intellect.

There was an interesting double symbolism in this picture. The Proud Tower was another kind of phallus often associated with the heavenly Father's establishments on earth: the obelisks, temple pillars, herms, crosses, sacred trees, campaniles, and other "erections" supposed to embody his virile spirit—at times more frankly, at other times less so. The biblical God himself was called a "high tower" (2 Samuel 22:3). The lightning bolt attacking the tower signified the god of the future destroying the god of the past: a classic Oedipal drama in metaphor. Significantly, the lightning spirit's first appearance in the Bible was as a "son of God" (Job 1:6).

Though phallic implications of these symbols were glossed over by Christian authorities, who would claim not to understand them, it was freely admitted that lightning stood for "light-bringing" Lucifer or Satan. It couldn't have been denied, when Jesus personally bore witness to it (Luke 10:18). As "Prince of the Power of the Air," Satan was believed to hurl destructive lightning at church towers. Bishops complained in 1783 that, over the previous 30 years, the Devil's lightning had damaged 400 churches and killed 120 bell-ringers in Germany alone.[9] There seemed to be no help in the preventives the church called infallible: bell-ringing, prayers, sprinkling of holy water, vigils, and processions around churches during rainstorms.

The phenomenon proved theologically embarrassing. Why was God unable to protect his churches from the Devil's lightning? Naturally, heretics whispered that the churches belonged to a false god, on whom the true god's wrath must fall. In a way, this heretical idea found favor, since to this day any damage by lightning is legally styled an act of God. But no one explained why God should attack his own houses of worship.

Lightning continued to strike tall church towers, until the arch-infidel Benjamin Franklin invented the lightning rod. Even then, many ecclesiastical authorities resisted this "ungodly" solution for a long time.[10]

Among the more peculiar canonical notions about lightning protection was the belief that bells bearing the name of St. Barbara would keep lightning away from their bell towers.[11] Her Christian legend claimed the "virgin martyr," Barbara, was tortured and killed in a tower by her evil pagan father for adhering to her Christian faith. A little too late, God struck the man with a retributive lightning bolt and reduced him to ashes, to teach him a lesson.[12] From this sequence of events it was somehow concluded that St. Barbara absolutely controlled the lightning.

Unfortunately, it was later discovered that St. Barbara was no saint after all, but "the Barbarian" Goddess of Round Mountain, near Pozzuoli. Like many other magic mountains throughout Europe, this was one of the entrances to the underground pagan paradise of Fairyland. Inside the mountain dwelt the heathen ancestral dead, whom churchmen described as "bewitched men and women who spent their time in dancing and lechery until Judgment Day."[13] In earlier times, the site was a sacred omphalos, with a tower on its summit to attract the lightning that was thought to represent the mating of heaven-god and earth-goddess.

Perhaps a memory of just such ancient shrines, which the Greeks called "places of coming," contributed to the imagery of the Tarot card. It was widely believed that the second coming of the lightning god would fertilize the womb of Earth, which was symbolized by the Cauldron of Regeneration or the Holy Grail—even by their derivative, the church's baptismal font, which was likened to the "womb of Mary" and said to be rendered fertile by the candle plunged into its water.[14] A stroke of lightning was supposed to bring forth from "infinite depths" the living waters of cosmic fertility, in both the spiritual and the literal sense.[15] This explains why some old Tarot packs transformed the lightning bolt into a leafy or flowering branch.[16] Living waters appeared on the next card of the trumps, in a design that featured the Naked Goddess and could hardly be mistaken for anything other than a promise of creativity restored.

17

The Star

17. The Star

The Goddess called Mistress of Earth and Sea reappeared on the seventeenth trump. Her earlier counterpart, the Empress, was clothed, but now she was fully revealed, naked, or in the Tantric phrase, "sky-clad" (*digambara*). Design of the Star card seldom varied. Virtually all packs showed the Naked Goddess pouring out living waters on land and sea, from her two jars (or breasts), while seven stars shone in the heavens with one large star in their midst.

The card was also the Star of Isis, symbolic of the annual Nile flood that brought the food of life to all the land of Egypt.[1] Isis became the source of the Waters of Life for all souls who journeyed to the starry heaven. She was pictured pouring out her waters for souls as they came before her.[2] After being initiated into her Mysteries, her devotees were promised, "Thou shalt appear in heaven, thou shalt traverse the sky, thou shalt be side by side with the gods of the stars."[3]

Hermetic texts invoked as Mother Isis the same Star-goddess, known in Carthage as the Celestial Virgin, or Astroarche, Queen of the Stars. It was usual for the Goddess to be accompanied by seven priestesses, as the large star of the Tarot card was accompanied by seven smaller stars. Prophecies from the Carthaginian seven were circulated throughout the Roman Empire, rivaling even the authority of the Cumaean sybils.[4] Seven oracular priestesses also attended Astarte in Syria, Ishtar in Babylon, Esther in Elam, Ashtoreth in Palestine, Ostara or Eostre in northern Europe—all these names meaning the same "Star," and the last of them being the origin of our "Easter."[5]

The oracular seven were the original Seven Sages of Arabia, who were said to be female.[7] They were also known as the Seven Pillars of Wisdom, and their wise sayings were Wisdom's "pearls." The Bible still speaks of the Goddess of Wisdom, who has "hewn out her seven pillars" (Proverbs 9:1).

The holy Seven Sisters on earth had their counterparts in heaven. A seven-star constellation was regarded as the repository of their souls, which descended to earth in the form of doves, to possess the priest-esses at the moment of their ordination. Pleiades, "a flock of doves," was the Greek name for the Seven Sisters.[7] Herodotus said seven holy women called Doves founded the oracles of Dodona, Epirus, and Theban Amon.[8] Some said the Pleiades were all daughters of Aphrodite—whose totem was a dove—under her alternate name of Pleione, "Queen of the Sea."[9] Another of her titles, Stella Maris, "Star of the Sea," was later copied by Christians and applied to the Virgin Mary. The image of the Holy Spirit descending on Jesus at his baptism in the form of a dove was another copy from the iconography of the ancient Goddess.

One of the Greek Pleiades was Maia, called "the Grandmother" or "the Maker," who gave birth to Hermes the Enlightened One. She was descended from Kali-Maya, the Creatress, who gave birth to Buddha the Enlightened One.[10] In India, all the Pleiades were emanations of Kali. They were known as Seven Mothers of the World, or Krittikas, meaning "razors," "cutters," or "judges," who "critically" judged men.[11] Their name gave rise to Greek *kritikos*, or "judge."

The reason why the primitive Hindu Pleiades were "razors" might be found in central America, where a whole nation was named after Maya, and the Pleiades occupied a curiously significant position in the heavens. On the last night of the sacred Great Year, a savior called Our Lord the Flayed One was offered to the Pleiades on the Hill of the Stars. Like the Hindu "red god" Rudra, and his Greek counterpart Marsyas, or Mars, the victim was flayed with razors and his skin was worn by the high priest. The Mexicans believed that if this ceremony were not performed in due season, the constellation of the Pleiades would halt at the zenith, and the world would come to an end.[12] His blood set free the waters of spring.

The annual Tibetan festival of "setting free of the waters of springs" is still announced by the rising of the Dog Star, a god named Rishi-Agastya.[13] The rising of the same star announced the setting free of the waters of the Nile to the people of Egypt. They called the star Sothis (Sirius), the soul of Osiris in heaven between his incarnations. Osiris was dismembered rather than flayed, but he was a typical savior whose death brought new life to the world. The rising of his star was heralded by the Three Wise Men, or Magi, that is, the three stars in the belt of Orion, which point toward the Dog Star. "Star of the Magi" was also another name for the Tarot Star.[14]

Thus it may be that the Tarot embodied a tradition of vast antiquity, common to India, Greece, Egypt, and even pre-Columbian Mexico, connected with the renewal of "waters" or of fertility. Jesus too was born of "waters" (*maria*), or the Goddess Mari-Ishtar, the Star of the Sea once worshiped in Jerusalem as the spouse of God.

In Asia Minor the Star-goddess was named Artemis Caryatis, and often worshiped in the form of a pillar. Portraits of her seven priestesses were the *caryatides*, original "pillars of the church," carved in the shape of women. Examples are still to be seen on Greek temples. Artemis governed all the star-souls in heaven until Zeus, god of the patriarchal Hellenes, usurped her authority.[15] As Goddess of Animals she sometimes put on the shape of a she-bear, appearing in the heavens as a larger seven-star constellation than the Pleiades, namely Ursa Major, the Great Bear, now familiarly known as the Big Dipper.

This constellation was greatly venerated by the ancients, because of its commanding position at the summit of heaven, circling the pole star. Seen from northern latitudes it was a hub of the galactic wheel, never dipping below the horizon like the zodiacal constellations. Since Artemis was also the moon, the seven bright stars of Ursa Major were probably viewed as her attendants, nymphs, or Horae, guarding the *axis mundi*, Polaris. Not only the Greeks, but other Europeans such as the Helvetii worshiped Artemis. She was Artio, the Berne ("She-Bear").[16] Her portrait still appears to this day on the Bernese coat of arms.

Through this and other mythic images one can trace the ancient Goddess, who ruled the stars when they were thought to be blessed souls in heaven—heroes, gods, martyrs, deceased sacred kings and saviors, animal deities, and oracular spirits revealing the fates of men through their mysterious movements. The Goddess dictated their movements. Some she sent to earth to be born in human bodies. Some she took up to heaven when their earthly cycles were fulfilled. In rural areas it is still said that a falling star betokens a soul coming down to earth, to be conceived or to be born.[17] The mystics' "astral body" is literally a star-body, based on the ancient notion that one's inner spirit was, or will be, a star. Greeks called the astral body "ethereal," that is, made of ether or star-stuff, a fifth element thought to be more rarified than the element of fire.

After the destruction of the House of God, the Goddess's reappearance in the Major Arcana may be interpreted as a wish-fulfillment symbol of the post-revolutionary world, when the Goddess would be restored to her rightful place. Perhaps Gnostics taught that she would be kinder to the souls in her care than the church's God, who made it so difficult to get into heaven. Like the old "Star of the East," Astarte, she was "the true sovereign of the world . . . presiding over the perpetual renewal of life by means of love and regeneration."[18] Her picture on the card of the Star seemed to show the "green pastures and still waters" of the paradise of Isis and Osiris, first mentioned in Egyptian scriptures and later translated into a biblical psalm. She was certainly not a Christian image, but her appearance seemed to convey a feeling of peace and serenity.

18. The Moon

18

The Moon

It is curious that none of the Major Arcana—not even Death or the Devil—aroused so much fear as the card of the Moon. More evil connotations were given this card than any other. Among the least of its dire predictions was the dark night of the soul, "a crisis of faith."[1] What could have been so crucial or so frightening about a picture of the full moon, two dogs, and a crab or crayfish in a pool? So extravagant a reaction seems to demand explanation.

At the outset, it must be understood that the moon was a primary symbol of the Great Goddess, long before there were any solar gods or any notion of a "supreme" male deity.[2] Chaldean inventors of astrology ignored the sun, and based their system on the celestial movements of the maternal moon.[3] Moses Maimonides said moon worship was the religion of Adam.[4] An old name for Egypt was Khemennu, "Land of the Moon," and Egyptian priests addressed the moon as Mother of the Universe.[5] Throughout Africa, ancestral rulers of the tribes were said to have been incarnations of the moon.[6] Africans as well as Basques called all divine beings "moons."[7] Polynesians called the moon the primordial Virgin Mother and Creatress; she gave birth to all humanity.[8] Plutarch said the power that nourishes the human body and makes it grow is the moon, from the beginning when a mother's "coagulum" of lunar blood forms the child in her womb.[9] It was once believed that "blood" relationships were only matrilineal, because moon-given uterine blood created each new life, and males could have nothing to do with the process.

These beliefs, and other related ones, were never wholly extinguished even by patriarchal Christianity. In the Middle Ages it was said that any woman who desired special divine help should pray, not to God (who was the enemy of her sex, according to the Bible), but to her own deity, the moon.[10] Peasants in Portugal and France never ceased to worship the moon, which they called "Our Lady" and "Mother of God."[11] According to the Digby Mystery Play, even Jesus sang hymns to "the Moon, his Mother, the vessel . . . in whom he rested before he ascended to the Sun."[12]

If a woman dreamed of her own image in the moon, it was taken as a sign that she would bear a daughter.[13] Nursery chants of the Loire

121

district showed a continuing belief that the moon was the real source of children. An Orkney Island bride would not consider herself properly married until she went at night to pray for fertility in a megalithic stone circle, locally known as the Temple of the Moon.[14] Ecclesiastical hostility was demonstrated by the common belief among clerics that if a woman exposed herself naked to moonlight, she would conceive and give birth to a vampire or devil.[15]

The moon was regarded as the source of conception because, according to the ancient, worldwide concept of reincarnation, the Moon Mother constantly received souls and sent them back to earth to be born again. "The crescent-moon worn by Diana and used in the worship of other Goddesses is said to be the Ark or vessel of boat-like shape, symbol of fertility or the Container of the Germ of all life."[16] The Vedas say all souls after death return to the moon whence they came, to be devoured by "maternal spirits."[17] The Greeks often located the Elysian Fields in the moon.[18] Romans said the souls of the just are purified in the moon, a pre-Christian model of purgatory.[19] The ivory crescent worn by Roman nobles represented a residence in the moon after death.[20] The Gnostics said the souls of enlightened ones are drawn up to the moon, while souls of the ignorant are reborn as animals.[21]

> The idea of the journey to the moon after death is one which has been preserved in the more advanced cultures. . . . It is not difficult to find themes of the moon as the Land of the Dead or as the regenerating receptacle of souls. . . . This is one reason why the moon presides over the formation of organisms, and also over their decomposition.[22]

The Isle of Man (Moon) was once a northern European "Isle of the Dead," sacred to the Moon Mother Mana, ruler of heaven—which the Teutons knew as Manavegr, "Moon's Way."[23] Moon Mother Mana was also queen of the ghost world, Manala, in Finnish mythology; and the Mother of Fate in Arabia; and the mother of the ancestral spirits known to the Romans as *manes* or *maniae*.[24] Mother Mana of the Moon-isle kept souls of the dead in "pots turned upside down."[25] East Jutland passage-graves contained large numbers of "soul receptacles" in the form of upturned pots.[26] A similar custom was recorded among South American Indians who said the moon carries souls away and keeps them under inverted pots.[27] In Southeast Asia, all life-giving fluids were likened to soul-stuff whose "pot" was the moon: "Water, sap, milk, and blood, represent but differing states of the one elixir. The vessel or cup of this immortal fluid is the moon."[28]

All versions of the triple Moon Goddess show the same patterns of connection with birth, death, and rebirth, particularly her Crone form, which was most feared by men. A classic Crone was Hecate, who became Christianity's dreaded "queen of witches" because her ancient priestesses claimed to control the moon—even to draw it down from the sky by their magic words.[29] Actually, "drawing down the moon" consisted of calling the lunar spirit to inhabit a human being, as when a priestess was ordained, in the same kind of ceremony later copied by Christians as a "calling down" of the spirit of God. Porphyry wrote: "The moon is Hecate . . . her power appears in three forms, having as symbol of the new moon the figure in the white robe and golden sandals, and torches lighted; the basket which she bears when she has mounted high is the symbol of the cultivation of the crops which she made to grow up according to the increase of her light."[30]

The Tarot card of the Moon was sometimes called Hecate, or the Dogs of Hecate—which brings up the matter of its two dogs howling at the moon.[31] Throughout Europe, the superstitious insisted that dogs howling at the moon gave omens of death, because dogs could see the Angel of Death (Hecate) approaching.[32] The usual design of the card showed two pylons of a gateway beyond the dogs, a road leading between them. This was a classic image of the Gate of Death. Vedic poets, and most other Indo-Europeans, believed the Gate of Death was guarded by dogs. The Irish maintained that mourners must not wail too loudly, for fear of disturbing the dogs at death's gate, and inciting them to attack the departed soul.[33]

The Goddess as Crone was mother or mistress of the death dogs. The Vedas called her Sarama, that is, Sara-Ma, Mother Sara, a divine huntress, the same as the gypsies' Sara-Kali.[34] The Venidad said the soul arriving in heaven meets the beautiful lunar lady "with the dogs at her sides."[35] A Norse version of the Crone was Angurboda, "Hag of the Iron Wood," who gave birth to Hel and to the packs of wolf-dogs, led by Managarm, "Moon-Dog."[36] They helped carry the dead to Valhalla.

Dogs, jackals, and wolves, like vultures, were everywhere associated with death because they eat carrion. As companions of Mother Death, they were canine gods. The pre-dynastic name of Egypt's jackal god Anubis was Mates, "He of the Mother."[37] The name of Shiva, like that of Anubis, meant a jackal. He accompanied the Goddess in jackal form.[38] The Gallo-Roman bearer of the dead was a wolf god known as Lupus, or Feronius, or Dis Pater. To the Greeks he was Apollo Lycaeon, "Wolfish Apollo," once mated to Artemis as Mother of Animals.[39] The Lyceum or Wolf-Temple where Socrates taught was dedicated to him. Persephone also, the "Destroyer" aspect of the same Goddess, had as her gatekeeper the dog Cerberus, "Spirit of the Pit."[40]

The dogs of the Moon card may well have been traditional guardians of Death's gate, but Death had already appeared as #13 of the Major Arcana. The Descent into Hell and the meeting with the Devil were also pictured earlier. What was different or more disturbing about the Moon card? The answer lies with the crab in the foreground. Through this symbol, the card represented not only death, but man's most catastrophic projection of death onto the external universe: doomsday.

Cancer, the Crab, was a zodiacal sign of water, and always ruled by the Moon.[41] Thousands of years ago, early Chaldean astrologers announced that the world-destroying Deluge last occurred when all planets came together in the constellation of Cancer. When, in the course of time, the planets would again enter the sign of the Crab, the present world cycle would end. Everything would be swept back into primal chaos, to prepare a new creation. This doctrine permeated India, Egypt, China, Persia, the Middle East, Europe, and the pre-Columbian Americas.[42]

Here is the dread secret of the Moon card. The Crab announced the last coming of the Crone who would devour the earth, the gods, the elements. Kali-Bhavani, Being, would return to her "dark formlessness" as Kali-Uma, Not-Being—that is, the primordial Deep, symbolized by the Crab's pool of water. This was a dark night, not of the individual soul, but of the cosmos. It may have been the secret that the Moon's alter ego, the Papess, read in her book. She too sat before a gateway.

Innumerable superstitious fears were fueled by hoary intimations of the moon's destructive powers. "Mania" and "lunacy" were derived from the Moon Mother's names (Mana, Luna) because churchmen accused her worshipers of insanity. The custom of sleeping in closed rooms was rationalized by Victorian doctors as a need to shut out unhealthful night air; but in earlier times it was to shut out moonlight. Roger Bacon solemnly wrote: "Many have died from not protecting themselves from the rays of the moon."[43]

What Christians forgot about the lunar doomsday was that the old religions did not follow it with eternal stasis in heaven or hell. It was not a true end. New life came out of every death, even the cosmic death. Destruction was a necessary preliminary to creation. The ancient apocalyptic myths bore this implication—and so did the Tarot's Moon card with its new Sun following, bringing a picture of Eden-like youth, innocence, and joy.

19. The Sun

19

The Sun

Traditional Tarot decks placed two naked children on the Sun card, a boy and a girl, dancing together in front of a garden wall. Perhaps the most accessible interpretation is found in myths of northern Europe, where extremely old Aryan beliefs saw the Sun as a female deity, Glory-of-Elves, who would give birth to a new daughter Sun after the death of the present universe. This new young Sun Goddess would preside over a new and better creation. In the primal garden of the next Eden, the first two human beings would grow up together. The girl would become the next Mother of All Living, a woman named Life (Lif). The boy would be her mate, a man named Desirer-of-Life.[1]

These two seem to have been not only future incarnations of the pre-biblical Adam and Eve, but also projections of the solar-lunar twins common to most Indo-European mythologies. For example, Isis and Osiris were twins who mated even in the womb of their Mother, and produced offspring, the elder Horus. When Isis gave birth to the younger Horus, who was her brother-spouse reincarnated, she said, "The fruit I bore has become the sun."[2] When she appeared in the guise of the celestial Moon-Cow, he was her Golden Calf—the same one whose cult the Israelites brought with them out of Egypt.

Apollo and Artemis were a similar pair, joined in the womb of their mother Leto, or Latona, another personification of the primal darkness. Apollo mated with his sister Artemis on the altar of his temple at Delos. The Lemnian Cabiri annually celebrated his rebirth at the winter solstice by carrying "new fire" from this altar to relight their hearths.[3] The ceremony of the new fire was adopted by Christianity and is still performed every year on Mount Lycabettus. The Cabiri worshiped the holy male-female twins as Gemini, which was an alternate name for the Tarot Sun card.[4] When he matured, their Sun god was "made flesh" in the person of Heracles, by way of the usual virgin birth. Both the god and his earthly incarnation carried the surname of Savior (Soter).[5]

Diodorus quoted the historian Hecateus on the subject of the Moon temple on the Hyperborean island where Latona was born. Every nineteen years, Apollo visited this shrine of his Mother Night.[6] Two spans of nineteen years each—that is, two solar "great years"—plus a lunar "great year" of eighteen calendar years, completed one of the fifty-six-year cycles in which movements of sun and moon coincide. The numbers matched those of the Sun and Moon cards in the Tarot, not by coincidence alone. Possibly the Tarot's solar twins suggested the double nineteen-year solar cycle of the Great Year. Hecateus's Hyperborean island was certainly Britain, where megalithic temples like Stonehenge clocked the Great Year in circles of fifty-six markers.[7]

In Cornwall, temples of the Sun god included nineteen stone posts in a circle.[8] At Kildare, nineteen priestesses of the Celtic Moon-goddess Brigit tended a sacred fire which, like the fire on Vesta's altar, was never allowed to go out, because it magically supported the light of the sun. Christianity converted Brigit into a phony saint and her temple into a convent, "but did not dare quench the fire, which kept burning until the days of the Reformation some one thousand years later."[9] Some of Brigit's enthusiastic devotees even insisted that she was the mother of Christ.[10]

In Norway, the Sun-Moon twins were associated with doomsday (Ragnarok) as forces of creation and destruction, called Hjuki and Bil—from *jakka*, "to assemble or increase," and *bil*, "to break up or dissolve." These powers were personified by two divine children taken up to heaven by their mother Mana, the Moon. They drew the Water of Life from "the well Byrgir, in the bucket Soegr, suspended from the pole Simul, which they bore on their shoulders." These names were derived from a list of constellations. Hjuki and Bil represented star-souls of the next universe, for they tumbled down again from the heaven-mountain, like falling stars, to carry the seeds of birth-and-death to the new world. Their cosmic myth was trivialized by Christian storytellers, and they became the familiar nursery pair, Jack and Jill.[11]

The pagan paradise, the Christian paradise, and the new Eden of the next cosmic cycle were often confused in the medieval mind. Some said souls went to heaven to become angels or stars. Others said they would be reborn in the new creation. Others said they went west, to the Great Mother's fairyland of eternal youth, where the Sun went to rest. Sun gods and solar heroes generally went west to the paradise of many names: Land of the Westerners, Fortunate Isles, Avalon, Elysium, Garden of the Hesperides, Isle of the Dead, and so on. Even St. Thomas Aquinas believed in the western paradise, and affirmed that Elijah and Esdras still lived there.[12]

The Tarot children also suggest this western land, which the Irish called the Country of Youth (Thierna na Oge). Its magic fountain, a lunar-menstrual symbol of the "blood of life" that overflowed once a month, was believed to give eternal vitality to those who drank of it. Ponce de Leon actually thought he could find this Fountain of Youth by sailing west. He even claimed to have discovered it in Florida.[13]

"Youth Eternal," the blessing bestowed by the wonderful fountain, was also another name for the Tarot card of the Sun.[14] On the card, the children danced in a walled garden—the *hortus conclusus* or "enclosed garden" representing the womb of the Virgin Mother in both her pagan and her Christian disguises. Oriental scriptures spoke of her as the Naked Goddess whose "mayik vesture" is the Sun, the "most glorious symbol in the physical world."[15] Copied into the Bible as "the woman clothed with the sun" (Revelation 12:1), she was identified with the Virgin Mary. However, she was originally the virgin form of the Dooms-day Crone, or Mother Night, from whose "enclosed garden" the children of the new creation must come.

Commentators say the Tarot Sun children represent emergence from the Womb of Darkness, that is, the dark night of gestation between the death of one life and the rebirth of the next, according to Oriental views of cyclic reincarnation and perpetual re-creation of worlds.[16] Since the Moon card was supposed to represent the Dark Night of the Soul, and its lunar nature obviously symbolized a uterus, it could only have been followed by a card of rebirth. The children were seen as the young lunar-solar twins of a new creation, dancing in joyous innocence within a new Eden, called the Hidden Garden of the Soul.[17] Mythic symbolism everywhere shows identification of infantile existence with the primal paradise, the *hortus conclusus*, and a state of bliss.

The mundane counterpart of the Sun children was the Magician (Trump #1), whose connection with Hermes the Psychopomp provided a mythically sound relationship to newborn souls. As a wizard-demigod conducting the Self through a complicated initiatory symbol system, he could have been showing these children as a pre-ordained revelation, withheld during earlier stages, because it could not have been understood until after certain other matters had been taught.

20. Judgment

20

Judgment

On the face of it, the card of Judgment looked like the most Christian of the Major Arcana. It showed an orthodox picture of the Last Trump —though the card is actually the next-to-last trump. An angel, sometimes identified as either Michael or Gabriel, blew his trumpet from heaven. At the sound, the dead rose from their graves to face the final reckoning. The card's number, 20, stood for completion of the two decades. Or, was its message subtly mocked by its numerical connection with the Fool (#0), and by the fact that this was not the Tarot's final statement at all?

In fact, the Last Judgment scene was not originally Christian. It was yet another borrowing from Indo-European paganism, via Essenic sects that copied Persian-Mithraic apocalypses. To trace the idea backward from its most recent manifestation in Christian Gospels:

Jesus announced the end of the world within his hearers' own lifetimes (Luke 9:27; Matthew 24:34), and identified himself with the Mithraic "Son of Man" who made this same announcement centuries earlier, and whose second coming was already described before 70 B.C. in the Book of Enoch.[1] Jesus explained in Enochian style how he would return "in the clouds with great power and glory," and would "gather together his elect from the four winds, from the uttermost part of the earth to the uttermost part of heaven" (Mark 13:26–27).

For the Jews, such ideas evidently began with the Essenic communities of the first century B.C., each of which appointed a perfectly human "Christ" to serve as a scapegoat for the community's sins, as well as an equally human "Messiah."[2] Christ and Messiah were common titles for any self-styled holy man. The Essenes believed Persian stories of such holy men, and also stories of the Son of Man (Mithra) who told mortals of the impending "War of the Sons of Light with the Sons of Darkness," a model for the biblical Armageddon.[3] But the title Son of Man was not Essenic in origin, nor even Persian. It came from one of the oldest Aryan phallic gods, Vishnu, whose worshipers called him Son of Man (Narayana) to prove he had no mother. However, in an earlier incarnation as Mitra, the Vedic forerunner of Mithra, he was a son of the

Sun Goddess Aditi and one of the spirits who were supposed to "reveal their light at Doomsday."[4]

The Persians' Mithra was also motherless, begotten by "fire from heaven" and born from a rock, the *petra genetrix*, on the twenty-fifth of December—the old winter solstice. He was adored by shepherds and Magi. He was called Light of the World and Sun of Righteousness. He healed the sick, cast out demons, preached, and partook of a Last Supper with his twelve disciples. He died and rose again at the spring equinox (Easter). His church had seven sacraments, communion cakes marked with a cross, and a celibate priesthood. After being "washed in the blood" of the Mithraic bull at the Taurobolium, his worshipers were "born again for eternity."[5] In Rome, where Mithra was officially declared Protector of the Empire early in the Christian era, his cult was Christianity's most successful rival as well as an obvious model for imitation.[6]

After descending from the oldest Indo-European mythologies of doomsday and the Last Judgment, Mithraic-Essenic-Christian versions made an important change. They no longer postulated constant cyclic destruction and renewal. They became linear and static, preaching one doom for ever, with nothing to follow but eternal bliss or eternal torment. There was to be no new creation.

A purer form of the original Indo-European myth was preserved in Northern countries, which remained pagan for a thousand years beyond the initial Christianization of the Roman world. Norse priestesses created apocalyptic literature of better quality than the Revelation of pseudo-John, (signed by a false name, as was Christian custom at the time), enshrined in the New Testament. The *Voluspá* (Priestess's Prophecy) tells of the oncoming cataclysm, the battle at the end of the world, the sailing of the ship of death, the falling of stars from heaven, and the destruction of the earth by fire and flood. This Ragnarok, or Götterdämmerung, would be announced not by an archangel, but by the god Rig-Heimdall, who would blow the Last Trump on his "ringing horn," the Gjellarhorn.

Rig-Heimdall was the primordial father of the three castes, by way of his three sequential marriages with the trinity of Mother Earth, Edda the Great-Grandmother, Amma the Grandmother, and Modir the Mother. Like Scyld, Merlin, Arthur, and other Saxon heroes, he was born of the ninefold Sea-goddess—sometimes called Mari, Morgan, Minne, or Maerin—who deposited him on the shore in her ninth wave. He was "born in days of old, filled with strength, of the race of gods; nine bore him, daughters of giants, on the edge of the earth. . . . He was made strong with the force of the earth, with the cold sea and the blood of the sacrificial boar."[7]

Rig-Heimdall's "race of gods" were the Aesir, meaning "Asians."

His name meant "son of the Sea-mother," the same as the title of the Dalai Lama.[8] The doomsday he announced came to be called Götter-dämmerung, the Going-into-the-Shadow of the Gods, sometimes inaccurately translated "Twilight of the Gods." This rendering was inaccurate because the Shadow was not an impersonal twilight, but an entity who swallowed the gods, namely the Goddess Skadi—Gothic *skadus*, Old English *sceadu*, "shadow, shade"—the Great Mother in her black, destroying Crone phase. Here we find a link with Hindu antiquity. Skadi was none other than Kali the Destroyer, the black Goddess who reabsorbed the universes and devoured all gods when they became corrupt and violent, learned to misuse their power, and taught men to do likewise. The Goddess therefore laid her death-curse on them and drew their universe back into her own illimitable darkness.

In short, Skadi pronounced her Mutspell (Mother's Curse) on the world, and on the warlike gods who flouted her law. To destroy them, she summoned evil spirits all the way from her ancestral home, "the hot lands of the south," which the Vikings called Mutspellheim.[9]

These traditional beliefs, spreading across the Eurasian continent from southeast to northwest with the earliest Aryan migrations, showed that the idea of doomsday was older than Mithraism or Christianity. It belonged to the root religion of black Kali, whose wrath fell on gods and men during the Kali Yuga or Last Age, because they neglected her commandments of love, peace, and unity. They chose to fight others of their own kind, to violate the bonds of family and clan, to tyrannize women and children, to cheat, steal, and kill. The World's End would come, according to the ancient notion, because the angry Mother would no longer sustain a universe for the sake of such evildoers. So she devoured all that she had created: "As white, yellow, and other colors all disappear in black, in the same way . . . all beings enter Kali." Hindu sages explained that after the dissolution of all things, Kali would resume her "dark and formless" aspect, remaining alone "as One ineffable and inconceivable," until in the fullness of time she would speak the primal word, Om, and create again.[10]

Thus, the Tarot's angel of Judgment was probably not Michael or Gabriel at all, but Rig-Heimdall or his Tantric counterpart, announcing destruction of all the world except the Mother's chosen ones—seeds of the next creation, who would be saved on Manu's ark. Symbolically, in the Tarot system the saved approached the real Last Trump, #21, the Goddess herself seen naked and "face to face." This was a decidedly un-Christian final revelation, and its position in the Major Arcana implied a female-oriented, cyclic cosmology. Therefore, the card of Judgment may have meant, not the judgment of men by God, but the judgment of gods by the Mother.

The twentieth trump has been called the card of the regenerated Self, not in the Christian sense of resurrection in the flesh, but in the sense of a new being discovered within the present physical body.[11] This new being, in turn, was the one capable of understanding the final lesson of the Major Arcana: not a lesson about heaven, but a lesson bearing the very mundane name of the World.

21

The World

21. The World

The true Last Trump had many names, like the Goddess it pictured. It was called Eve, Shekina, Sophia, Mother Nature, Truth, the Bride, the System, the Major Fortune, the Anima Mercury, the Universe, or the World.[1] The Goddess representing all these things was a western version of the World Soul, Mahadevi, Kali-Shakti, known to European mystics as "the feminine Ultimate Reality."[2] Her archetypal form was described by Jung as the Lady Soul embodied perforce in every mother and every beloved, an "omnipresent and ageless image, which corresponds to the deepest reality in a man."[3]

Some of her "thousand names" in the East were: Kali, Sarasvati, Lakshmi, Gayatri, Durga, Annapurna, Sati, Uma, Parvati, Gauri, Bagala, Matagini, Dhumavati, Tara, Bhairavi, Kundalini, Bharga, Devata, Maheshvari, Maya, Cunti, Kurukulla, Hariti, Savitri, and many others.[4] As Shakti, she represented Cosmic Energy, the power source of every deity and every living thing. Shakti meant "ability, capacity, faculty, strength, energy, prowess; regal power; the power of composition, poetic power, genius; the power of signification of a word or term; the power inherent in cause to produce its necessary effect . . . *shakti* is the female organ; *shakti* is the active power of a deity and is regarded, mythologically, as his goddess-consort and queen." Psychically and physically, to plug into this power was the goal of every mystic. "The possession of her, the cosmic Shakti, the living embodiment of the principle of beauty and youth eternal, is the ultimate quest, the very highest prize. She it is who is ever desired, won, and lost again."[5] And she was what the Major Arcana presented at the end.

Oriental scriptures demonstrate the sages' reverence for "Her who is pure Being-Consciousness-Bliss, as Power (Shakti), who exists in the form of Time and Space and all that is therein, and who is the radiant Illuminatrix in all beings." They declared, "All is the Mother and She is reality itself. 'Sa'ham' (She I Am) the Sakta says, and all that he senses is She in the form in which he perceives Her. It is She who in, and as, him drinks the consecrated wine, and She is the wine."[6] She was the original "Alpha and Omega" that Greek Neoplatonism eventually transmuted into the Christian Logos; in her formless phase she was "the Generative Womb of All, the Beginning and End of Beings."[7]

Two thousand years ago, the philosopher Plotinus adapted the Oriental vision of the Mother to his own concept of the Universal Soul, or Psyche, a transliteration of Shakti. Projecting her own images or reflections into the lower world of matter, he said, she "gives rise to the phenomena of the sensible universe."[8] To realize her essence, the mystic must progress stepwise from "the sight of a beautiful lady," perception of individual female beauty, toward contemplation of the Universal Beauty.[9] Her mystic trinity, like Kali's, was made up of time, matter, and spirit, performing together "the great dance of the universe."[10]

The cosmic dance is implicit in the pose of the Tarot's World Goddess, as she bends one knee like the figure in the Egyptian hieroglyphic symbol of dancing—the same pose adopted by the Hanged Man in his death-like trance of contemplation. Egyptians, like Hindus, conceived the active principle or heartbeat of the cosmos as a dance created by the Goddess they called Isis, or "the One Who is All."[11] More than three millenia ago, Egyptian hymns were addressed to her in terms similar to those honoring Kali-Shakti:

> Thou who art pre-eminent, mistress and lady of the tomb, Mother in the horizon of heaven. . . . Praise be unto thee, O Lady, who art mightier than the gods, words of adoration rise unto thee from the Eight Gods of Hermopolis. The living souls who are in their hidden places praise the mystery of thee, O Thou who art their mother, thou source from which they sprang, who makest for them a place in the hidden Underworld, who makest sound their bones and preservest them from terror, who makest them strong in the abode of everlastingness.[12]

When the cult of Isis reached Rome, and was disseminated from there to all parts of the Empire, many of her devotees recognized in her the same principles embodied in other forms of the Goddess, and worshiped her in terms that Christians later copied. On initiation into the congregation of the Goddess, Lucius wrote a hymn whose phrases were to recur in Christian writings:

> O Thou holy and eternal Savior of the human race, ever lavish in Thy bounties to mortals. . . . Thou bestowest a mother's tender affection on the misfortunes of unhappy men. Nor day nor night, nor even a moment of

time passes which is not replete with Thy benefits. . . . Thou dispellest the storms of life and stretchest forth Thy right hand of salvation, by which Thou unravellest even the inextricably tangled web of Fate. . . . Thou turneth the earth in its orb; Thou givest light to the sun; Thou rulest the world; Thou treadest Death underfoot. To Thee the stars are responsive; by Thee the seasons return and the gods rejoice and the elements are in subjection. At Thy command the winds blow; the clouds bestow their refreshing; the seeds bud and the fruits increase. The birds that range the heaven, the beasts on the mountains, the serpents lurking in their den, the fish that swim the sea, are awe-inspired by Thy majesty. . . . I am too feeble to render Thee sufficient praise, and too poor in earthly possessions to offer Thee fitting sacrifices. . . . Thy divine countenance and most holy deity I shall guard and keep forever hidden in the secret place of my heart.[13]

The Christian father Origen—who missed canonization because after three centuries his church decided to call his views heretical—adopted the same Universal Soul mentioned by Plotinus, calling it (or her) by the feminine name of Psyche. He wrote, "As our body while consisting of human members is yet held together by one soul, so the universe is to be thought of as an immense living being which is held together by one soul."[14] This was precisely the same as India's vision of Kali-Shakti, and Rome's vision of the female world-soul Anima, who "makes to live." To Byzantine mystics she was Sophia, the Goddess who first framed all living forms "in the Heavens above the Stars," as her own *I-deas*, which meant "Goddesses-within."[15]

One of the expressed goals of alchemical mysticism was to release the Anima or *I-dea* imprisoned in matter, like the goal of ancient sages who yearned to see the Naked Goddess face to face.[16] The same result seemed to be promised by the Tarot's Last Trump, whose number evoked the twenty-one emanations of Mother Tara, as the Great Shakti was sometimes called. A Tibetan hymn said:

Hail! O verdant Tara! The Savior of all beings! Descend, we pray Thee, from Thy heavenly mansion, at Potala, together with all Thy retinue of gods, titans, and deliverers! We humbly prostrate ourselves at Thy lotus-feet! Deliver us from all distress! O holy Mother! We hail Thee! O revered and sublime Tara! Who are adored by all the kings and princes of the ten directions and of the present, past, and future.[17]

This verdant Tara was the same as Ireland's Tara, or Rome's Terra—Mother Earth—whose worship continued in secret through the Middle Ages. As late as the twelfth century A.D. she was still addressed in an English herbal as the divine Goddess "who dost generate all things," and to whom the spirits of the dead would return, Great Mother of the Gods, "source of the strength of peoples and gods; without thee nothing can either be born or made perfect; thou art mighty, Queen of the

Gods."[18] These were strange utterances for an allegedly Christian society.

The Goddess arose once more on a Tarot card as the culminating "Great Secret," flanked by symbols of the seasons, bearing the rods of power, dancing the dance of life: one more representation of the archetypal, ineradicable image in the mind of every mother's child. Despite the efforts of patriarchal sects the world over, she does not seem to be stamped out yet. Swami Vivekananda said, "One vision I see clear as life before me, that the ancient mother has awakened once more, sitting on her throne rejuvenated, more glorious than ever. Proclaim her to all the world with the voice of peace and benediction."[19]

Perhaps that was what the Tarot was designed to do.

In any event, the final revelation of the Major Arcana was surely not a Christian deity—not even the new Christian version of the Great Mother. The Celestial Virgin of the medieval church never appeared naked. The unveiled Goddess, however, represented a basic, primary symbol of creation and re-creation, her eternal cycles not to be comprehended through Christian cosmology with its one-way, linear perception of time. The Tarot seemed rather to point out that the World Soul and the World Womb were essentially identical. The mandorla-shaped wreath encircling the Goddess was a common womb symbol, leading naturally to the next card, the Fool, symbol of the newborn child.[20] In effect, it referred to the old doctrine of reincarnation, a type of rebirth idea that was alien to, and opposed by, patriarchal religious systems, which demanded "permanence and not change, eternity and not transformation, law and not creative spontaneity."[21] Patriarchy transmuted the Great Mother into a demon, for the very reason that she was man's "undoing" as well as his "doing." In this process of diabolization, a very large portion of nature's reality was lost. Some believe that humanity has been blindly searching ever since for that lost feminine reality.

Part III

The Lesser Secrets

Begin, Sicilian Muse, a lofty strain,
The voice of Cumae's oracle is heard again.
See where the cycling years new blessings bring;
The Virgin comes, and he, the long-wished king.

—Virgil

Cartomancy
and
Individualism

The cartomancer's relationship to the Minor Arcana (Lesser Secrets) was always more creative than strictly interpretive. Until the beginning of the twentieth century, when Tarot decks with a picture on every card were first designed and put into circulation, only the court cards and the Major Arcana used to be illustrated. Aces through tens were pip cards, as in the regular bridge deck. Lack of specific imagery on these cards left considerable scope for the card reader's own visualizations.

Therefore, methods of reading the Minor Arcana differed from methods of reading the Major Arcana. Interpretations in the existing literature show more variety in the pip cards than in the trump cards. The Minor Arcana seemed to encourage the free play of imagination, essential to the diviner's art.

Certain flexible boundaries were imposed by the qualities associated with the four elements, and the life-areas supposedly ruled by them. Cups (water) pertained to matters of the heart: love, sex, romance, marriage, children, family relationships, feelings, emotional problems. Wands (fire) pertained to matters of power, politics, commerce, conflict, success or failure, winning or losing: the games of life. Pentacles (earth) pertained to property and possessions: money, real estate, inheritances, Lares and Penates, giving and receiving. Swords (air) were generally accorded the dire meanings of danger and death: illness, grief, injury, accidents, hostile forces, setbacks, and sorrows.

Within these boundaries, the sequence of cards from ace to ten was usually envisioned as three triads or triangles of increasing complexity, summed up by the tenth card which encompassed the whole, like the final statement of a theme. The graphic sign of such a system was the so-called Dragon's Eye: a triangle, divided into three smaller triangles by three straight lines drawn inward from each angle to meet in the center. Ace-two-three, four-five-six, seven-eight-nine made three triangles. The ten was a summation of the life-area governed by each suit.

In divination, court cards were usually taken to represent people, though they could also be seen as spiritual entities symbolizing affective influences. Standard court-card sequences of three males and one female—page, knight, king, and queen—may have been patterned after the Christian all-male Trinity with its peripheral, officially nondivine Queen of Heaven. However, some early minchiate packs showed an even balance of the sexes, after the classic pattern of two male and two female elements. Knights were matched by ladies, not pages. Some modern designers used a similar system of sexual balance. Crowley's deck had knights, princes, princesses, and queens. The Golden Dawn Tarot had kings, queens, princes, and princesses. This arrangement is followed in the present work, as more in keeping with the "elemental" theme.

In any given layout, each card is influenced or modified by other cards in its immediate vicinity, and by its own position in the design. Some cartomancers invert a card's usual meaning when it appears upside down in the layout. Others interpret each card the same way, whether it is upside down or right side up, on the ground that a Tarot layout is double-ended, facing both the diviner and the querent. These are individual preferences, indicative of the creative latitude allowed in nearly all phases of interpreting Minor Arcana. Most Tarot experts emphasize the importance of following one's own feelings about the cards. No two people read cards quite the same way. Probably the best approach is to study as many different authors as one can find on the subject, impress their various ideas upon one's mind, then relax and let one's unconscious take over as in a waking dream.

Laying out cards has long been regarded as an aid to both divination and meditation: two poorly defined mental activities with no very clear distinction between them. Generally, meditation is supposed to lead to genuine insight, while divination verges on the more vulgar connotations of fortune-telling, often open to suspicion of fraud, or at least of frivolity. Some say the cards should never be read for money, any more than the common sacraments of a church are performed for money, unless it be a genuinely voluntary donation—and even that may be suspected of subtle coercion. "Pure" or non-commercial meditation on the cards may afford real help in allowing the mind to focus on a problem. Just as a dream may suddenly provide answers to questions that the conscious mind couldn't resolve, so the ritual of placing cards and considering their relationships may suggest a fresh outlook and a consequent solution.

Card readers recommend a certain amount of preliminary ritual. Like any religious ritual, this may look like silly mumbo-jumbo on the surface, yet may help quiet the mind and focus attention on the matter at hand. Suggestions include the following: fast for seven hours before consulting the cards; observe a certain time of day or phase of the moon, or take out the cards only after sunset; spread a black silk cloth on the card table; light incense; burn two candles, a black one to the left hand, a white one to the right; wear special clothing, such as a robe; place the reader's chair with its back toward due north; recite a verbal invocation; sip water or wine from a silver goblet (the lunar metal); hold the cards until they are warmed; breathe on them; raise them three times above the head; place them against the forehead and close the eyes for seven seconds—and so on, through whatever formal gestures the individual reader prefers.

When one person reads cards for another, the reader may ask the querent to join in the verbal invocation or share the drink of wine or water; to place the hands on the deck for seven seconds; to lay both hands on the table with thumbs touching the deck; to cut the deck seven times with the left hand only; to blow on the cards three times, and so on. Participation in such rituals need not indicate a superstitious credulity about the "magic" of the cards. Like art, ritual serves a number of psychological purposes. Human beings, both believers and unbelievers, evolve rituals as naturally as they breathe. The mere performance can induce a calm, receptive mental state.

Laying out cards is a ritual in itself, as any compulsive solitaire player knows. Cartomancers have devised many different ways to do it. We are already familiar with the square, "elemental" or "holy mountain" layout; the lemniscate infinity sign or double "wheels of becoming" layout; and the triangular "yoni yantra" layout. Another common arrangement, perhaps the most popular, is the so-called Ancient Celtic spread. It is probably neither ancient nor Celtic, but rather a short form evolved by Golden Dawn cartomancers. It uses only ten cards. Six are laid in the shape of a cross, four in a vertical column to the right.

Traditional interpretation of the Ancient Celtic spread runs as follows. Card #1, placed at the center of the cross, stands for the querent, his immediate situation, or the problem that concerns him. Card #2, placed horizontally across card #1, represents a difficulty blocking or modifying a present situation. Card #3, placed above the first two (at the head of the cross), is the short-term goal: the best that can be achieved under present conditions. Card #4, placed beneath the first two (at the foot of the cross), represents influences from the deep past that affect a present situation. Card #5, at the right arm of the cross, represents an influence from the more recent past. Card #6, at the left arm of the cross, is a projection for the near future, supposing that other factors remain constant. Card order traces the Hermetic or backward version of the sign of the cross, like a figure 4.

The last four cards are placed in a vertical column from bottom to top, at the right of the cross. Card #7 stands for the inner self, secret wishes and desires, the basic personality affecting a current situation. Card #8 stands for environmental or family influences, including a place of residence, either real or spiritual. Card #9 indicates the unexpected stroke of fortune, good or bad. Card #10 sums it all up like the tens of the Minor Arcana, indicating a probable conclusion.

There is a handy mnemonic charm for laying out cards in the Ancient Celtic design. As the cards are placed, say: "One finds you, two crosses you, three crowns you; four beneath you, five behind you, six before you; seven for your hopes and fears, eight for your house and home, nine for what you don't expect, ten for what is sure to be." The very syntax of this charm expresses the Dragon's Eye pattern of the triple triad.

It is not recommended that a card reader try to memorize the multitude of meanings attached to each card in the deck, word for word. It is better to gain a general impression of the spectrum of ideas belonging to each, to know how they overlap, and how they might be modified by accompanying cards. Thus, it is possible for each card to be interpreted somewhat differently every time it appears in a layout.

The best purpose of cartomancy is not to "tell fortunes" like a gypsy trickster, but to learn how to activate and trust one's own intuitive processes. Pictures of any kind are always useful for this. Like dreams, pictures communicate with the pre-verbal mind. Tarot pictures are especially useful because they show mythic archetypes that human minds and hands have repeated and reshaped for many centuries. Such archetypal visions are never wholly identical, but they follow the same basic patterns over and over. Therefore, the figures of these Lesser Secrets are often the same as the figures of myth, intended to suggest the same overtones and meanings as myths themselves. Most readers are likely to find this system highly evocative and stimulating to the individual vision—as Tarot cards were intended to be from the beginning.

The Suit
of Cups

Ace of Cups:
Love

Ace of Cups:

Love

The Goddess Minne, whose name meant Love, was the patron of medieval *minne*singers: another incarnation of the Great Mother known to pre-Christian Europe as Aphrodite, Venus, Isis, Freya, Mari, Mana, Maerin, Mene, Diana, Juno, and many other variants of these. Minstrels called themselves her honorary sons, celebrated her in their poetry, and devoted themselves to her worship through *minnedienst*, the "service of women," which churchmen regarded as a heresy, even a form of devil worship.[1]

Minne was often represented as a mermaid. She inherited the piscine symbolism of the Mother of Waters, giver of love, life, and fertility: the *vesica piscis* or Vessel of the Fish, emblem of female genitalia; the water-producing full moon called Pearl of the Sea; the single or double fish tail, shown by the alchemical Siren in both pagan and Christian iconography; and the cup or grail identified with her Sacred Heart, the link between cups and hearts in the cards. In earlier images of the Holy Grail, her vessel of waters, the Goddess personified the Heart of the World. Saxon chroniclers spoke of the mystic paradise "where Venus lives in the Grail."[2]

Fish were eaten "for love" on Venus's day, Friday, named for her northern counterpart Freya. Christians continued the pagan practice, pretending it was a fast in honor of Christ. But in some areas even today, people retain the older Goddess-oriented belief that fish are aphrodisiac food.

Christians also claimed the Goddess's fish sign was invented by the early church to symbolize Christ. However, long before Christianity, this sign referred to the Mother in her orgiastic aspect as divine Salacia, with "fish-teeming womb."[3] The fish was one of her oldest totems. Women's sexual odor was widely compared to the odor of fish. The salacious Goddess was described in India as "a virgin named Fishy Smell, whose real name was Truth."[4] As Matsya, the cosmic fish carrying the ark of Ma-Nu through the womb of chaos between worlds, she bore a name like that of Egypt's Mother Maat, whose name also meant Truth. Patriarchal Brahmans redefined Matsya as an incarnation of their phallic god Vishnu; but in Egypt, the fish retained its feminine connotation as the yoni that swallowed the phallic god.[5] Maat-Isis, as the Fish of the Abyss, was sometimes called Ma-Nu, sometimes Abtu. In Greece, both the Delphic oracle and the sacred dolphin *(delphinos)* were named after the Goddess as Delphos, Greek for "Womb."

Greeks used to celebrate orgiastic festivals called Hysteria—another word for "Womb"—in honor of the Goddess whose cosmic maternity inspired every form of love: sexual, parental, tribal, social; the bondings of siblings, lovers, friends, and so on. Under the Goddess, sexuality and sensuality were associated with affectionate feelings rather than with the fear, guilt, or aggression characteristic of patriarchal attitudes.

Water, the element of the suit of cups, was once a common metaphor for the all-embracing, all-surrounding essence of love. The ancients said love, like water, takes the shape of the vessel that contains it, and is infinitely flexible, but it can never be squeezed, compressed, or coerced. Any attempt to clutch it tightly in the hand only makes it disappear. Held gently, it remains with its life-giving virtue.

A water-personifying form of the Goddess appropriately introduces the first suit of cups, hearts, grails, and so on. Water represented the Creatress, whose womb was the primal Deep. It was once believed that mothers brought forth out of their own internal fluids, stimulated by the impulse of love in their hearts, just as the Great Mother brought forth the universe. The ace of cups has always suggested ideas related to this concept: birth, beginning, fruitfulness, pleasure, happiness, home, nourishment, satisfaction, and caring. It is a benevolent card par excellence. In a divinatory layout it may be regarded as an enhancement of other good influences, or a mitigating power over bad ones—for any trouble is easier to bear with the help of love.

Two of Cups:

Romance

Two of Cups: Romance

Lovers came to be regarded as "couples" after pledging their troth in cups (French *coupes*). So in the Tarot, a pair of cups naturally suggested a male-and-female pair committed to each other by a sexual-romantic bond like the *drudaria* celebrated by medieval minnesingers.

The common people never tired of these troubadours' love songs, even though church authorities condemned the songs as heathen and sinful (because they were dedicated to the Goddess), and tried to forbid them by law.[1] Some of these songs, still extant, describe the minstrels' power to turn people away from the church, and make them forget the priests' teaching, that love must be equated with sin.[2] Churchmen insisted that God would punish lovers in hell, with eternal roastings over fires fed by their earthly passions.[3] Yet the romantic poets, indirectly inspired by Eastern Sufis and Tantric sadhakas, strongly hinted that man's spiritual fulfillment must be sought by the path of sexual love.[4]

Minnesingers were supposed to know of certain secret places formerly sacred to the Goddess—grottoes, groves, hidden temples—where lovers could hold their trysts without fear of discovery.[5] These were sometimes identified with the earthly paradise called "terrestrial place of pleasure" *(locus voluptatis terrestris)* or "paradise of joy" *(pratum felicitatis)*.[6] Spenser's Fairie Queene presided over such a Bower of Bliss, centered on the feminine Rose of Love, a sexual symbol much revered by the bards' Arabian precursors, who called the sexual paradise a holy Rose Garden.[7]

Love songs were "romans" in southern France, home of the heretical courtly-love movement later extinguished in the bloody Albigensian

Crusade. Love affairs came to be called "romances" because they were celebrated by the poetry of this movement. A typical poem was the medieval romance of Aucassin and Nicolete, star-crossed lovers thwarted by ecclesiastical guardians in all their efforts to unite. Aucassin, who was really a Western version of the Arabic "prince of lovers," Al-Kasim, renounced the teachings of the church and declared that he would rather go to hell with his beloved Nicolete than to Heaven with the "halt old men and maimed" of the Christian community. At last, he and his sweetheart were united in the pagan paradise, a fairyland called Torelore, where love was encouraged instead of condemned.[8]

Like romance literature, the Tarot card sets lovers in an isolated place, hidden from all but the Moon Goddess who kept their secrets. Meanings assigned to this card include trust, sympathy, consummation of desires, vows, promises, engagements, marriage, and intimate friendship. When the unified concept of Love (as in the ace) becomes a duality, all permutations of active partnership are suggested.

Three of Cups:

Grace

Three of Cups: Grace

Christianity borrowed the concept of grace from pagan votaries of the trinitarian Goddess, whose special blessings were collectively *charis*, "grace," dispensed by her three emanations, the Charites or Graces.

According to Pausanias, the Charites were worshiped at Orchomenos in the form of three very ancient sacred stones.[1] Their cult was older than Greek civilization. Homer's name for the leading Grace was Cale or Kale, perhaps none other than the triple Kali.[2] The classic image of three naked Graces dancing together was found also in the statuary of Hindu temples as well as Greek ones.[3]

An old word for manifest signs of the Goddess's favor was *charisma*, literally "Mother's Grace," a gift from the Queen of Heaven. To Romans it was sometimes *venia*, the blessing of Venus (which, to later Roman Catholics, designated a type of sin). Julian wrote, "The three-fold gift of the Charites comes to us from heaven, from the circles of the stars."[4] The Gnostic author Marcus called upon the ancient Goddess under the name of Charis or Grace: "May She who is before all things, the incomprehensible and indescribable Grace, fill you within, and increase in you her own knowledge."[5]

Like Hindu *karuna*, grace used to mean a combination of feminine qualities such as sympathy, sensitivity, responsiveness, loving-kindness, goodwill, intelligence, and personal magnetism; also, physical grace, sexual attractiveness, and unabashed sensuality. Ascetic Christianity radically altered the original idea of *charis*. In the New Testament, *charis* is translated either "charity" or "love," neither of which conveys the flavor of the earlier, female-oriented idea of grace. A copy of a pagan hymn to Charis in 1 Corinthians 13 says, "Now abideth faith, hope, charity, these three; but the greatest of these is charity." This passage helped convince early Christians that giving away money to the poor was the best way to reserve a privileged place in heaven for one's self. But the older *charis* meant a great deal more than giving away money. It was the epitome of all forms of love, based on mother-love, the root of them all, exemplified by the Goddess.

Faith and Hope were also emanations of the Goddess in her many triadic forms. As Bona Fides, "Good Faith," she invented the Roman legal system and governed codes of honor, contracts, and agreements.

According to some classical writers, the Graces were Aglaia, "Brilliant"; Thalia, "Flowering"; and Euphrosyne, "Rejoicer of the Heart." Others confused them with the triad called Horae, the heavenly whores Eunomia, Dike, and Irene—Order, Justice, and Peace—whose sexual rites were said to "mellow" the violent behavior of men.[6]

Traditional interpretations of this Tarot card suggested the old Goddess's gifts of grace rather than the orthodox Christian concept. They included celebration, fruition, joy, satisfaction, healing, solace, fulfillment of hopes. Sometimes the Romantic two of cups was said to be completed by the Gracious three, as a couple may be completed by the birth of a child. It used to be said the ability to give birth was the most dramatically visible sign of the Goddess's grace—which she bestowed, of course, on women only. The patriarchal God of Genesis transformed this blessing into a curse, and Christians maintained it was a sign of female sinfulness. Then, *charis* was removed from the series of ideas related to mother-love, and came to mean the giving of money instead of the giving of love. Thus "grace" became another kind of fruition in the patriarchal sense. Still, three dancing female figures on the card continued to recall the older idea of the Graces as agents of kindly fate, in northern Europe identified with the Norns, who were "three rosebuds" in the mystic garden of Love.[7]

Four of Cups:

Decline

Four of Cups: *Decline*

In the ancient sacred drama, the period following consummation and fertilization brought the death of the god, who descended into the underworld like the declining sun. Similarly in the Tarot suit of the heart, following the fulfillment of the first trimester, a new cycle would be initiated with a decline from grace and a regression of happiness. The four of cups thus carried a regressive or negative meaning.

Ancient Middle-Eastern traditions associated the period of the god's decline with Salome, or the Goddess Salma, a Crone aspect of Mari-Ishtar, who pronounced the ceremonial word of "farewell" (shalom, or salaam) to the god entering the underworld. The Bible's version of her "dance of seven veils" was a trivialized re-interpretation of the high priestess's sacred dance, which originally portrayed the removal of the Goddess's magical garments at each of the seven underworld gates, as she descended to bring the dead god's spirit back to his next rebirth.

This was widely regarded as a dangerous and sorrowful period. Babylonian scriptures said neither human beings nor animals could copulate or reproduce during this time.[1] According to even older Sumerian versions, it was a time of wailing for the vanished savior and of praying for the return of love and fertility to the land.[2] Romans also looked upon this period of decline as a loss of the love-spirit personified by Aphrodite (Venus) and her slain lover Adonis. While the world was not illuminated by their love, all forms of emotional bonding—friendship, family ties, sexual relationships, loyalty of parents and children—suffered depletion.[3]

The same seven veils, stoles, or magical ornaments adorned many versions of the descending Goddess, in addition to their biblical derivative, Salome. Inanna, Ishtar, Maya, Venus, and Isis wore them.[4] Originally they represented the seven spheres of earthly or heavenly appearances, hiding her true nature behind the seven colors of the rainbow. Neither god nor man could be properly reborn until he had penetrated the veils and beheld the Naked Goddess face to face. Salome danced for the king, because a king was invariably apotheosized; and her removal of the veils symbolized his god-like destiny.

146

In the biblical version, the ceremony was performed for King Herod while a surrogate or "sacred king," in the person of John the Baptist, suffered the royal death formerly meted out to kings themselves at the end of each cycle. Gnostic traditions sometimes insisted that the true sacrificed Christ—a sacred "King of the Jews"—was not Jesus but John.[5] An early Greek hymn said it was John's blood that fructified the reproductive powers of Jerusalem ("House of Salom"), as it was ritually sprinkled on its mothers and children.[6] Yet, Salome was present not only at the death of John, but also at both the death and the birth of Jesus, according to Mark 15:40 and the *Protoevangelium.*[7]

In Canaan and other nations that served as sources for biblical subjects, the term usually allotted to each king in antiquity was seven years: a "magic seven" combining, as in the Tarot, the three of grace with the four of decline. Salome's dance overturns the last cup: the king's fatal year. Throughout the Middle East, to turn down an empty cup was a common symbol of death, as is still shown by the familiar phrase from Omar Khayyam's *Rubaiyat:*

> And when like her, oh Saki, you shall pass
> Among the Guests Star-scattered on the Grass,
> And in your joyous errand reach the spot
> Where I made One—turn down an empty Glass!

Interpretations of the four of cups focus on the stage in any relationship known as the end of the honeymoon: decline, some hint of disillusionment, satiety, disappointment, or lack of appreciation; a stagnant period, when nothing much seems to happen. However, the element of naked revelation hints at new insights to come, in view of the belief that decline and death are cyclic, so that every dissolution leads eventually to a rebirth.

Five of Cups:

Regret

Five of Cups: Regret

Tarot fives generally bore dire connotations, perhaps because of a half-remembered link with the Egyptian sign of the underworld, a five-pointed star in a circle, standing for the nadir of the sacred king's mystic journey.[1] Under this sign of the five-pointed star (or pentacle), the god lay dead in the earth's "pit," waiting for the time when the Goddess would resurrect him. These were dark days of lament and regret. Also, symbolically associated with such a period was the overturned cup spilling the sacred blood or wine of happiness, implying a deadly impotence.[2] In the cults of Canaan, for example, the god now took the names of Death and Sterility.

Since the suit of cups represented emotions in particular, the five was often interpreted as a card of alienation, poverty of feeling, frustration, loss of pleasure, or disturbance of a formerly harmonious relationship through a failure to live up to expectations. Marriage without real love was a common implication. The five usually indicated a union once intended to be satisfying, unfortunately found wanting in some essentials, and therefore a source of regret.

The five-pointed star of the underworld, the spilled cup, and a couple united only by mutual avoidance appear as appropriate symbols of this rather discouraging card. Withdrawn from her partner, a woman gazes at her own element, the sea. A man sulks, brooding over his own trouble. An observer of such a scene usually leaps to the conclusion that these are lovers or spouses who quarreled, and who have killed their love. That most people would make this same interpretive leap in itself says something about our own cultural predilections. In fact, there are many other possible ways of looking at the apparently angry pair. The woman, whose face is invisible, may stand for any sort of abandonment or indifference; the man for any annoyance. There is also a sense of turning away from old ties and looking outward to new interests, needs, and meanings. Something comes to an end, and there is a hiatus of regret; but that too ends in time.

Six of Cups:

Childhood

Six of Cups: Childhood

In the philosophies of antiquity, endings usually implied a return to origins where a new beginning could be made. The Tarot's six of cups suggested a psychic return of this kind, reverting to childhood memories either as a nostalgic inner pilgrimage or as a new light shed on the events of life's yesteryears.

Mythology presented this idea as a return to the primal Age of Giants, or Golden Age, which the collective human mind projected onto its past. Giants appeared in such myths because the universal experience of childhood is that of living among people much bigger than one's self.

Hindus defined this "first age of the world" as the Satya Yuga, when human beings grew to enormous size, strength, and wisdom, and were without sins—as adults appear to very young children. During the Satya Yuga, human lives could last a thousand years because their vital energies were still "centered in the blood" of the Great Mother whose menstrual outpourings created life in the first place.[1] The Bible copied and preserved some of this same idea of "mighty men" and "giants in the earth" during a long-ago time (Genesis 6:4). Human lives became shorter and less virtuous, the Hindus said, as additional generations slowly diluted the potency of the Goddess's original Blood of Life. Thus, the Bible portrays the earliest semi-divine ancestors living not quite a thousand years, but more than 900 years at least. There were also Hebraic traditions maintaining that the early patriarchs were of gigantic stature.[2]

Northern Aryans called their gigantic ancestors *risi*, a derivative of Sanskrit *rishi*, which meant the sages of the elder race. These ancestors were governed by their mothers, the giantesses or Afliae, "Powerful Ones."[3] Even Thor, the mighty Thunder-bull, had to undertake a pilgrimage to their mystic land in order to acquire his divine powers. This myth of many meanings incorporated the idea (later elucidated by Jung) that emotional progress toward maturity depends, in part, on a symbolic return to the "children's land" to re-activate hidden memories.[4] Many mythic heroes returned in some way to the Golden Age, or to the long-lived race: the faraway places and times when fatherhood was unknown, and human life was traced through the matrilineal blood bond.[5] To learn of these matters was a fundamental passage into the heart of the Mystery.

Greeks called their primordial giants Titans, who were ruled by Mother Rhea, the Universal Goddess of prepatriarchal Aegean civilization.[6] She was often depicted as big as a mountain. Phrygians called her Panorma, the Universal Mountain Mother. Indo-Iranian myths also identified her with the Holy Mountain who supported all the gods. When medieval Europe characterized the elder deities as "fairies," the Divine Mother became Titania, Queen of the Fairies, after her ancient mountain shrine of Titane.[7] Symbolic reduction of the gigantic Titans to small-sized fairy people reproduced, in popular mythology, the typical change of viewpoint during growth and maturing, when parental figures seem to shrink from giants to ordinary humans.

Following the failure of love associated with the five of cups, the six tended to suggest a psychic return to early experiences of love and faded memories of the deep past—just as longings for the lost Golden Age of (singular) childhood or (collective) pre-civilization could be mythologized as nostalgia for a primal paradise under the giants' rule. This card was usually associated with a mother figure, maternal influences, first formations of character, old loves or fears, living in the past. A new interest in things of antiquity could be necessary for refreshment of vital energies. As in Oriental mysticism, the true source of all vital energies was expressed in the image of Mother-as-giantess or Goddess-as-power.

Seven of Cups:

Dream

Seven of Cups: Dream

The symbolic return to the children's land, signified by the six of cups, led naturally to the seven's implication of pre-verbal modes of thought: the rich depths of the unconscious, tapped by dreams and archetypal imagery. Here dwelt inspiration—literally "breathing-in" a spirit—and idea, literally the Goddess-within.

Greek myth said the Mountain Mother brought forth the Muses: female spirits of inspiration and creative ideas. Their blessings generated music, poetry, dance and all other arts.[1] They were either a trinity or a ninefold emanation of the Goddess herself, the "nine maidens" of Teutonic myth; they/she provided all human "I-deas."

All over the world, ancient religions viewed the source of inspiration as a feminine spirit, even in a masculine host. By Tantric definition, the Way of the Muses was the Left-Hand Path, also called the Way of Woman (Vamacara), or simply Marga, "the Way," another name for the Goddess herself.[2] The Chinese called it Tao, "the Way."[3] Chinese sages described Tao by many metaphors applicable to their idea of the primal womb. Tao was a vessel, or a divine ancestress of every life, or an inexhaustible source of things, or an unfathomable deep. It—or she—existed before God.[4]

The same vessel generating life and inspiration in pre-Christian Europe was the cauldron with all its synonyms: cup, grail, fountain, well, sacred heart, Source. The bard Taliesin spoke of the creative Word emanating from the cauldron, kindled by the breath of "nine maidens" (the Muses).[5] Taliesin himself was said to have received his Grace of Inspiration from the cauldron of his mother, the Goddess Cerridwen, one of the female trinity called "source of life, and receptacle of the dead."[6] She too was linked with the Left-Hand Path under her other titles as Mother Earth, or Tara. By pagan tradition it was forbidden to move "righthandwise" around her shrine.[7] One could only take the left-hand way, moving widdershins or moonwise (counterclockwise), the direction later associated with witches.

The Goddess, as source of inspiration, appeared to her lovers in opaline veils, the "rainbow veils" of Nature's appearances, as Hindus called them, created by the magic of Maya-Kali the Cosmic Shakti. Among her Latin names was Ops, the Earth-mother of the Opalia.[8] Her sacred gem the opal was supposed to contain a magical essence of her many-colored veils. Because of its former association with Goddess worship, Christians came to regard the opal as an unlucky stone.

For similar reasons, patriarchal religions described Nature's appearances as false illusions created by the Goddess's "glamor." They said one should not worship Mother Nature, but only the God who somehow dwelt *in* Mother Nature—as a child in the womb. His devotees insisted that he was more real than things that could be seen and touched. From this notion came a patriarchal habit of belittling dreams and inspirations from the Goddess as "fairy favors" that would soon disappear, just as treasures received in a dream would melt out of the hand upon awakening.

Medieval folklore said a man could receive rich favors if he found a statue of the Goddess in one of her ruined temples and made it his ladylove, like Pygmalion of the olden time. If he embraced her, ejaculated semen on her, and promised her that he would never enter a

151

church again, she would become his Fate, dwell in his dreams, and tell him secrets, such as where to find buried treasure.[9] Forgetting that the Muse's buried treasures and hidden gems once symbolized her wisdom, the simpleminded took such stories literally. As their dreams of glory faded in morning light, men called the Goddess of the Left-Hand Path an artificer of false hopes. Their priests claimed her promises of Paradise/Fairyland were devilish delusions.

Thus, the seven of cups may reflect men's ambivalent attitude toward mystical experiences and inspirational dreams. On one hand, the card is associated with true vision, poetic sensibility, talent, insight, and revelation.[10] On the other hand, it is a card of fantasy, illusion, unrealistic attitudes, or wishful thinking. Interpretation can only be decided by the context.

Eight of Cups:

Loss

Eight of Cups: Loss

The classical Greek shrine of the Muses was the Helicon, "Willow-Stream," which encircled their sacred mountain of the same name.[1] As the mountain-mothers of inspiration, the Muses were sometimes combined as a single Goddess under the name of Helice, "Willow," a virgin form of Hecate. A shape-shifting nymph, Helice could take the form of a willow tree. Her lover was Pan, the Arcadian goat god, whose name meant "All-father," and whose cult was once universal throughout the Aegean.

Pan appeared in classical mythology as a deified goat-king fathered by Hermes and carried up to heaven, where he became the zodiacal Capricorn. Pan was a master of magic, and an invincible warrior. His spellcasting battle-cry produced "pan-ic" in his enemies. Once he had numerous followers in Palestine. As the goat god Azazel he received each Yom Kippur sacrifice. At the source of the Jordan was a cave dedicated to him as Baal Gad, "Goat Lord."[2]

Naturally, Pan became a leading model for the Christian idea of the goat-footed devil, after churchmen insisted that his worship must cease. Nevertheless, the cult of Pan and Helice survived underground,

Ace of Cups, Love

Two of Cups, Romance

Three of Cups, Grace

Four of Cups, Decline

Five of Cups, Regret

Six of Cups, Childhood

Seven of Cups, Dream

Eight of Cups, Loss

Nine of Cups, Happiness

Ten of Cups, Salvation

Princess of Cups, Elaine

Prince of Cups, Galahad

Ace of Wands, Power

Two of Wands, Alliance

Three of Wands, Fate

Four of Wands, Success

Five of Wands, Impasse

Six of Wands, Glory

Seven of Wands, Challenge

Eight of Wands, Fall

Nine of Wands, Defense

Ten of Wands, Oppression

Princess of Wands, Atargatis

Prince of Wands, Dugon

Ace of Pentacles, Reward

Two of Pentacles, Change

Three of Pentacles, Work

Four of Pentacles, Avarice

Five of Pentacles, Hardship

Six of Pentacles, Charity

Seven of Pentacles, Failure

Eight of Pentacles, Learning

Nine of Pentacles, Accomplishment

Ten of Pentacles, Protection

Princess of Pentacles, Nimue

Prince of Pentacles, Merlin

Ace of Swords, Doom

Two of Swords, Balance

Three of Swords, Sorrow

Four of Swords, Seclusion

Five of Swords, Defeat

Six of Swords, Passage

Seven of Swords, Opposition

Eight of Swords, Disillusion

Nine of Swords, Cruelty

Ten of Swords, Ruin

Princess of Swords, Skuld

Prince of Swords, Tyr

many of its details preserved by "witches" with their sacred wands of willow wood and their dances in honor of the Horned God.

The old traditions lasted all the way up to the nineteenth century when poets romanticized them into a new vitality. Byron wrote regretfully of the death of "the great Pan." Oscar Wilde exclaimed, "O goatfoot god of Arcady! This modern world hath need of thee!" Shelley wrote to his friend Thomas Hogg: "I am glad to hear that you do not neglect the rites of the true religion. Your letter awoke my sleeping devotion, and the same evening I ascended alone to the high mountain behind my house, and suspended a garland, and raised a small turf-altar to the mountain-walking Pan."[3]

Poets were especially sensitive to the implication of creative sterility in the mythic loss of Pan and his Willow-goddess Helice, who personified the inspiration of the Muses. Like the eight spilling cups representing Loss in the Tarot, the tears of the deposed god, weeping for his vanished nymphs, provided a poetic metaphor for loss of true inspiration, in what the poets called an age of ignorance and shallow materialism. Helice too became a "weeping" willow, the gift of the Muses immobilized and rooted to one spot, for according to the later patriarchal revision of her myth the transformation of the Willow-goddess was permanent. Both male and female deities here represent loss or bereavement.

The eight implied cups of devotion poured out uselessly; abnegation of physical energies; turning away from the vital forces of nature that Pan and Helice once stood for. The card bore connotations of abandonment, severing links with the past, rejection of the Muse's gifts, desertion of old loyalties, and similar changes of viewpoint accompanied by feelings of sadness, melancholy, or helplessness. The eight also could imply unavoidable regret at leaving behind something valuable, during a passage into a new phase of life.

The Secrets of the Tarot

Nine of Cups:

Happiness

Nine of Cups: Happiness

As the nine Muses symbolically tripled the power of the Triple Goddess, so Tarot nines symbolically intensified the central theme of their suits. The nine of cups was seen as a full expression of the suit-theme of love, and its usual interpretation was Happiness.

According to pagan belief, the epitome of earthly happiness was to be found in the sacred moon-groves, *nemetonae* or *nimidae*, that used to serve as open-air temples everywhere in Europe. In such groves, the Goddess and her God coupled over the mystic Rose of Love, which later appeared at the central point of the Fairy Queen's magic garden.[1] The Fairy Queen was another form of the many-named Goddess, who was also Diana Nemetona (Diana of the Grove), Ops, Maia, Artemis, Hecate, Brigit, Tara, Cerridwen, Mana, Marian, Nimue, Viviane, Luna, Venus, and so on. Her consort too had many names. He was Dianus, Faunus, Dionysus, Consus, Zeus, Jove, Orpheus, Merlin, Iasus, Hippolytus, Sylvanus, and Mars. He was once the god of the oracular oak trees, the sky, and the lightning. He was still worshiped in Russia as late as 1874, when a sacred oak grove was decorated with wax candles while an Orthodox priest chanted, "Holy Oak Hallelujah, pray for us." The service was followed by an orgy.[2]

The orgy was a primary sacrament of the Old Religion and the main reason for its diabolization in the Middle Ages. Christian writers spoke of "heathen abominations" in the sacred groves, and insisted that the oracular oak trees should be cut down and the altars buried.

Still, the old names of the Goddess's greenwood shrines persist in place names such as Medionemeton in southern Scotland, Nanterre (formerly Nemetodurum) in France, and Nemetobriga in Spain—that is, the *nemeton* of the Goddess Brigit, whose empire of Brigantia once occupied the whole Iberian peninsula.[3] Even Christian cathedrals borrowed symbolism from the pagan groves. The upper vaultings of Gothic churches are still technically known as "the forest."

The groves were appropriate locations for sexual unions that were supposed to promote world fertility, for each nation's principal grove was viewed as the genital center of Mother Earth. The implanted sacred pillar, obelisk, or tree stood for her consort's phallus. Worshipers' orgiastic rites were both an imitation and an encouragement of the all-important union between male and female deities.

Modern religions suppressed the ancient connection between religious and sexual "bliss," now distinguished as two separate—even inimical—kinds of happiness. By the Judeo-Christian definition, religious ecstasy was a supreme good, sexual ecstasy a supreme evil even within marriage. St. Augustine declared, and his church ever afterward confirmed, that sex was the medium of transmission of original sin from every generation to the next.

Yet, folk traditions and the sad literature of witchcraft persecutions show that the old connections were not forgotten. In Gnostic lore as in the Tarot, "happiness" was akin to the Tantric *karuna*, amalgamating sexuality and sensuality with kindness, goodwill, contentment, fruitfulness, physical health, and emotional stability. The benign outlook of the nine of cups encompassed every happiness of flesh or spirit, without the taint of sin or fear that often poisoned life's enjoyments for the orthodox.

Ten of Cups:

Salvation

Ten of Cups: Salvation

Ten cups were said to sum up the qualities of their suit, suggesting attainment of the earthly paradise in harmonious love, security, peace, union: the true salvation from men's greatest fears: loneliness or abandonment. The underground religions of Europe mythologized this paradise as Fairyland, or Joyous Gard, or Venus's Mount (*mons veneris*), or Torelore, or the Castle of the Holy Grail on Montsalvatch, the Mount of Salvation.

Some accounts placed this legendary temple-castle in the Spanish Pyrenees, where real Catharan heretics sought their final refuge from papal Crusaders at Montségur in the fourteenth century. Other accounts placed the Grail temple-castle in the East, under the rule of a Fairy Queen or high priestess named Repanse de Joie (Dispenser of Joy), an old title of the Goddess Venus.[1] Semi-Christianized Arthurian Grail legends identified the mistress of the divine castle as Elaine or Elen, an ancient Celtic name for the Virgin Moon-goddess.

Legends show that the natural guide to the Mount of Salvation would have to be the western equivalent of a Shakti—either the Fairy Queen herself, or her representative, an "emanation" embodied in the hero's mystic ladylove. She would conduct her postulant across the River of Blood (corresponding to the menstrual Styx), and show him the way to the magic mount. All this had a genital symbolism as well as a spiritual one. An early traveler on the romantic journey was the Celtic hero Peredur Paladhrir, that is, the Spearman with a Long Lance, later called Perceval—that is, He Who Pierces the Valley. Again the symbolism was sexual. Peredur's ladylove was undoubtedly a Shakti, for she told him to seek her in India.[2] Her colors were the same sacred *Gunas* displayed in India by "the divine female Prakriti:" virginal white, maternal red, funerary black.[3]

Salvation through "joy" or sexual bliss was a tenet of both Oriental and European religions, until Christian missionaries taught that salvation must be won by renouncing earthly joys. Hidden doctrines of Gnostic heresy in myth and folktale hinted at the older ideas of salvation. Roland's paladins, who resembled the warrior-lovers of Saracen romance more than Christian knights, used as their battle-cry the word *Montjoie*, a synonym for Montsalvatch of the Grail cycle.[4] The same slogan was adopted by a fourteenth-century peasant leader who also adopted the Goddess's three-lobed lily, and used the suggestive surname of Cale or Kale.[5]

Conventional readings of the ten of cups implied attainment of any long-sought goal as well as salvation through love: achievement of concord, honor, and reputation; realization of dreams; a kind, benevolent person looking after one's interests as devotedly as a mother. The Tarot's salvation might be equated with the Christian concept of a heavenly reward, but its earth-rooted Mount and female guide betokened a religion of priestesses, not of priests.

Another common meaning of this card was a good marriage, lasting many years: a lifetime of contentment. In general, the Tarot's "salvation" was not the orthodox dream of heaven, but a practical solution to the perennial human problems of fear, alienation, loneliness, or disconnectedness. This was a literal, immediate, and human reading of salvation through love.

Princess of Cups:

Elaine

Princess of Cups: Elaine

The primary meaning of the princess of cups was like that of the Virgin Moon-goddess, keeper of the Grail temple. Celtic pagans called her Elaine the Lily Maid, divine queen of Britain—also known as Elen, Helen, Hel, or Hel-Aine. Even the Christianized knights in the later Grail myths encountered the holy vessel in her castle, where she wove the tapestries of life, death, and fate.[1]

Some Christian writings frankly described the Holy Grail not as the chalice of Christ's Last Supper, but as a *basina* or *escuele*—a cauldron.[2] It was a medieval transformation of the most sacred womb-symbol in European paganism: the Great Mother's Cauldron of Regeneration.

Like the Lily Maid, the princess of cups presides over a cauldron showing the same scene as the famous Gundestrup Cauldron, manufactured in the first century B.C. The central design showed a high priest plunging a sacrificial victim headfirst into a shield-shaped, double-lobed yoni, in preparation for his rebirth. The female gate of death and rebirth was attended by the usual wolf or moon-dog, Hound of Hel-Aine. In the original, a line of warriors approached the sacred vessel on foot as sacrificial victims, and departed from it as heavenly hosts, crowned, mounted on spirit-horses, transformed into gods.[3]

The Lily Maid resembled the *Mabinogion's* fairy woman from India, associated with the mystic Court of Women where slain warriors were daily resurrected from the sacred cauldron.[4] Her miraculous vessel appears in some form in nearly every mythology, dispensing youth, life, healing, wisdom, apotheosis, rebirth, or transformations in general. "As its primal image, the Grail takes the place of the mother."[5] The Lily Maid was an aspect of the Triple Goddess who was Snow White and Rose Red, virgin and mother, as well as the black Crone of death. According to the older religions, her womb was the cauldron in which living forms were continually recycled.

The mystery of the Grail myths is resolved by the realization that the holy vessel in the Maid's castle was not Christ's chalice after all. Christian knights would have had no reason to go questing for that particular cup of divine blood. The church's doctrine of transubstantiation insisted that it was literally present all the time, at every altar. What was lost was not the Christianized version of the Grail, but the pagans' old beloved symbol of rebirth, the cauldron, which later became the symbol of witchcraft. A Salic Law of the eighth century spoke of certain witches charged with the sacred duty of "bearing the cauldron" to their ceremonies.[6] Frensham Church in Surrey preserved one of these vessels, "an extraordinary great kettle or cauldron" supposed to have been donated by the fairies.[7]

As a guardian of such deep mysteries of the fairy world, the princess of cups was not only a "Dispenser of Joy" but also a source of hidden knowledge, poetic inspiration, mystical insight, inner truths, and the gift of wisdom. Hers was a cup of mystery, to be sampled only by those whose intuitions were prepared and trustworthy. She could symbolize a need for such gifts, or a person possessing them, or a hint that in certain circumstances such modes of thought can be essential.

Prince of Cups:

Galahad

Prince of Cups:
Galahad

Often associated with Elaine the Lily Maid was the hero known in his younger phase as Galahad, in his elder phase as Lancelot or Lanceor, "Golden Lance"—the lightning. Arthurian legends said young Galahad was raised by the Fairy Queen or Lady of the Lake, who changed his name to Lancelot of the Lake when he reached his maturity, and sent him on his quest for the Grail (or Cauldron). The mother of Galahad-Lancelot was called Queen Elaine.

As Galahad, the hero discovered the sacred vessel in Elaine's castle, symbolic of the Moon-goddess's realm. As Lancelot, he lay with her younger aspect the Lily Maid Elaine, and begot on her his own reincarnation, Galahad. This was the same kind of cyclic reincarnation of the father-son figure found in all the mystery religions including Christianity: Jesus was both son and father of himself, born of the Queen of Heaven who was both Bride of God and Mother of God. Indeed, Galahad was sometimes equated with the Christian version of the father-son. Some medieval writers said Galahad was the only knight worthy of the Grail quest because he was the only knight in Arthur's court who had never loved a woman; moreover, he "came of the ninth degree from our lord Jesus Christ."[1] In thus revising Celtic legends to a Christian context, the monkish chroniclers overlooked the implication of this genealogy—that "our lord Jesus Christ" must have loved a woman at least once.

It was a Christianized, virginized Galahad who renounced the traditions of courtly love, pulled the magic sword (phallus) out of the sacred omphalos-stone (yoni), and became one of the few men of his time who "believed in God perfectly" by giving up female companionship and the system of matrilineal blood kinship. However, the original Galahad was one of the pagan sacred kings who reigned for one lunar "year and a day," then met a sacrificial death. This detail remained intact even in his Christianized story. At the end of his span of kingship, Galahad suddenly died at the altar, in the very moment when he received a vision of the Grail. He was carried to heaven by angels. In like manner, each heathen sacred king was ceremonially slain, and then rode to heaven on the horse of the gods after his immolation.[2]

The oldest roots of this king-knight-hero lay in the land of Galatia in Asia Minor, early home of the Gaels or Gauls, who traced their descent from a union between their ancestral Goddess Galata and the immolated king-for-a-year, Heracles.[3] Another of his names was Phoenix, the dying-and-resurrected "Phoenician." The real Phoenicians called him Pumiyathon, consort of Astarte. The Greeks corrupted this name to Pygmalion, consort of Aphrodite in the guise of her own milk-white image, Galatea—that is, the same milk-giving Moon-goddess worshiped in Galatia, in Gaul, and in the Lily Maid's Britain.[4]

The prince (or knight) of cups was supposed to represent the qualities generally associated with complex heroes like Galahad: gallantry, gentleness, self-sacrifice, sensitivity, courtesy to women. His influence in the Tarot was like that of a visionary, a bringer of ideas and of inspiration, a messenger, or a man well in touch with the "feminine" aspects of his own being.

Queen of Cups:

Virginal

Queen of Cups: *Virginal*

Long before Christianity evolved its paradoxical virgin-mother figure, the Virgin and Mother aspects of the Goddess Kali merged in the Mother of the Gods called Durga the Inaccessible.[1] Beautiful, but formidable as a mother defending her offspring, Durga was said to be invincible in battle. Glacial and remote, she lived in the highest mountains of heaven, the uttermost Himalayas.

Personifying mother instinct, Durga was called "virginal" because she was inaccessible to males, like any animal mother preoccupied with her young. The sexual indifference of the pregnant, breeding, or lactating mammalian female used to be a codified law in primitive human cultures. It was the rule for men to refrain from making sexual advances to any nursing mother—wife or not—until her infant was weaned. The custom still prevails in parts of Asia.[2]

Western medieval poets had their own version of Durga the Inaccessible. They called her Virginal the Ice Queen, a divine fairy of the high mountains. German minstrels said Virginal once descended to the lowlands to marry a German prince. But she soon wearied of him and returned to her lofty ice cave among the clouds, in the realm of eternal snow, where she still rules as a supreme Goddess.[3]

Like Virginal the Ice Queen, the queen of cups represented water in its frozen forms: cold, crystalline, perfect, untouchable; the image of the nonsexual virgin mother. Like the high mountains Virginal inhabited, she stood above the petty concerns of men. As Durga personified the inaccessibility of the nursing mother, so Virginal combined indifference to men with a strangely maternal nourishing of their world—an idea long ago derived from milky glacial streams flowing down from mountains to bring life and fertility to the valleys. The inaccessible Goddess of the Himalayan "Mounts of Heaven" had this dual function, which is why her white peaks received names like Nanda Devi (Blessed Goddess) and Annapurna (Great Breast Full of Nourishment).[4]

The queen of cups traditionally represented an ethereal, otherworldly person of the highest ideals, perhaps unattainably high. Her purity and brilliance are symbolized by an empty crystalline cup on a mountain summit. Like all Tarot queens, she could be identified with a standard *persona* of the Goddess. She was the remote, uncaring one that men found especially threatening—as if they never truly outgrew the infantile fear of potentially lethal maternal indifference.

Patriarchal society was at pains to establish many legal, economic, and cultural safeguards against women's possible indifference to men. Yet, mythic figures like Virginal the Ice Queen (and her Christian counterpart, the Virgin Queen of Heaven) continued to haunt men, eliciting their worshipful placatory gestures, to avert the feared abandonment. Frigid, meaning sexually indifferent, became an opprobrious word of criticism, by males, of the female who would not respond. Somewhere within every man lay a fear of her, just as somewhere within every woman lay the unattainable Durga whose love objects did not include male adults. A noted psychologist observed that any woman might suddenly show this aspect of her character: "obstinate, cold, and completely inaccessible."[5]

Yet, the Ice Queen and her counterparts inspired almost abject reverence. Goethe prayed to his own interpretation of Virginal-Mary: "Supreme and sovereign mistress of the world. . . . Oh Virgin, in the highest sense most pure, oh Mother, worthy of all our worship, our chosen queen, equal with the gods."[6]

King of Cups: Dewi

King of Cups:

Dewi

The Celtic sea king Dewi was not really a name but only the title, "God," from Indo-European *deu, dewi, devi,* or *deva,* a deity. Dewi, the ancient Lord of the Abyss, was eventually Christianized as St. David, the patron saint of Wales, because David was the biblical name most easily identified with his old title. Welsh sailors familiarly called him Davy Jones, and went to "Davy Jones's locker" when they were buried at sea. Another popular name for St. David-Dewi was the Waterman.[1] His pagan shrine, now the city of St. David's, used to be called Menevia, "the Way of the Moon."[2] David-Dewi was once married to the Moon Goddess under her Viking name of Mardoll, "Moon Over the Sea," or her Welsh name of Mab, the Fairy Queen.

This god-king of the sea had other names as well. Some said he was Manannan, son of Llyr, or Lir, who became Shakespeare's King Lear. Manannan kept the souls of the dead in his undersea palace in "pots turned upside down."[3] Like most ancient gods, as well as the Christian ones, Manannan and Llyr were father-son alternating aspects of the same endlessly reincarnated being.

Another name for Dewi was Bran the Blessed, a masculine twin of the Goddess Branwen, who was part of the primordial trinity of Matriarchs guarding the original Cauldron of Regeneration.[4] It was Bran who carried the precious cauldron up from the bottom of the Lake of the Basin.[5] In the Christianized mythology of the Grail, he became a custodian of the sacred cup, a mysterious Fisher King or Rich Fisher named Bron.[6] Although these revisions of the Grail romances called Bron a brother-in-law of Joseph of Arimathea, he was still the old sea god, patron of sailors and fishermen, gazing forever from his seaside throne out across the ocean that had been his ancient home.

Men who sailed the seas never wholly forgot their old deity, even though they saw him in various aspects as a saint, giant, spirit of the deeps, ancient king, or Fisherman of Souls guarding the Holy Grail, like the gate-guard Peter, another "fisherman." Sailors tended to be superstitious because of their dependence on the whims of the "elements." They required their Waterman to listen to prayers in time of need. Some of the sea-king's attributes invested the Tarot's king of cups, another Waterman. He was interpreted as a figure of ageless power and strength, reliably protective of the needy. Like the sea, he was gigantic in comparison with puny mankind. Like water, he stood for a quality of irresistible force underlying a calm surface.

The Suit of Wands

Ace of Wands: Power

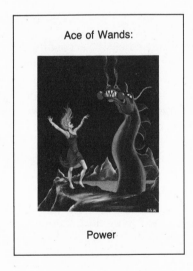

Ace of Wands:

Power

Mythology's ubiquitous image of raw power was the fiery dragon or lightning-serpent. Pre-Jahvistic Hebrews worshiped him under the name of Leviathan (Wriggly), or Nehushtan, whose image was made by Moses (2 Kings 18:4). The latter name originated with the Vedic serpent-king Nahusha, who once ruled heaven, but was cast down to the underworld by a later god, Indra.[1] Some Jewish sects continued to worship the serpent, and claimed the post-exilic God was only a demonic usurper who wrongfully stole the Wise Serpent's kingdom.[2]

The archetypal rivalry between the serpent, or Great Dragon, and the patriarchal god was a real power struggle dating from prehistory. Both were originally phallic deities. The fiery serpent was the older of the

163

two, and often called the firstborn of the Goddess. Various myths said she created him out of clay, to "churn" the abyss of her womb. This story was based on the primitive notion that males' only part in conception was to provide a movement that would stimulate women's mysterious reproductive magic.

The Goddess had power over the serpent. She could make him rise up and stiffen, like women's power over the phalli of men, who displayed lively anxiety about the other sex's inexplicable command of their own flesh, exerted even at a distance. As an expression of this power, Akkadian priestesses bore the title of "snake charmer," later inherited also by male priests.[3]

Vedic creation myth called the primal serpent Vasuki, who churned the mother-symbolic sea to bring forth living things. Stiffened, Vasuki became the *axis mundi,* a phallic shaft planted in the Earth's middle, reaching to the poles, the still point at the center of the turning heavens. The *Mahabharata* said the pole where the "yoke of the world" was fixed was "the supreme snake, Vasuki."[4]

Five thousand years ago, the pole star was Alpha Draconis, the Dragon's Eye.[5] Precession of the equinoxes since moved the north celestial pole to the constellation of Ursa Minor, the Little Bear. This subtle precession was interestingly personified in Celtic myth. King Arthur's name has been derived from Welsh *Arth Vawr,* Heavenly Bear. His predecessor was Uther Pendragon, which means "Wonderful Head of the Dragon."[6]

Incarnations of the celestial Dragon once came to earth, according to the Bible, as *seraphim,* the angels called "fiery flying serpents."[7] Like Lucifer, they seem to have represented lightning bolts descending to stimulate fertility in the abyss or the earth. In the underworld, they became the fiery dragons underlying volcanic mountains. They were immortal because they dwelt close to the source of all birth, the mighty cauldron of the nether regions (Hel).

The fire-breathing phallic dragon also represented the "sacred fire" of sexual desire. The Goddess, priestess, or witch who controlled the dragon was the same as Eurynome-Eve who controlled the serpent, her first consort, whom she created but then cast down to the underworld when he arrogantly pretended to be the Creator.[8] Eve had been such a Goddess. Several noncanonical sources stated that the Serpent was her first consort. As the earthly "father," like Hermes or the World Serpent Ouroboros, he became the eternal rival of the Heavenly Father. They struggled for power over the world.

Like the serpent or dragon, the Tarot suit of wands stood for power and the masculine element of fire, with its connotations: heat, vigor, aspiration, contest, enlightenment, avidity to consume. The dark side of power was suggested by the clubs, symbol of tyranny, the common suit marker substituted for wands or rods. Cards in this suit represented both constructive power and the power to oppress or destroy. As the Goddess controlled her phallic serpent, so the cards also suggested the power to control significant or even fearsome forces.

Two of Wands:

Alliance

Two of Wands: Alliance

Traditional meanings of the two of wands indicated a partnership of two powers having different individual capacities, such as male-female, moon-sun, thought-action, and so on. Mythic symbols of such an alliance may be found in the androgyne composed of such male-female twins, spouses, or mirror images as Artemis-Apollo, Isis-Osiris, Yami-Yama, Hermes-Aphrodite, Freya-Frey, Diana-Dianus, Mashya-Mashyoi. Even Adam and Eve were said to be combined as an androgyne before God tore them apart. In some parts of the world, the androgyne is still worshiped as the creative principle of the universe, like the Dahomean deity Nana-Buluku, the Moon-Sun.[1]

Apollo the sun and Artemis the moon were born together from the womb of Night; but Night herself was called a daughter of the moon, Phoebe in pre-Hellenic Greece, an original female owner of the oracular temple at Delphi, "the Womb." Apollo had to take on the surname of Phoebus, "Moon-god," before he could claim the Delphic oracle for his own. Such myths attest to the precedence of feminine moon worship over the later cults of the sun god.[2]

Apollo got the art of divination from his earlier female counterpart, the Moon-goddess, who ruled all types of prophecy and soothsaying from prehistoric times. The wand or "divining rod" was sacred to her priestesses in antiquity, and to their medieval descendants the witches, who made their wands from the Goddess's special trees: holly, hazel, willow.

Some of the ancient divinatory magic was still used by Christians in the Middle Ages. The Fourteenth Law of Frisons mentioned a divinatory "Lot of Rods," whereby criminals could be discovered by laying wands or divining rods on the church altar.[3] It was believed also that magic wands could discover underground water, concealed weapons, buried treasure, and many other hidden things. Possibly the Tarot suit of wands stood for power because medieval people still thought of magic as a real and effective form of power.

Magic power came to Oriental gods only when they were properly united with their feminine halves, souls, twins, or Shaktis. Similarly, it was said of a sun god like Apollo that he beheld his true soul in the mirror of the Abyss, that female-symbolic Deep that reflected his feminine alter ego as a moon. The idea of a reflection-soul was very old. Dionysus's soul became immobilized in a mirror before he was torn to pieces by the Titans (one of whom was Phoebe, the Moon). Another myth called the same god Narcissus, whose soul was caught in the nymph's reflecting pool.[4] In a medieval variation, she was transformed into the death-dealing witch Mara, who trapped the soul of the Enchanted Huntsman in her magic mirror and stole it away.[5] The Goddess of the reflecting Deep had power to cause the sun god's death because he died every day when he sank into her depths.

The two of wands shows an androgynous combination of solar and lunar powers, each one reflecting the other, their wands meeting at the interface between their respective realms. The basic idea of this card was that alliance is necessary if anything is to be truly accomplished, and each partner must be reconciled to the different qualities of the other.

Three of Wands:

Fate

Three of Wands: Fate

Shakespeare's three witches were "Weird Sisters," from Anglo-Saxon *Wyrd*, "Fate," the female Trinity once credited with absolute power over all lives, even the lives of gods. Beowulf said Wyrd was "the ruler of all men." No one escaped the final bed "where Wyrd has decided to nail him."[1] Here might be seen a reason behind the yogi's traditional "bed of nails": a symbol of total submission to Fate's power.

This trinitarian Fate-goddess appeared everywhere. She was the Greek Moerae, the Celtic Morrigan, the Roman Fortunae, the Norse

Norns, all of immensely old Asiatic roots. Kali as the female Creator, Preserver, and Destroyer provided the initial image of all-powerful Fate (karma) called virgin-mother-crone, past-present-future, birth-life-death, spinner-measurer-cutter, and so on. In Tibet, her composite being is still known as the Three Most Precious Ones.[2]

An element common to most images of Fate was her color symbolism. What Indian mystics called her *Gunas* or "strands" were white-red-black. Kali-Maya, "the divine female Prakriti" corresponding to Greek *Physis*, Mother of Nature, governed birth, life, and death through color magic.[3] The Virgin's pure white was *sattva*; the Mother's royal red was *rajas*; the Crone's funerary black was *tamas*; they stood for the progress of life in nature from light to darkness.[4]

Older religions of the West colored the Fate-goddess's trinity the same way. Theocritus, Ovid, Tibullus, and Horace said the colors of the life-threads are white, red, and black.[5] Io the Moon-cow changed her color from white to red to black because "the New Moon is the white goddess of birth and growth; the Full Moon, the red goddess of love and battle; the Old Moon, the black goddess of death and divination."[6] Celtic myth assigned the same three colors to maidens in the Grail temple. Peredur's mystic trance resulted from a sight of crow's feathers and blood on snow; he remembered that his ladylove had snow-white skin, hair black as crow's feathers, and blood-red spots on her cheeks.[7] The colors also figured prominently in medieval magic and alchemical texts which called them the colors of purity, passion, and darkness.[8] Because these colors were widely associated with Goddess worship, Dante gave his Lucifer three heads colored white, red, and black.

Like Dante's Lucifer, the Goddess had sometimes assumed one body with three heads. Egypt's Mother Mut often had one head wearing the plumes of Maat, the Virgin of Truth; a second head wearing the royal crowns of the Two Lands, representing World-Mother Hathor; and a third head painted black, wearing the vulture feathers of Nekhbet, Mother Death.[9] Her sacred hieroglyph showed three cauldrons.[10]

Hera, the pre-Hellenic Queen of Heaven, merged with the Moerae or the trinity of Hebe-Hera-Hecate, worshiped as Child, Bride, and Widow.[11] Mary, the Christian Queen of Heaven, resembled the Moerae in several respects. Like the Norns standing at the foot of Odin's sacrificial tree, three Marys stood at the foot of Jesus's cross. The *Gospel of Mary* said all three were one and the same.[12] A Coptic *Discourse on Mary* plainly represented her as the Fate-goddess. Like Clotho the virgin spinner among the Moerae, Mary conceived Jesus at the moment when she began to spin a blood-red thread (of life) in the temple.[13] Some said the constellation of Orion was Mary's distaff; but centuries earlier, Norse pagans called it the distaff of Freya as the Norn who spun the destinies of men.[14]

The Moerae, Norns, or Weird Sisters were popularly supposed to visit the cradle of every newborn, to set the child's fate in the life ahead. Even many Christians implicitly believed in these emanations of the ancient Goddess.[15] Folk customs and fairy tales show parents making propitiatory offerings to these "fairy godmothers" on behalf of a child's future.[16]

The Tarot's three of wands also represented the Three Sisters' absolute power to control the events of men's lives. In conjunction with other cards, the three implied that it would be impossible to change what the other cards indicated. The meanings of the three alone included powers of creation, invention, commercial enterprise, and good fortune; also, rewards or punishments, in the karmic sense.

Four of Wands:

Success

Four of Wands: Success

Four wands were once equated with the four corner-posts of the earth, signifying a home place, security, and the sacred marriage. Egyptian kings won the crown of apotheosis or divine approval from the hands of the Goddess by marrying her earthly representative, the queen, under the bridal and coronation canopy called *senti,* "tent," on its four posts.[1] The canopy was copied by the Jews, who use it to this day for wedding ceremonies, calling it *huppah,* "tent." In the ancient period of Semitic matrilocal marriage customs, the *huppah* represented the bride's home place. The wedding meant official permission for the bridegroom to enter her tent.[2] Pre-Islamic Arabian wives used to be able to divorce their husbands by turning their tents around so the entrance faced another direction; then the cast-off husband was forbidden to enter.[3]

Achievement of a marriage meant worldly success for a man or king, in the days when landed property belonged to women, and a queen represented her whole country. As in the matrilocal marriage system of fairy tales, Greek youths used to leave the homes owned by their mothers and sisters, to seek their fortune—which meant a bride and her "matrimony" or mother-inherited wealth.[4] "Patrimony" was a later variation introduced by patriarchal gods (actually, by their priesthoods).

King James quoted an ancient precedent by calling all of England his "lawful wife."[5] Medieval bards said the Roman emperor acquired Britain only by marrying its Goddess-queen, Elen; and Llefelys became king of France only by marrying the Gaulish queen.[6] Before patriarchal laws were fully established in Europe, it was said a woman and her fief were inseparable.[7]

For a man, hero, or god, ultimate success was embodied in the *hieros gamos* (sacred marriage) that insured his resurrection or immortality. Its original model may have been the *svayamara* ceremony of India, in which the virgin aspect of Kali (Sati) chose Shiva to be her bridegroom, signifying her choice by placing a wreath of flowers over his head.[8] Sometimes the chosen male was given an apple, that ubiquitous symbol of Goddess-given immortality, the real meaning of Eve's much maligned gift. Norse pagans maintained that all the gods would die without the Apples of Rejuvenation donated by Mother Idun.[9] Celtic queens offered apples to their bridegrooms to show postmortem acceptance into the Goddess's western Apple-land (Avalon).[10] Men made sacred marriages in Persephone's "bridal chamber" at Eleusis, which guaranteed them a blessed afterlife.[11] The Hellenic myth of the Judgment of Paris was mistakenly deduced from an icon showing the Triple Goddess presenting her apple to the hero of her choice.[12] Gypsy girls selected their lovers by tossing apples at them; gypsy myths told of the Actaeon-like hero converted into a sacrificial stag, then into a god, by magic apples he received from his ladylove.[13]

Apple, wreath, and the canopy supported by its four rods figure in the Tarot picture of a sacred marriage, suggesting the card's traditional meanings: success, the reward of effort, the first establishment of a secure position in the world. Like any wedding, this *hieros gamos* implied that the initial security would be of a provisional nature, with much knowledge still to be acquired, and many future challenges to be met.

Five of Wands: Impasse

Five of Wands:

Impasse

A time of trial and difficulty, an inability to stand up to hostile powers, were indicated by the five of wands. The situation might be symbolized by the sacred king's *pathos* or Passion, following his *hieros gamos*. Having been chosen, he was then expected to die for the sins of others, as Shiva the Bridegroom of Kali-Sati became Shiva the Condemned One.[1] Jesus too became a "Bridegroom" (of Zion) prior to his immolation. The pattern was common to all mystery religions and salvation cults throughout the world.

One of the druidic rituals surviving to the present century in Scotland and Ireland was a Mummers' Dance known as "The Rose." Five men with swords or cudgels danced around a sixth, called The Fool, who was symbolically slain, then resurrected with a magic elixir, the Golden Frosty Drop. At times, he was said to represent Christ, at other times, the devil. His death-and-rebirth dance was accompanied by a chant, "The Dewdrop in the Rose," a western version of Shiva's "Jewel in the Lotus." This mystic phrase had many overlapping meanings: the lingam in the yoni, a drop of semen in the vulva, a fetus in the womb, a child safe in its mother's care, a soul embedded in the natural world, a corpse entombed in Mother Earth: any male in some way enclosed in the female. According to Meister Eckhart, the Dewdrop in the Rose represented Christ within the body of Mary the Rose, by analogy at least: "As in the morning the rose opens, receiving the dew from heaven and the sun, so Mary's soul did open and receive Christ the heavenly dew."[2]

The Rose was a universal symbol of the Goddess as nubile nymph and mother. In pre-Christian Rome it was the emblem of Venus.[3] Related to the five-petaled apple blossom both botanically and mythologically, the rose signified the Goddess's paradise that Tantric sages called Jambu Island, land of the rose-apple tree.[4] Sacred dances like that of the Mummers expressed the mysteries of the journey to paradise. The same dance was called *Ringel-Ringel Rosencranz* in Germany, Ring-Around-A-Rosy in England.[5] The last phrase of the chant, "All fall down," was the inescapable behest of Death, a necessary prelude to any resurrection.

The Fool in the Mummers' rose-dance was obviously descended from the sacrificial victim in the midst of his *pathos,* trapped in the magic pentacle formed by the Rose's petals, helpless to escape the five priestly figures whose duty it was to dispatch him. As at Abdera in the early Christian era a man was solemnly excommunicated and killed each year "in order that he alone might bear the sins of all the people," the Fool was cast out, depersonalized, turned into a hunted animal by his ritual isolation, and destroyed by those his blood would save.[6] For him, the situation seemed hopeless. Like the similar pseudo-victim in the similar round-dance game of Blindman's Buff, he could see no way out of the trap.

In the suit of power, the dire five indicates powerlessness. Earlier security collapses into acute insecurity. Even though the impasse may serve a higher goal not immediately apparent, it feels agonizing to its victim of the moment.

Six of Wands:

Glory

Six of Wands: Glory

Glory, victory, and triumph were among the usual interpretations of the six of wands, which followed the impasse of the five as resurrection followed the sacrifice. It meant the triumphant acclaim of a hero: one who had been obliterated, and rose again like the sun.

Disappearing and re-ascending solar heroes were likened to the sun in nearly every ancient mythology. With the glory of sunrise, their worshipers chanted, "He is risen." The Hindu solar hero, "most supreme Heruka," may have been a prototype for Egypt's solar Heru, or Horus, called Ra-Harakhti when he became the elder, setting sun; and for his Greek counterpart Heracles, whom the Romans called Hercules; as well as for the word *hero* itself.[1]

Tantric Buddhists call Heruka a Knowledge-Holding Deity and an Asvin, or centaur.[2] The ancient Greeks also regarded the centaurs as "knowledge-holders." Each solar "savior" supplanted a predecessor in the guise of a centaur—a godlike horse-rider capable of galloping to heaven. Heracles supplanted the centaur Nessus and wore his royal garment, which burned him like the flames of a pyre.[3] Flames themselves were sometimes viewed as fiery horses on which the hero's soul rode to the sky, to become one with the gods.

When Heracles arose to glory, he became one with his heavenly father, and was called Light of the World, Sun of Righteousness, King of Glory, and similar titles later adopted by Christians for their own hero. Julian said the demiurgic and perfective power to rule the elements belonged to Heracles, "whom the great Zeus has begotten to be the Savior of the Universe."[4]

Heracles was a popular model for many saviors including the Christian one. Heracles was god-begotten and born of a virgin who was married but untouched by her husband.[5] He performed twelve miracles, corresponding to the "houses" of the zodiac that the sun traversed in his year-and-a-day. He died, descended into hell, and rose again. His resurrection was announced by the temple women. He ascended into heaven and took his place among the stars, next to the constellation of Orpheus's lyre (Lyra).

Impersonating Heracles, men sacrificed themselves each year in St. Paul's home town of Tarsus, which is why Paul thought it very virtuous to give one's body to be burned (1 Corinthians 13:3). Each victim was assimilated to Heracles and, consequently, to the sun. Pausanias said the sun's surname is Savior, "the same as Heracles."[6]

Apparently most men who offered themselves to die did so willingly, for the sake of the hero-god's brief year of glory on earth, and his promised immortality in heaven. In the third century A.D., the annual custom of burning "men who were gods of light" was still maintained in Carthage.[7] The killing eventually ceased, but the ceremony lingered on in Egypt up to the nineteenth century, when kings were burned in effigy, and a living man crawled out of the ashes to represent the reborn god.[8]

Such short-lived glory as that of the sacred king was suggested by the six of wands: either a personal or a vicarious experience of adulation and fame, a sense of victory with all adversaries conquered and all blockages overcome. But the triumph was usually described as a "period," meaning that it would come to an end, or that its glory would shift to some different meaning, perhaps less glorious and more perilous.

Seven of Wands:

Challenge

Seven of Wands: Challenge

After achieving his glory, a sacred king faced the necessity of holding it against challengers. The apparent security of his eminence was actually a dynamic equilibrium preserved only by constant risk, like a juggler's performance.

To keep their subjects convinced of their ongoing usefulness, ancient god-kings often pretended to control the movements of heavenly bodies by manipulating their magic wands or scepters: to make the sun rise, for example, by raising the correct rod at the correct moment. If the people doubted the king's ability to perform this cosmic juggling, he might be killed at once, and replaced by another candidate who seemed more in tune with the forces of nature.

The legend of Damocles was a well-known illustration of the precariousness of royal rank. Like the name of Heracles, his name meant either "glory of the Lady" or "glory of the blood." In classical myth, Damocles was described as a courtier of a Syracusan king "Dionysus" during the fourth century B.C. As owner of the divine name, the king represented the god on earth and so, according to the Orphic pattern, was expected to suffer the same fate as the god.[1] Kings serving as "sons of God" became sacrificial victims at the end of the allotted reign, or were deposed by a stronger candidate and ceremonially killed. To escape this fate, some kings were able to choose a surrogate victim to die for them.

The legend says the Syracusan god-king chose Damocles, who willingly offered himself because he envied the king's glory and wanted to taste it for himself. He was given his chance, but he soon learned that the privileges of royal rank carried compensatory penalties. The king's doom was symbolized by Damocles's discovery: when he sat on the throne, a sword was suspended over his head by a single hair.[2]

This symbolic sword may be connected with the deadly moon-sickle representing Time (the lunar calendar) that slew kings throughout the ancient world. The biblical King Belshazzar was terrified by the fatal lunar word Mene, Mene (Moon, Moon) written on the wall of his banquet hall (Daniel 5:25). Babylonian kings sometimes escaped their fate by substituting a condemned criminal during the Sacaea festival, the time when every king faced the condemnatory word Mene spoken by

173

the Moon-goddess in her Crone aspect. The substitute king occupied the throne and exercised all the royal prerogatives for five days. Then he was stripped of his finery, scourged, and hanged or impaled.[3]

A similar threat of dire fate in the midst of glory characterized the seven wands, whose card shows a princely juggler desperately manipulating too many objects while a moon-sickle hangs above his head. The card warned against the challenges of high ambition, always vulnerable to threats from both above and below. Possession of power is always envied by those as yet ignorant of its risks; but the possession of power can be held only by sustained effort, skill, and courage—the juggler's dynamic equilibrium.

Eight of Wands:

Fall

Eight of Wands: Fall

The expression "riding for a fall" was appropriate for the eight of wands, which signified careless haste, driving energy, excessive speed, over-aspiration, or pride. These added up to the *hubris* that figured prominently in myths of the deified heroes who rode the divine horse to heaven. One Greek name for this celestial animal was Arion, "Moon-creature on high," the magic horse ridden by Heracles when he became king of Elis. Another was Pegasus, the winged horse of the Muses, whom Bellerophon tried to ride up to heaven "as though he were an immortal."[1]

As punishment for his unauthorized use of the magic horse, which he stole from the Nymphs of Inspiration called Pegae, Bellerophon was thrown down in midflight. He fell back to earth and landed in a thorn bush. He was blinded, lamed, accursed. His story represented an early failure of male priests to take over the fount of inspiration on behalf of their god. Pegasus was a female symbol even in Hellenic myth. He was born of the blood of Medusa, who was also Metis (Female Wisdom), and symbolized the power of the all-knowing Crone.[2]

Pegasus may have had an Egyptian origin. His hoofprint made the famous Hippocrene or "Spring of the Horse" on Mount Helicon, which was tended by the Pegae. They, in turn, derived from the priestesses of the sacred spring Pega at Abydos, Egypt's oldest Osirian shrine.[3] The holy women there preserved the god's mummified head and received oracles from its mouth. Osiris was one of the early Lords of Death capable of carrying mortals to immortality in heaven—as Pegasus did. In fact, Osiris's worshipers claimed that he was the only god with the power to make human beings born again in heaven.[4]

Another hero who fell because he tried to fly too high was Icarus. In a parody written by Lucian, Icarus received a Pegasus-like steed, the horse Ikaromenippos (Moon-Horse of Icarus). This beast could fly up to the sphere of the moon, cross over to the sphere of the sun, then rise on eagle wings to the citadel of Zeus at the summit of heaven.[5]

Early shamanistic religions considered a flight to heaven on the Moon-horse essential to the enlightenment of the sage. Classical writers were more concerned about the "sin" of trying to be godlike. Rather than recounting a safe trip to the celestial otherworld and back again, their hero-tales often resulted in a disastrous fall during the attempt.

Interpretations of the eight of wands generally followed the classical pattern. An important journey, changes of scene, motion, and progress were implied, but all could be ruined by overeagerness, overconfidence, or excessive activity. This card was often considered a warning against the pride that goeth before a fall.

Nine of Wands:

Defense

Nine of Wands: Defense

The nine wands were connected with suspicion, insecurity, inner doubts, barriers, and a hidden position.

In ancient myths, a male spirit closely associated with this constellation of meanings was the Egyptian god Seker, a Lord-of-Death aspect of Osiris, tutelary deity of the Sakkaran necropolis which bore his name.[1] Babylonians called him Zaqar, a messenger from the lunar realm of the dead.[2] In the eleventh century B.C. he was incarnate in kings of Byblos under the name of Zakar-Baal. From his name came the Arabic *zekker,* "penis," and the Hebrew *zakar,* "male."[3]

Seker was sometimes called Amen, "the Hidden One." His hieroglyph was a pregnant women's belly, because he dwelt in the womb-symbolic "divine subterranean place," the pit at the bottom of the Tuat, "filled with blackest darkness."[4] From this lightless, unassailably safe place he would be reborn, to face once more the perils of life and sacred kingship. He would mature, and again become the phallic god Osiris-Min, "who impregnates his mother."[5] In other words, he stood for the archetypal wish-fulfillment fantasy of cheating death by re-entering the maternal womb to be born again.

Some myths hinted that Seker was reluctant to come forth from his secure hiding place, as an infant would resist—if it could—coming forth from the security of the womb. The nine of wands suggested a position like that of the god in his quiescent phase, both dead and fetal at the same time, when he lived within a dark cave of complete protection, suspicious of the outside world and ready to defend his fortress at any cost.[6] But insofar as no position of defense can be held forever, the card also indicated an expectation of change, accompanied by trouble and difficulties.[7]

An alternative implication of this card was literally inside-out. The threatening danger might lurk within, not without. The fortress might be a prison, containing something savage or uncontrollable. This description might apply to an element of the unconscious, hidden deep in the mind, closed away and dark to everyday perception. Nine wands might interlace to form a barrier; but every barrier has two sides. It keeps things out, and it keeps things in. It was up to the interpreter of the cards to decide which description might be more applicable to any given situation.

Ten of Wands:

Oppression

Ten of Wands: Oppression

Christian fathers like St. Augustine, Athanasius, Origen, Basil, Aquinas, and Albertus Magnus declared that pride was the sin of Lucifer, because a certain passage in the fourteenth chapter of Isaiah represented his fall as the consequence of hubris. The passage said:

> How art thou fallen from heaven, O Lucifer, son of the morning! . . . For thou hast said in thine heart, I will ascend to heaven, I will exalt my throne above the stars of God; I will sit also upon the mount of the congregation, in the sides of the north; I will ascend above the heights of the clouds; I will be like the most High.

What the Christian fathers didn't know about this passage was that it was plagiarized from a much older Canaanite scripture describing the ambition of the Morning-star god Shaher, son of Helel the Earth-goddess, to emulate the brightness of the Sun-god Elyon. Each day with the rising of the sun, Shaher's light was overpowered and he disappeared from heaven with his ambition unfulfilled. The Canaanite priests addressed him:

> How hast thou fallen from heaven, Helel's son Shaher! Thou didst say in thy heart, I will ascend to heaven, above the circumpolar stars I will raise my throne, and I will dwell on the Mount of Council in the back of the north; I will mount on the back of a cloud, I will be like unto Elyon.[1]

Lucifer the "Light-bringer" was a title of the same Morning-star god, also known as Venus-in-the-Morning. The ancients saw that the planet Venus is both morning and evening star, heralding the sunrise, and also following the sun into darkness at day's end. The same god acted as the sun's messenger to the living on earth, and to the dead in the underworld. A verse attributed to Plato called the god Aster (Star), recounting his daily progress: "Aster, once, as Morning-Star, light on the living you shed. Now, dying, as Evening-Star you shine among the dead."[2]

As a result of the Isaian plagiarism in the Bible, the pagans' allegorical description of natural events was theologized into a War in Heaven

177

and a demonic Fall that all pious Christians were expected to believe literally. Lucifer, the Light-bringing "Son of Morning," became king of the underworld, and later its chief devil.

Yet, Gnostic sects continued to revere the Light-bringer and to deplore God's injustice toward him. They claimed the Heavenly Father was a tyrant whom Lucifer rightly defied in a heroic attempt at revolution against forces that were magically superior, but morally inferior. God won the day by a ruthless exertion of power.

The ten of wands expressed meanings similar to this Gnostic view: a triumph of tyranny, misuse of power, selfish authority demolishing its opposition, excessive pressure, punishment of ambition. Oppression of this magnitude could only generate resentment or mutiny.[3] The final pip card of the suit of power indicated power triumphant, supreme, unchallengable—but by that very token unjust. If power corrupts, and absolute power corrupts absolutely, as the saying goes, then an omnipotent God could only be absolutely corrupt. The oppressed could only suffer, hope, and wait.

Princess of Wands:

Atargatis

Princess of Wands: Atargatis

The Philistine name for the fish-tailed White Goddess was Atargatis. Her Syrian name was Astarte. Her Babylonian name was Ishtar. At Der she was called Derceto, "Whale of Der," the great Fish-mother who swallowed the phallic god Oannes, prototype of the biblical Jonah. Even Judeo-Christian Scriptures admitted that Jonah's whale was female, and he spent three days in her "womb" (not stomach) prior to his rebirth.[1]

The myth of the swallowing was really a sexual allegory. The fish was a common symbol of the yoni, as Egyptian Isis took a fish-form in the guise of Abtu, the Abyss, to swallow the penis of Osiris and give him rebirth. While Atargatis and similar manifestations of the Goddess were worshiped as fish-tailed mermaids, they were also dreaded as instances of that ubiquitous castration figure ever apparent in men's dreams and myths: the *vagina dentata* (toothed vagina), worldwide emblem of male sex fears. It, or she, could swallow up man or god, root and branch, as the sea swallowed the lightning bolt and never let it out again.

This Goddess figure tended to evoke the power of the female over the male. It was he, not she, who was "eaten" or "devoured." Ancient writings speak of the male sexual function as "putting forth" or "being taken," as opposed to the modern patriarchal terminology.[2] In many primitive languages, the words for "copulate" and "eat" are the same; the male is the one who is eaten.[3] Men of Malekula said women's genitals have a spirit "which draws us to It so that It may devour us."[4] Chinese sages claimed women's genitals are gateways to immortality, and also "executioners of men."[5] It is a well-known principle in psychiatry that both sexes fantasize a vulva as a mouth.[6]

In addition to the *vagina dentata*, another common symbol of the devouring female was the Goddess's spider incarnation, whom the Greeks called Arachne. The revised myth said Arachne was only a mortal maiden turned into a spider by jealous Athene, because she could spin better than Athene herself. Earlier, however, Arachne-the-spider was only another incarnation of Athene as the Goddess who spun the web of Fate, and caught souls as a spider catches flies. In fact, the fly was the usual symbol of the soul swallowed by a female, to be given rebirth.[7] One of the consorts of Atargatis was Baal-zebub or Beelzebub, "Lord of Flies," which meant he was a psychopomp who conducted souls like his Greek counterpart Hermes. Atargatis or Astarte was called mother and ruler of all *baalim* (gods).[8] In due season she swallowed them all, and gave them rebirth.

Like Atargatis, the princess of wands might be regarded as a mysteriously dark, irresistible power, possibly representing a compulsion fraught with peril. She stands for a great force which might be misused or misunderstood. As the symbol of a personality, she was one who would be a valuable friend but a dangerous enemy.

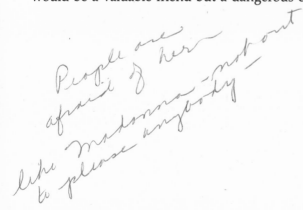

People are afraid of her like madonna—not out to please anybody

a brig "gy" creativity

Prince of Wands: Dagon *The fire*

Prince of Wands:

Dagon

A Philistine consort of Atargatis was Dagon, known in biblical tradition as a "devil" because he was opposed to the cult of Yahweh. A shape-shifter, like most other Middle-Eastern gods, Dagon could present himself as a serpent, goat, bull, merman, or a Jonah-like entity emerging from the mouth of the Great Fish, which gave him the appearance of a human torso with a fish's tail. Like Lucifer, he also represented the fertilizing fire descending into the watery abyss, so he bore the symbols of phallic scepter and uterine cauldron in token of his sacred marriage.

Biblical writers pretended that Dagon and Yahweh were implacable enemies, but earlier myths show that Yahweh's followers actually adopted many of Dagon's attributes for their own deity. Another name for Dagon was Phoenix, "the one from Phoenicia," especially as the god immolated in fire and regularly resurrected. In the Phoenician city of Tyre he was called Melek, "the King." In the Bible he was Molech, "King." The Bible says it was once a custom of the Israelites to "make their children pass through the fire to Molech" (2 Kings 23:10), dedicating them as firstborn sacrifices to the god. Yahweh also commanded, "Sanctify unto me all the firstborn . . . both of man and beast; it is mine" (Exodus 13:2).

Still another Semitic name for Dagon-Phoenix-Molech was Yamm. Under this name he became the Great Serpent of the nether waters, slain by his alter ego Baal in eternal cyclic competition for the favors of the Goddess. Yamm was probably related to the Hindu Yama, lord of the nether world, who was united with the Goddess Mari as the androgynous Yamamari, incarnate in the Dalai Lama as "Slayer of the Death King."[1] The Middle-Eastern male-female deity was Mari-Yamm or Meri-Yam, the same name applied to the mother of Jesus by early Christians.[2] Jehovah took the name when he was worshiped together with the Sea-goddess Mari, or Miriam, or Mariamne. Sacred medallions of the second century B.C. showed Jehovah with a sea-serpent tail like the marine aspect of Dagon.[3]

The many facets of this complex deity make him an appropriate symbol for the prince of wands, representing all that is unexpected, startling, unpredictable, or unconventional. His dual nature—fire above, water below—echoes the ancient images of all gods, even Yahweh, as simultaneously good and evil, light and dark, sometimes fertile, sometimes sterile. The biblical God announced that he was the creator of evil (Isaiah 45:7) after the manner of all his contemporary colleagues who "punished" erring worshipers with evil or hurtful "acts of God."

Whenever the prince of wands appeared in a card layout, he was supposed to introduce an element of chance or change, often seeming irrational, but having a deep underlying consistency. Often a knowledge of myth is required to interpret the apparent irrationalities of the unconscious, which usually turn out to be quite logical when properly understood.

Queen of Wands:

Hel

Queen of Wands: Hel

The most appropriate Goddess of the ancient world to play the role of the Tarot's queen of fire was the same Goddess after whom hell, the realm of fire, was named: Mother Hel, ruler of the fiery cauldron of regeneration in the underworld.

Hel's cauldron under the earth was not the torture chamber it became in later Christian mythology. It was a place of purification and rebirth. All the dead went there, to be purged of their memories of former lives, and to be reconstituted in Hel's sacred fire. Like the Volcano-goddess Pele in the Pacific islands, Hel gathered the souls of the dead under fire-mountains. The Helgafell in Iceland is still said to be a home of the pagan dead.[1] Even Odin, the heavenly father himself, was buried in "Hel's Mount."[2]

Cave-temples called *hellir* were the pagan purgatories where souls were cleansed for a ritual rebirth while still on earth.[3] Sacred springs or wells within such enclosures gave rise to legends like that of Dame Holle's Well, which gave birth to all the world's children.[4] *Hella cunni* or "kindred of Hel" were ancestral ghosts supposed to rise out of the earth and ride the winds at Halloween. This name was corrupted into Harlequin, the classic Fool of the medieval mystery play.[5]

Hel's name had many variations: Holle, Helle, Halja, Holde, Hild,

Hellenia, Nehellenia, Brunnhilde ("Burning Hel"), or Matabrune, "Burning Mother."[6] Among the places sacred to her were Helsinki, Heligoland, Helstadt, Holstein, Holderness, Holland. She was the Hyldemoer or "Hel-Mother" to whom the Danes prayed at their holy elder trees, known as elven-trees or Hel-trees.[7]

Another plant sacred to Hel was the "holy" holly, bearing her name, displayed especially at the Yule season when the sun was said to be reborn from her underground womb. Holly berries represented drops of her divine blood, while the white berries of mistletoe stood for her divine milk. The Druids' name for mistletoe was Guidhel, the Guide to Hel. It was the same Golden Bough that led many heroes—including Aeneas and Virgil—safely through the chambers of the netherworld.[8]

Those chambers were not always fiery. Hel also ruled the dark land of shades, or of shadows. Ghosts of the dead were often supposed to become shadows of their former selves. As Queen of Shades, Hel was sometimes called Nifl (Nef-Hel), Goddess of Niflheim within the earth, mother of the Niflungar or Nibelungs, who were ancestral shadows.[9] A Greek cognate was Nephele, the shadow twin of Hera. Her name meant mist and darkness.[10] The same Queen of Shades was known to biblical writers as the mother of the *nephilim*, ancient giants born of a great power called Soul of the Earthly World.[11] Her consort, the great Serpent of Darkness, dwelt with her at the foundations of the earth.

Hel was not to be distinguished from any other manifestation of the underground Goddess: Nephthys, Hecate, Persephone, Eresh-kigal, or Kali the Destroyer. The fires of Hel lighted the place Romans called Infernus, literally an oven in the earth. Their proverb said, "The oven is the mother."[12]

As another female underground power ruling the realm of fire, the queen of wands was said to have fiery characteristics: warmth, illumination, benevolence, domestic utility with a certain danger of sudden shifts into destructiveness or cruelty. She represented a person of hot passion and sharp wit, having the fire's capacity to bite the hand that feeds it, unless it is treated with all due respect.

King of Wands: *Valraven*

King of Wands:

Valraven

According to shamans of the Chuk-chi, a god named Big Raven first gave the secrets of magic to men, after he won them by sacrificing his manhood to the lunar Death-goddess.[1] According to the Danes, this god became Hel's king and a lord of the underworld, Valraven, sometimes known as King Morvran, which meant a sea-raven.[2] A raven was his totem and also the soul-shape in which he could appear to his followers.

Valraven may have been the oracular "little bird" who told occult secrets. Ravens were especially sacred in many Indo-European mythologies as bearers of messages from the otherworld, or as psychopomps. The Valkyries could transform themselves into ravens to consume the bodies and souls of dead warriors. The skalds' term for blood shed on the battlefield was "the raven's drink."[3] Sigurd understood the secret language of birds, because his mother was the Valkyrie Brunnhilde ("Burning Hel"), whose other name was Krake, "Raven."[4]

Icons of the Orphic Mysteries showed a raven perched on the shoulder of a novice as he entered the temple, indicating the imminence of a mock death preceding his ritual rebirth.[5] Raven was the name given each new initiate of the Mithraic Mysteries, when he attained the first of the heavenly spheres, that of the Moon-goddess. After this he became a Bridegroom.[6] Fairy tales of the princess and the magic raven were drawn from such traditions. More often than not, the raven turned out to be a man in disguise.

Like the Phoenix bird, a raven was said to be reborn in fire. He was associated with this "element" and also with the sacred tree, whose wood some oriental alchemists regarded as a fifth element.[7] The alchemical symbol for wood was the same trefoil that now appears as the standard club in cards.[8] In older Tarot decks, wands were wooden rods or rough wooden clubs, sometimes with leaves still attached, such as might be set alight for torches. When the alchemical symbol replaced the literal picture of a club, modern cards inherited a design that looks more like a shamrock. This was derived from Arabic *shamrakh*, the trefoil that was once another sign of the ancient Triple Goddess.

The king of wands was always seen as a powerful person, of a fiery nature: energetic, active, hard to control, attractive but sometimes dangerous. Like the Valraven, he would be a bearer of hidden information. As Hel's man he would be familiar with the earth's secrets, having much to teach. He would have the totemic form of the raven, the symbolic bird of doom, and the shamrock emblem of his suit, in addition to the wand of kingship. All these were symbols of considerable numinous power, suggesting magical and practical knowledge.

The Suit
of Pentacles

Ace of Pentacles: Reward

Ace of Pentacles:

Reward

A natural model for the magic pentacle was the five-pointed star in the core of an apple, revealed by cutting the apple transversely. Gypsies called this the Star of Knowledge. To the ancient Greeks, it was the revelation of Kore, the Virgin Goddess in the heart of the Earth (represented by her mother, Demeter). In Egypt it meant the female regenerative spirit in the womb of the earth.[1] The Egyptians' five-pointed hieroglyph became the symbol of St. Anne, mother of the Virgin Mary—formerly the pagans' Grandmother-goddess Anna, mother of the virgin Mari.[2]

Christian mystics claimed the Virgin Mary was a reincarnation of the Apple-goddess Eve, who was once worshiped as the soul of the earth. She was Hvov in Persia, Hebe or Hebat in Anatolia, Eveh in Assyria,

Hawwa or "Life" in the land of Hatti. Babylonians called her "Goddess of the Tree of Life," or "the divine Lady of Eden."[3] The Bible's version of her gift of the apple to Adam was a distortion of earlier symbolism, which showed the Mother of All Living bringing the first man to life with her magic fruit, while her serpent hung in the tree behind her.[4] Gnostic Gospels showed why Adam called Eve the Mother of All Living. She gave him life, and sent her serpent to teach him knowledge, defying Jehovah who wanted to keep Adam and his descendants ignorant.[5]

Many myths hint that Eve's apple with its inner pentacle once represented not original sin, but the original gift of life. The Norse Goddess Idun kept the gods alive with apples from her western garden.[6] Similarly, Morgan le Fay gave Celtic heroes eternal life with her magic apples from Avalon. Mother Hera preserved the lives of Olympian deities with fruit from her Hesperian apple tree, which was guarded by her great serpent.

Gypsies said a woman could restore life to a corpse by placing an apple in its mouth, as the apple magically represented the "heart-soul." A Circe-like gypsy maiden transformed her dead lover into a pig, and put an apple in his mouth to raise him from the dead, as the Vikings put an apple in the mouth of the Yule pig to insure its regeneration.[7] The original sacrificial pig was Vishnu in his boar incarnation, dying and rising again to save the world.[8] Gypsies also used the apple as a heart symbol in affairs of love. A gypsy girl chose her lover by tossing an apple at him. When an "occult couple" engaged in a sexual sacrament, they cut an apple to reveal its pentacle and fed it to each other, saying, "I am your nourishment. You are mine. We are the feast."[9]

Thus, the reward of knowledge implied by the pentacle was carnal knowledge, a revelation of the mystery of life emanating from woman and the earth. To the gypsies, earth meant reward, fertility, abundance, or riches—the Sanskrit *artha*—which may be why the suit of pentacles was associated with money, and made alternatively a suit of coins, denarii, or diamonds. Dia-mond meant literally Earth Goddess, from whose womb came gems and precious metals, hidden as the pentacle was hidden in Eve's apple. In Tantric Tibet, the Earth Goddess is still the Diamond Sow, consort of the sacrificial boar.[10]

The ace of pentacles meant creation and giving; the birth of *material* wealth from the *mater*, Earth or Eve. Pythagoreans called the pentacle a prime symbol of beginning, because its endless angles repeated the birth-letter Alpha. They called it Pentalpha, emblem of creation.[11]

Beginning the suit of possessions and rewards, the ace indicated propitious fortune. Connections with the Goddess's apple also hinted at sexual knowledge, deplored by patriarchal writers as Eve's "sinful" gift to Adam. The ace meant the things most men desire: opportunities in the worldly sense; stable foundations for future building; security, ownership, and real property, the rewards of practical effort in the world.

Two of Pentacles:

Change

Two of Pentacles: Change

The two of pentacles was a particularly important card. As modern cardmakers chose the ace of spades, early Tarot cardmakers chose the two of pentacles to carry their trademarks, with ornate or oversized pips. The "deuce" may have descended from *deus*, "god," via the Gaulish deity Dusius, whom St. Augustine called a lascivious incubus.[1] Demons who seduced women were still called Dusii or "deuces" up to the fifteenth and sixteenth centuries.[2] There may have been a connection with the phallic serpents of the Hermetic "ca-duceus," who appeared on the two of pentacles swallowing each other's tails while their bodies formed the same lemniscate infinity sign that the Major Arcana featured twice. Two circles or pentacles linked by the serpentine figure eight sometimes showed contrasting light-and-dark, yang-and-yin hues, like the mysterious alchemical emblem called "the Sun and Moon linked by the Dragon."[3]

Flamel wrote of this emblem: "These are snakes and dragons, which the ancient Egyptians painted in the form of a circle, each biting the other's tail, in order to teach that they spring of and from one thing. These are the dragons that the old poets represent as guarding sleeplessly the golden apples of the Hesperian maidens. . . . These are the two serpents that are fastened around the herald's staff and the rod of Mercury."[4]

Golden apples were the typical symbols of the Earth Mother's gift of life, with their mystic pentacle within. The presence of the infinity sign at this important spot in the suit of pentacles suggested an appeal to the Earth Mother for "salvation." Like the endlessly curving Oriental yang-and-yin, the endless line of the serpents' figure eight hinted at the eternal alternation of opposites in the cycles of becoming ruled by the ancient Goddess. While the Christians' (and pagans') cross may have represented a direct ascent to heaven, the figure eight enclosing pentacles of life and death stood for existence folded back on itself, reincarnation without beginning or end—like the endless line creating the very form of a pentacle.

Serpents guarded such graphic mysteries in the old religions, and the secret books that set them forth. The legendary Book of Thoth (often identified with the Tarot) was said to be guarded by serpents under the sea.[5] Similarly in India, the Nagas or serpent-people guarded "books of secret teachings in underwater palaces."[6]

Interpretations of the serpent-guarded deuce focused on the concept of Fate (karma) as an alternative to the Christian concept of a simple choice between good and evil. Two pentacles meant cycles and fluctuations, fluidity, perpetual change. As the earth sign, a pentacle referred to the natural world of matter, where transformation was the rule: light turned dark, dark turned light, winter became summer and vice versa; youth and age, death and life were thought to alternate too.

Change, therefore, was the basic meaning of the two of pentacles. One serpent merging with the other, one pentacle sliding into its opposite, suggested gain where there was loss, or vice versa; difficulty where there was ease, or vice versa; growth, alteration, new directions, new ideas. Like the timeless wisdom of the yang-and-yin yantra, the two of pentacles hinted that opposites are illusions, and all things are ultimately different forms of the same thing. Knowledge of this sort was the seeker's reward, and the gift of hope.

Three of Pentacles:

Work

Three of Pentacles: Work

Works, crafts, and skilled labor were common reference points for the three of pentacles, which presaged progress toward commercial success through effort and training. This card hinted at a connection between Tarot symbolism and that of Freemasonry.[1] The traditional illustration showed masons at work on a Gothic cathedral, one of those curious medieval "Palaces of the Queen of Heaven" whose masonry incorporated so many pagan figures and symbols.

The pagan origin of such figures and symbols is suggested here by a runic shrine. The central figure from the Gundestrup Cauldron shows Cernunnos, the Horned God, in modified lotus position with his torc and serpent. On the Cauldron he was accompanied by one of the funerary lunar wolves, possibly the "moon-dog" Managarm, whose image strongly resembled that of the Sabine wolf-mother Lupa, said to have nurtured the founders of Rome, Romulus and Remus.[2]

Three pentacles suggested the number 15, long associated with the three Matronae (Mothers), or Triple Goddess worshiped in conjunction with Cernunnos. The Celts calculated the ages of Virgin, Mother, and Crone in multiples of 15. On earth, the first of the trinity was represented by a damsel "fifteen winters of age, wearing a wreath of flowers"; the second member twice that, "thirty winters of age, wearing a circlet of gold"; and the third member twice that again, "threescore winters of age, wearing a garland of gold."[3] Fifteen was a feminine magical number, which may have been why it was assigned to the female-breasted Devil of the Tarot.

The oldest myths said it was the Triple Goddess who first gave humanity a knowledge of the sacred runes. The heavenly father Odin himself knew nothing of writing and reading until he won this feminine knowledge by an act of self-immolation. The Goddess who invented runes was the same Goddess who kept the divine apples of regeneration, with their inner pentacles. She made her consort Bragi a master of magical poetry by engraving her runes on his tongue. Like all mythologies, Norse mythology called the alphabet a female invention. Thus, the writer of sacred runes on the three of pentacles is a woman, whereas less scholarly labors are performed by a man.

Among the secret symbols on the card are: the moon, swastika, triangle, Cross of Wotan, lemniscate, Nordic Triceps, Greek cross, alchemical sign for wood, and sigils of Mercury, Athene, and Vesta. From a mythic past come also monsters, gods, warriors, sailors of the dragon ship, and magic-working mothers.

Such a place of meditation might well refer to the symbols of paganism and their philosophical implications, which have been almost forgotten.

The three of pentacles referred especially to work undertaken or performed together with others: a joint effort, a partnership, with male and female components functioning harmoniously. The card either predicted, commended, or advocated a productive effort of teamwork.

Four of Pentacles:

Avarice

Four of Pentacles: Avarice

While the three of pentacles implied material gain as a result of creative skills, the four warned against the danger of working for material gain alone. Joy of craftsmanship might be forgotten under the pressure of excessive desire for its rewards. This could mean entering the barren landscape of avarice, dominated by the stronghold of Money, simultaneously a fortress and a prison.

It is a curious fact that the word Money used to mean a warning from the divine Mother. Rome's Queen of Heaven, Juno, had the surname of Moneta, "Admonisher," in her lawgiving aspect. Her temple housed the Roman mint, where silver and gold coins were struck, bearing the Goddess's image and blessing —a custom copied by Christian Rome in its manufacture of holy medals. Such coins were styled Moneta after the Goddess. Eventually the term became "money."[1]

Gold was a favored metal for currency, not only because temple-manufactured coins carried the Goddess's blessing, but also because the incorruptibility of gold suggested eternal life. Tombs and funerary furnishings throughout the world give ample evidence that ancient peoples thought human flesh could partake magically of the qualities of gold, which could not "die"—that is, rust, corrode, crumble, tarnish, rot, decompose, or otherwise show its age. When "twice-born" Brahmans passed through their ritual of second birth, they were dragged through a giant yoni of gold, signifying rebirth from the eternal womb of Earth (Kali-Tara).[2]

The same implication of Mother-given life attached to the cowrie shell, which was often used as currency because it was universally desired, due to its universally recognized resemblance to female genitalia. Romans called the cowrie *matriculus*, "little matrix," a womb-gate invested with miraculous powers of fertility and healing.[3]

On a deep psychological level, the phenomenon of miserliness may include the mythic connections between wealth and the desire to control such maternal powers as birth-giving, nurture, and healing. But, as the miser's card implies, greed is ultimately barren. Accumulated wealth must be protected, but in the process of protecting it, the miser becomes its prisoner and its slave.

Such was the warning of the four of pentacles. Interpretations included hoarding, covetousness, selfishness, suspicion, mistrust, inability to let go of anything or to delegate authority. Blockages of thought and action would naturally follow from excessive devotion to the piling up of material rewards, and the provisions for guarding them.

Five of Pentacles:

Hardship

Five of Pentacles: Hardship

Pictures on the five of pentacles card customarily showed ragged, sick, poverty-stricken people on a wintry night, outside a church, whose warmly lighted window suggested comfort within, not available to those without. During the Middle Ages, beggars did gather outside churches, hoping the more affluent would be inspired to give them something when passing in or out. Beggars were not allowed inside. On a winter night, the church's warmth was for those who could pay.

Thus, symbolized in the middle of the suit of money was a vital ideological issue, bitterly debated in the fourteenth century when Tarot decks were becoming popular. The church was then at a peak of its accumulated wealth. Clergymen as a group were the richest people in Europe.[1] Some heretics objected, citing the Gospels on the subject of giving away one's worldly goods to the poor. Jesus said it was easier for a camel to pass through a needle's eye than for a rich man to pass into Heaven. He commanded his disciples to own nothing, after the manner of Buddhist ascetics, and to depend on charity for their daily bread.

The churchmen's official response to this implied criticism was to deny the poverty of Jesus and his disciples. The bull *Cum inter nonnullos* of Pope John XXII declared it heretical to discuss or believe in the poverty of Jesus.[2] Such rules maintained the priests' right to their riches, in an age when the church had little inclination to help the poor out of its own funds, though laymen were urged to be charitable.

A popular story from the Rhineland underscored the resentment of poor folk, who believed their Holy Mother would have been kinder than the male-dominated church that usurped her image. When a starving beggar played his fiddle before a statue of the Virgin, she gave

191

him one of her gold shoes. He was caught with the treasure and sentenced to death. However, as he was being taken to execution, he prayed to the Virgin again. She exonerated him by publicly giving him her other shoe. The beggar's life was saved, but the priests took away the gold shoes and locked them up in the church treasury, "lest the Virgin should again be tempted to bestow them upon some penniless beggar who prayed for her aid."[3]

The five of pentacles was sometimes the beggar's card, implying hard times, worry, poverty, loss or lack of comfort. The struggle for survival would find no help from established institutions, not even those purporting to be "helping" agencies. Painful adversity may encounter only indifference from fair-weather friends. Insecurity may be worsened by failure of trust, errors of judgment, or enforced restrictions. A discouraging card, the five held out small hope for the future. Yet, like the Rhineland story of the Virgin, the following card suggested rescue of a sort.

Six of Pentacles:

Charity

Six of Pentacles: Charity

According to Gnostic Gospels, the principal dispenser of charity was not the clergyman but the harlot, who traced her Christian antecedents to the first "papess," Jesus's beloved, Mary Magdalene, who said, "Not only are we [harlots] compassionate of ourselves, but we are compassionate of all the race of mankind."[1] This philanthropic (literally, man-loving) expression might have been taken from prebiblical images of the Goddess's promiscuous priestesses, and of the Goddess herself, who announced, "A prostitute compassionate am I."[2]

The Italian word for a whore, *carogna*, may have come through Indo-European linguistic bypaths from the Sanskrit *karuna*, the quality of loving-kindness manifested in giving, as a mother gives to her child. Sacred harlots' once-revered gift of *charis, caritas,* or "grace" (depicted by the Tarot three of cups) became corrupted into Christian "charity," which meant giving money, not love.

192

Yet, even in this depersonalized version of feminine caring, the harlot often surpassed the churchman, as implied by the six of pentacles in contrast to the five. Folk traditions said well-to-do courtesans were most generous to the poor, either because they had felt the pinch of poverty and sympathized with its sufferers; or simply because they were women, with the female-maternal tendency to pity the helpless. Even today the "golden-hearted whore" is a favorite male fantasy figure, as men are wont to confuse the characteristics of love object and mother.

Oriental Goddess-worshipers detested theologians who talked of divine love but, unlike the Goddess, promulgated their deities' precepts by violence. They claimed the gods' laws were meaningless because they came from "the lips of those who hate and injure one another."[3] True religion, they said, is no more and no less than kindness. In pre-Christian times, the holy whores of the Goddess's temples dispensed kindness as *venia*, the grace of Venus, or *charis*, the grace of the Triple Charites.[4]

The Homeric word for gracious gift-giving was *philein*, "love."[5] This could also mean hospitality, welcoming the guest to the hearth—which from the earliest times was sacred to the clan mother and the ancient Goddess Hestia or Vesta, whose name may have been related to the Sanskrit *Veshya*, a sacred whore.[6]

Charity was seen as a feminine quality, as even now it is an exclusively feminine name. Under the sexual emblem of the hexagram on the six of pentacles, charity is represented by a sacred harlot rewarding a poor minstrel who has pleased her ears with music, just as the Rhineland beggar pleased the ears of the Virgin.

Other related meanings of the card are: patronage, gifts, philanthropy, material gain, help from someone favored by fortune. The card also warned against excessive expenditure of resources through misplaced generosity. Though a basically good quality, charity was not known to be dependable or steady for either giver or receiver; and possible impoverishment was suggested by the following card.

Seven of Pentacles:

Failure

Seven of Pentacles: Failure

The cultural anxiety of Europe's Middle Ages found expression in the symbol of *La Terre Gast*—the Waste Land—resulting from the knights' failure to find the Holy Grail. Pagan worshipers of the female principle long maintained that neglect of the Goddess and her nurturing Vessel would bring on "a landscape of spiritual death," and possibly the death of nature as well.[1] Bardic poets of *Minnedienst*, the service of the Love-goddess, warned against the dire consequences of her curse. Crusaders had seen a real Waste Land, Arabia Deserta, a country left waterless and dead where patriarchal Islam had rejected Arabia's ancient Mother of Fertility. Some feared the same result in Christianized Europe.

Bards told the stories of the rape of the Mother's high priestess and the theft of her golden Grail, crimes that led directly to the withering of grass, trees, and flowers, the drying up of waters, and the ruination of formerly fertile lands.[2] As Arabian mystics yearned for the Mahdi (one sent by the Moon) to come and restore fertility to their desert, so some Europeans insisted that if the Desired Knight did not come to find and restore the Grail, Europe would become a desert too.

Legends of the Grail were many. Some were Christianized. In both pagan and Christian traditions, however, the great quest petered out in ultimate failure. The Grail was never found. The Desired Knight never came to the "Castles of Damsels" where disinherited women awaited a champion to defend their old laws of mother-right and restore their properties. The pagan matriarchate crumbled. The Grail mystics died off. Eventually the great quest was simply forgotten. That was its true failure.

Seven pentacles suggest the Seven Sisters or Seven Sages of Arabian folklore, the seven female sages who prophesied the coming of the Mahdi. These could be identified with the "Seven Mothers of the World" or Pleiades, known as Goddesses who judged the qualities of men, and ruled the alternation of sacred kings in India and pre-Hellenic Greece. When the Pleiades set, the Seven Sisters announced the death of the sacred king.[3] In effect, they announced his failure—the same failure that came inevitably to every mortal man.

194

So the seven stars were associated with the failure of all quests. Their card meant frustration, inertia, alienation, lost opportunities. Seven pentacles were interpreted as a Waste Land in the spirit: deceived hopes, self-induced anxiety, dearth of reward leading to abandonment of vision. As the Grail myths faded away, losing their capacity to inspire, so the card of seven pentacles hinted at demotivation and ennui. A new vision would be required to overcome such deep-seated blockages.

Eight of Pentacles:

Learning

Eight of Pentacles: Learning

After the failure of the knights' Grail quest, in which women did not participate, the search for mystic enlightenment could well have taken a new direction toward the feminine sensibility. Gnostic traditions indicated a renewed impulse toward female-oriented perception and feeling, to tap life-affirming concepts hidden within the psyches of women. As an antidote to ennui and alienation, society would be forced to go back to the beginning and relearn the old wisdom that only the Mother could teach.

Such wisdom was thought to reside in women's "wise blood," which knew how to create life. This was often romantically symbolized by the Rose, and by its Christianized derivatives, the rose window and the rosary.

The first rosary was Kali's *japamala*, "rose-chaplet," and her official flower was the red China rose.[1] Sometimes this was called the Kula flower. When a girl menstruated for the first time, she was said to have borne the Kula flower; she was newly connected with the spiritual unity of the family, the ancestral mothers, and the ancient tribal loyalties and responsibilities "centered in the blood."[2] The rose was the symbol of both uterine blood and female self-knowledge, in which men might participate if carefully taught. Mystics of classical civilization understood the same symbolism. The rose was the Flower of Venus, worn as a token by her priestesses. Nossis said a man who never felt the love of the Goddess would live in darkest ignorance, not knowing "what flowers her roses are."[3]

Before it was adapted to the cult of the Virgin Mary, the rosary migrated into Europe by way of Arabian mystics who "told their beads" in connection with the mysterious secret of the Rose: "I think of nothing but the Rose; I wish nothing but the ruby Rose . . . the love of the Rose is enough."[4] The Arabian Goddess Al-Lat had been masculinized under Islam to Allah. Her feminine characteristics were assigned to Fatima, the alleged "daughter" of Mohammed—yet incongruously called Mother of her father, Womb of the Sun, Maker of Creation, Separater of the light from the darkness, Fate, Night, Moon, Essence of Being, and other titles of the Goddess herself.[5] She personified the rose garden of paradise, "the resting place of Allah."[6]

In Europe, the rosary was at first dedicated wholly to Mary as "Queen of the Most Holy Rosary."[7] Also dedicated to her was the rose window in the western, "female" facade of a church. The window at Chartres called Rose of France had "in its center the Virgin in her majesty," a source of rainbow light like the "earthly appearances" of Maya-Kali.[8] Rainbow light was also a manifestation of Fatima. Rose windows of eight medallions suggested the eight-petaled lotus, a yantra of Kali.[9]

Eight pentacles in a rose window could suggest inner wisdom passing from mother to daughter, from the red Rose Goddess to the white Lily Maid. The notion of a saving grace, hidden in female knowing, had its advocates in the Renaissance period of disillusionment with official or unofficial male "salvations." There were some men who claimed, however heretically, that men should learn from women.

The eight of pentacles was a card of learning, or relearning, secret doctrines. It suggested extension of understanding into new areas; an apprenticeship or a novitiate; a quest for the unstealable rewards of knowledge; and the serenity of true enlightenment.

Nine of Pentacles:

Accomplishment

Nine of Pentacles: Accomplishment

Tantric sages maintained that the ultimate aim of female-focused knowledge was comprehension of Kali in the guise of Maya-Shakti, "the world-protecting, feminine, maternal side of the Ultimate Being, [who] stands for spontaneous, loving acceptance of life's tangible reality. . . . She is the creative joy of life: herself the beauty, the marvel, the enticement and seduction of the living world."[1]

In Buddhist myth this divine principle was incarnate in the virgin Queen Maya, who gave birth to Buddha the Enlightened One under her sacred cherry tree. She was impregnated by the white elephant god Ganesha, whose name meant "Lord of Hosts."[2] In another incarnation she was also the mother of the same god, just as her western counterpart Mary was the mother of the same god who impregnated her, according to Christian theologians. Maya's cherry tree also passed into Western tradition with the Christmas "Cherry Tree Carol," along with the canonized form of Buddha (Bodhisat) as the apocryphal "St. Josaphat."[3]

Maya had her Western counterparts even before her characteristics were inherited by the Virgin Mary. Her older form in classical mythology was Maia, the mother of Hermes the Enlightened One. Her great age was shown by her multiplicity of forms. She was sometimes one of the Muses, sometimes one of the Pleiades. She was a virgin, incongruously known as "the Grandmother" or "the Maker," just as the virgin Kali-Maya was the Shakti of the universe.[4] In pre-Roman Latium she was the spouse of the primal fire-god Vulcan, or Volcanus, a derivative of the early Cretan god of fire-mountains, Velchanos.[5]

Northern European versions of Maya usually took the form of the May Queen, named May or Maj or Mai: Maerin in Norway, Maid Marian in the British Isles. To followers of the fairy-religion in medieval France, she was The Maid, or La Pucelle—a title said to be applied to one individual in every coven of witches, and significantly adopted by Joan of Arc. Renewing her virginity and her motherhood every year, the May Maiden represented the cyclic fertility of the earth. The flowering of her sacred tree was a promise of future fruit.

The nine of pentacles places nine five-petaled flowers on the tree, recalling the mystic Rose-Apple Tree of the Oriental paradise and its mythic connections with Apple-Eve and Rose-Mary—both of whom suggested links with Maya's multiple incarnations. The card meant accomplishment in the sense of gestation, productivity, careful cultivation, the establishment and nurture of beauty through learning. Love of nature was another common interpretation. Whatever god she gave birth to, the pregnant Goddess always personified Nature—including human nature, the true "mother" of gods. Further fortunate omens associated with this card were material well-being and an increase of wealth.

Ten of Pentacles:

Protection

Ten of Pentacles: Protection

The pentacle was widely regarded as a preeminent sign of protection, because of its "gateless" continuous-line construction, and because it was linked from the beginning with the protecting power of the Mother. The uncut line was likened to the uncut thread of the Fate-goddess, whose weaving went on for each individual as long as she chose to preserve his life. Magic charms for staving off death were essentially appeals to the Goddess to continue her unbroken weaving of the life pattern, such as the Slavic charm: "In the Ocean-sea, on the isle of Buyan, a fair maiden was weaving silk; she did not leave off weaving silk: the blood ceased flowing."[1]

One of the facts concealed by Homer's story of the wanderings of Odysseus was the fact that the hero's life was preserved only by the continuous weaving done by his alleged wife, Penelope, whose name was really a title of the Fate-goddess: "She Whose Eye is Behind the Web." Hellenic mythographers transformed her into the epitome of the faithful wife, fending off her other suitors by unraveling the thread of her web every night, so the weaving was never finished and the thread was never cut. Only in the light of older traditions it could be seen that the thread she never cut was the thread of Odysseus's charmed life; thus he could pass through many dangers without being harmed. Older stories of Penelope showed that she was really the orgiastic Goddess. She lay with all her suitors in turn; she married Hermes and gave birth to the Horned God, Pan.[2]

The red thread in the web was a universal sign of life embedded in the web of nature. In remotest antiquity it represented the mother-given blood bond, a soul connected to past and future through maternal heart's blood. Patterns of protection were associated with Penelope and other weaving Goddess figures, such as Persephone who conceived the savior Dionysus while she was seated in her sacred cave, weaving the threads of the universe; and Mary who conceived another Savior while she was seated in her temple, beginning to spin and weave a blood-red thread.[3]

Preservation of life by forming a pentacle of thread was the object of a popular gypsy healing charm called "measuring the pentacle." The patient was made to stand in the attitude of Microcosmic Man, with feet wide apart and arms extended to each side. The healer stretched a continuous thread (preferably red) from each foot to the opposite hand, from each foot to the head, and across the arms, forming a pentacle. Measuring various sections of the thread was supposed to give omens for the course or cure of the disease. Afterward, the thread was burned and the patient inhaled its fumes or drank water containing its ashes.[4]

Ten pentacles would have been a charm of surpassing power, and this design appeared occasionally in mosaic or sacred art, especially in the Middle East. Ten pentacles in the Tarot meant protection, especially in the sense of material advantages: inheritance, ancestral property, past foundations of present security. True to the tradition of the preserving Goddess, the protection implied by the ten of pentacles was not self-created but the work of someone else. The pattern that maintained continuity of the life-thread was a pattern established long ago, by the pre-Homeric Penelope, when the designs of the Goddess were seen in all things.

Princess of Pentacles:

Nimue

Princess of Pentacles: Nimue

One of the primary uses for the pentacle's protective magic was in occult invocations. It was almost universally believed that the operator must stand within a marked pentacle, as a defense against any demonic powers that might be summoned. Sometimes, standing stones formed the pentacle of protection, in certain places sacred to the Druids and other pagan ancestors.

Such places were formerly dedicated to the lunar Fate-goddess known in the early medieval period as Diana Nemetona, or Diana Nemorensis, queen of the *nemeton* (moongrove).[1] Another Greek name for the Goddess was Nemesis, the "doom" of gods. To pre-Christian Celts she was Nemhain, both a virgin and a death-dealing crone. To the Gauls she was Nimue, queen of the fairy-grove of Broceliande. She was the Nemesis or death-giver to the legendary Merlin, once a sacred king who, like other sacred kings, mated with the Goddess in the hour of his passing.

Patriarchal writers laid misleading interpretations on the story of Nimue's so-called betrayal of her lover. Christianized Arthurian romances claimed Nimue was not a divine personification of Fate but only a mortal harlot. By feminine wiles she managed to wheedle Merlin's secrets out of him; then she turned his own magic against him. She cast him into a trance of living death, and imprisoned him in the crystal cave at the heart of the fairy grove. It was said that one day he would awake and return to the world—a last vestige of the original myth of reincarnation.

The crystal cave was a mythic remnant of what the pagans envisioned as the heart of the world within the seven crystalline planetary spheres, sometimes called the seven-story mountain of paradise. Slavic fairy tales took the concept literally, as a mountain of glass belonging to the fairy queen or Moon-goddess. Slavs used to bury bear claws with their dead, to help them climb the slippery glass mountain in the afterlife.[2] A mountain in Britain carried the same name as Merlin in his pre-Arthurian character: Ambrosius. Before Christianity, this mountain was the seat of a famous college of Druidesses.[3]

Nimue was the deity of Druidesses, another version of their Triple

Goddess, as shown by some of her alternate names: Vivien, "She Who Lives," Morgan le Fay, the Lady of the Lake, the White Lady. Some identified her with Rhiannon.[4] Her emblem was a pentacle.[5] The oldest myths said Merlin learned his magic from her, not vice versa.

As the Muse, mistress of inspiration, Nimue stood for learning. Her pentacle meant magic learning specifically; but she was the patron of all bards, seers, and scholars who undertook to study her ancient mysteries. Her card has been interpreted as "the wisdom of the ages," or an apparent novelty of something actually known long ago. The card also meant concentration, desire to learn, and application to scholarly pursuits.

Prince of Pentacles:

Merlin

Prince of Pentacles: Merlin

This card indicated a person in command of powerful inner forces, naturally suggesting Nimue's consort Merlin, perhaps the most mysterious figure in the Arthurian cycle of legends. Like Heimdall, the primitive Scandinavian angel of the Last Trump, Merlin was born of the nine sisters of the cold sea, and cast up on the beach by the ninth wave.[1] The *Vita Merlini* identified his nine mothers with the Morgans of the Fortunate Isles. In German poems, the mystic nine ruled Meidelant, the "Land of Maidens," whence came many other heroes of romance.[2] The name Merlin means a child of the sea, though in medieval falconry it was applied to a type of hawk that could be flown only by a lady.[3]

Merlin was begotten by a god, probably the Red Dragon once worshiped as a phallic consort of the Sea-goddess in Caerleon. Legend said that as a child Merlin was sentenced to be sacrificed to the same god, to make his temple stand firm, according to the ancient custom of laying the foundations of any sacred structure in a victim's lifeblood. The stones of Vortigern's great temple on Salisbury Plain kept falling down during its construction. Two Druidic astrologers declared the structure couldn't be finished unless it was founded in the blood of a child who had no human father. Merlin was the obvious choice. He was saved by his own gift of second sight. He saw in the earth beneath the temple a great pit, where the Red Dragon of Wales struggled against the White Dragon of Britain, and lost, and was killed. Thus, Merlin prophesied the death of Vortigern at the hands of the Britons. After the fulfillment of the prophecy, the wizard himself completed the building of the temple which became Stonehenge, by singing the great stones into their places with his magic songs.[4]

Though Merlin was said to lie dreaming the centuries away in his crystal cave, folklore constantly predicted his second coming, perhaps to restore the old religion. Efforts were made to Christianize the old wizard, lest his legend become a rallying point for anti-ecclesiastical forces. The Merlin myth promulgated by the monasteries said he was begotten by the devil on a human virgin, with the object of making him the Antichrist. However, his mother's chastity overcame the power of evil, and Merlin was born virtuous. Robert de Borron claimed Merlin's magic powers were bestowed on him by God.[5]

Still, Merlin couldn't be dissociated from the images and symbols of paganism. He carried the willow wand and wore the conical cap or *apex* that used to crown pagan priests, and eventually became standard headgear for witches.[6] For centuries, the Merlin literature was used as an underground vehicle for criticism of the church. The Council of Trent placed such literature on the Index of Prohibited Books and burned all copies of it that could be found.[7]

In contrast to such policies of censorship, Merlin's Tarot card stood for the defense of free expression and such qualities as truth, honor, patience, and determination. The specialty of any famous seer was investigation of origins of things; Merlin might have investigated, by invocation, even the mysterious spirit supposed to have fathered him. His card then implied a fearless following of clues, regardless of possible dangers.

Queen of Pentacles:

Erda

Queen of Pentacles: Erda

Queen of the earth-elemental suit of pentacles could only be Mother Earth, the Teutonic Erda, worshiped by all primitive peoples as the universal life-giver and primary Muse. As the Kagaba Indians said, "The Mother of Songs, the mother of our whole seed, bore us in the beginning. She is the mother of all races of man and the mother of all tribes. She is the mother of the thunder, the mother of the rivers, the mother of trees and of all kinds of things. She is the mother of songs and dances . . . the only mother we have."[1]

This Mother was the only supreme deity known to European people for countless thousands of years.[2] Her images are traced all the way back to the Old Stone Age, the earliest typified by the famous "fat Venus" figurines found from Siberia to the Pyrenees, with their rudimentary heads and arms, huge breasts and hips. They are not only the earliest sacred art but the earliest artworks of any kind now known.[3]

All mythologies conceded that this Mother figure stood alone at the beginning of creation, under hundreds of variant names. She was Erda, Eorth, Ertha, Edda, Hertha, Hretha, Nertha, Urth, Urd, Wurd, Wyrd, or Weird in various areas of northern Europe.[4] To the Greeks she was Rhea or Gaea, "the deep-breasted, universal mother, firmly founded, oldest of divinities."[5] To the Romans she was Terra Firma, from the Aryan Tara or Terah, who also mothered the biblical *teraphim* (ancestral spirits).

A sense of connectedness with all forms of life arose from primary worship of the Great Mother who produced everything, according to the earliest beliefs. As the Indians said, when creatures came into existence, "It was just like a child being born from its mother. The place of emergence is the womb of the earth."[6]

A similar sense of connectedness invested the card of the queen of pentacles, whose traditional characteristics were like those of the immemorial Erda: generosity, opulence, overflowing fertility, compassion, comfort, support, abundance. The card was said to indicate a warm, nurturing personality: a Muse, able to create and to inspire creativity. Another interpretation often applied to the queen of pentacles was "answers to prayers." This would refer to the Tarot's non-Christian orientation, for Christian theory was unalterably opposed to the idea that the deity who answered prayers was the carnal, fleshly, *material*, earthly female. Still, bards of the romantic movement always invoked Erda's blessing on their works, not God's.

King of Pentacles:

Baal

King of Pentacles: Baal

Among the earliest mates of the Earth Mother were the mountain gods, collectively called Baal, "the Lord," in the ancient Middle East. Their real names were taboo and could be spoken only by their priests, who pretended to control the gods by the use of their secret names. Hence the biblical stricture against taking the name of "the Lord" in vain (Deuteronomy 5:11).

When men wished to commune with a Baal of the mountain, they climbed to the summit of his mountain throne, and waited there for the Lord's spirit to move them to vision, inspiration, or prophecy. Laws were supposed to have been handed down from sacred mountaintops in this manner. Moses climbed to the top of Mount Sinai to meet its resident Baal and learn his will. This was a common enough procedure, but the God of Moses was not originally the syncretic Jehovah he was to become in subsequent writings.

Mount Sinai was sacred to the Moon-god Sin, a son of the Queen of Heaven (Nanna). He ruled what the Bible called "the land of Sinim" (Isaiah 49:12), meaning the Land of the Lunar Mountain, an older form of the name of Zion.[1] Sin became assimilated to the volcanic mountain god of Jebel al-Aqra, in northern Syria, when Kenite or Cainite tribes of smiths migrated from there to settle in the land of Midian (Sinai).[2] Having brought their volcano-deity with them (symbolizing him by a pillar of fire by night and a pillar of smoke by day), the Cainites simply declared that he was the same as the Baal of Sinai, and worshiped his new throne. Moses was said to have married into the Midianite clans and inherited the priesthood of his father-in-law Jethro, one of the servants of Sin (Exodus 3:1).

The king of pentacles indicated a person with characteristics like those of the ancient mountain gods: stern, rocklike, authoritarian, heavy, tenacious. His good qualities tended to be earth-like, such as reliability, practicality, stability, and certain diamond-in-the-rough features, like the gems buried in rocks and known only to the primitive gods called Lords of Riches.

The wisdom of Baal, like those of other mates of Mother Earth, was signified by the "third eye" of insight: a shining pentacle of knowledge buried in the mountain as the pentacle of the Mother of All Living was buried in her apple of knowledge. Naturally, it was always supposed to be a long, hard climb for any man to reach the pinnacle where such a god dwelt, and to learn the significance of the hidden star.

The Suit
of Swords

Ace of Swords:

Doom

Ace of Swords:
Doom

Like the Tantric life-phase of *Moksha*, the suit of swords meant finalities and catastrophes: doom, death, ultimate fate. This suit was one of the most pagan parts of the Tarot. Paganism neither denied the fact of death nor imagined that death could be conquered, but advised acceptance of death even in its ugliest or cruelest forms because it was as much a manifestation of the Goddess's power as birth.

Among Celtic pagans, the death-dealing Crone aspect of the Goddess bore the name of Morgan or Morg-ana, the Anna of Death, with variations: Morgan le Fay, Morgan the Fairy, Morgan the Fate, Fata Morgana, Magog, Mugain, Morgue la Faye.[1] She carried dead heroes to her Fortunate Isles (or Avalon, the Apple-land), for she was the queen of the

207

western paradise.[2] Though Christianized Arthurian legends claimed Morgan le Fay was only King Arthur's witch sister, "a great clerk of necromancy," she also played the role of Lady Death: "Morgan the Goddess is her name, and there is never a man so high and proud but she can humble and tame him."[3]

Morgan was linked with the annual decapitation of sacred kings, shown by her management of the allegorical contest between Gawain and the Green Knight, who alternately cut off each other's heads at the New Year, like Horus and Set in Egypt, or like Njord and Frey in Scandinavia.[4] Early Celtic tribes used to preserve the heads or skulls of dead leaders and take omens from them. Hence the famous Green Man heads that developed into the ubiquitous carved "grotto-creatures" (*grotesques*) in old churches.

The ceremony of knighthood began as a modification of the old ceremony of apotheosis through decapitation, which sent a hero to Morgan's paradise. Touching each shoulder with a sword symbolically implied that the sword had passed through the neck. In a similar ceremony, Brauronian Artemis received drops of blood drawn from a man's neck with a sword, instead of his whole head as in former ages.[5] Artemis-worshiping Scythians used to represent a phallic god or hero by a sword plunged into Mother Earth and watered with blood.[6] As the Goddess's mate, he thus became Lord of Death.

Another symbol of Morgan's sovereignty over the dead was her magic mirror, where souls dwelt. The ancients regarded mirrors with awe, believing a mirror could steal the soul that was seen in the reflection: the same fate that befell Narcissus. A German story placed in the Valley of the Shadow of Death an enchanted hall of mirrors, where the Goddess kept souls in her magic glass. The place was called Wisperthal (Valley of Whispers), due to an old belief that ghosts lost their vocal cords and could speak only in whispers.[7]

Morgan appeared in various folkloric disguises in mysterious settings like the Wisperthal, sometimes as a destructive power, sometimes as an angelic queen who took her heroes to a more comfortable land. Since she wore the horns of the moon and presided over the lunar country of the dead (where her favored ones became stars), she was also a Queen of the Air. In the Tarot, her card would naturally lead the suit of doom, bearing meanings of finality and tragedy. But the ace of swords was also interpreted at times as a release, freedom from restraint, a new lightness, or a kind of salvation.

Two of Swords:

Balance

Two of Swords: Balance

The deuce of swords naturally set two potentially dangerous forces against one another, perhaps to cancel each other out. The image of a blindfolded female Justice with two swords, set against the sea and the moon, is traditional for this card.

In the early medieval period there were still female justices and magistrates, known to Christian chroniclers as the witches who were also judges, dating from pre-Christian systems of matriarchal *ius naturale* (natural law) based on tribal mother-right.[1] Ulpian said all justice must be founded on "the feminine nature principle, which has a profounder kinship with the *natura iustum* (that which is just by nature) than does the male sex, with its greater susceptibility to the principle of domination." Pythagorean mystics claimed that justice and equity were innate attributes of the feminine nature principle.[2]

The concept of balance in moral areas of life had its oldest roots in the Goddess's karmic law, which said in effect that every action produces a corresponding reaction; that benevolent acts bring benevolence upon the doer, and malevolent acts eventually cause their perpetrator to suffer, even though his punishment might be delayed until another life. This was the true origin of the Golden Rule, which some called the essence of Christianity. At first it was not a Christian idea, nor even a Jewish one, but an idea derived from ancient Egypt's law of the Goddess Maat.[3] Tantric sages were commanded to do unto others as they would have others do unto them.[4] The Buddhist version of the precept was "As ye sow, so shall ye reap," which was copied into Christian Scriptures 500 years later.[5]

The negative corollary of the Golden Rule was the harsh law of compensatory vengeance. If a man did to others as he would rather not be done to, he would get the same back. Human systems of justice were founded on this allegedly divine rule that two wrongs make a right: an eye for an eye, a tooth for a tooth, a life for a life. The ancient principle still operates in our own legal system. For example, it is believed that murderers should be slain, unless they are officially instructed to kill, as in a war.

Interpretations of the two of swords tended toward these more negative notions of karmic balance. One evil might offset another, as a surgical wound might cure the effects of an accidental wound. Balance of opposing forces could lead to stalemate, a temporary truce in the midst of strife, or a new equilibrium after difficult adjustments. The blinded figure also implied vengeful righting of a wrong with another wrong, due to inability to see future consequences.

Three of Swords:

Sorrow

Three of Swords: Sorrow

The dictates of natural law were not always easy to accept. Buddhism allegorized the opposing principles of attraction and repulsion in the figure of Kama-Mara, Love and Death, a "demon" who tempted the Buddha and almost caused a disastrous interruption of his meditation on the Middle Way.[1]

As the spirit of death and sorrow, Mara had many manifestations in Middle Eastern religious imagery: as the Syrian Mari, Hebrew Marah, Greek Moera, Celtic Maura, and so on. Like Oriental death-priestesses, the *dakinis*, she became the *mater dolorosa*—the wailing-mother in the temple, whose function was to perform the funeral hymns Greeks called *moirologhia* (Word of the Fates).[2] The dirges of death-priestesses were also known as *houloi*, "howlings." Herodotus said they originated in the Libyan temples of Athene.[3] Everywhere, laments for the dead were developed and performed by women, and tradition insisted that women invented them.[4] Even in patriarchal Jerusalem, the priestesses were the ones who wailed for the demise of the Savior every year in "the house of the Lord" (Ezekiel 8:14).

Temple women and their formal laments are suggested by the traditional interpretation of the three of swords as a card of "tears and woe" connected with a holy woman or with singing.[5] It was once believed that dead men had to be sung into the afterworld by feminine charms *(carmen)* expressing formal but not necessarily sincere grief. Even up to the present century, the Irish preserved the professional status of the keening-woman, hired to enhance a funeral and appease the departed ghost with loud wailing and ritual dramatizations of sorrow.

Keening lament was probably the "singing" connected with this card in the death suit, as though a balance of dangerous powers shown by the two might overtip one way or the other, resulting in a tragedy. The meaning was not rigidly interpreted as sorrow for death, but rather as sorrow for any cause; for any kind of bereavement or loss, any disappointment, any reason for self-pity. Blood on the three swords suggested a mutual destruction engendered by three contributing factors. Sadness and regret could result. There was also a sense of isolation, loneliness, imprisonment, or withdrawal into a restricted psychic environment representing endurance of inner pain.

Four of Swords:

Seclusion

Four of Swords: Seclusion

Dire events in general were associated with the Fatal Women, variously known as seeresses, pythonesses, mantes, valas, magia, stregae, or sybils—a derivative of the Goddess Cybele, whose name meant "cavern-dweller." Among the most famous Fatal Women in the ancient world were the Sybil of Cumae and the Pythoness of Delphi, who dwelt in sacred caves, and communicated directly with the oracular spirit of the earth.

The usual meaning of the four of swords was like the character of a sybil, set apart for an esoteric purpose; perhaps isolated by the sorrow of the previous card. Any four invoked the earth-sign of the square; and it was within the earth that the sybil's seat established magical connection between herself and the Mother of Fate. Oracular women often sat cross-legged on the ground, approximating the lotus position sacred to Kali's yogis. Medieval Christian authorities therefore claimed that sitting cross-legged was a form of witchcraft.[1]

Sitting on or touching the ground was a time-honored way of invoking Mother Earth.[2] Even Buddha touched the earth in his prolonged isolation, calling on the Mother's power to protect him from demons. The Enlightened One was not powerful enough to withstand evil forces without the intervention of the all-mothering Goddess. A Greek version of this idea was the myth of the giant Antaeus, son of Mother Earth, whose strength was irresistible only as long as he was in contact with his Mother's substance. Heracles defeated Antaeus by holding him up in the air, so he was prevented from touching the soil that gave him birth.

The oracular Goddess Earth was often characterized as a spirit of the Pit; and the four of swords implied a reference to her in connection with "graves and coffins."[3] This hinted at the dark side of the Earth-goddess whose spirit was supposed to inspire all the oldest oracles. Her deadly Serpent lived forever in her womb, and spoke secretly to her priestesses. Python, the prophetic Serpent of Delphi, mystic spouse of the Pythoness, was called the firstborn child of Mother Earth.[4]

The four of swords was a card of insight generated by seclusion, like the insight of Delphi's fatidic priestess. Sometimes it meant prophetic powers invoked in secret. Other related meanings included the seclusion of exile, imprisonment, convalescence, voluntary isolation, or rest and recuperation in the midst of adversity. The four of swords implied that consultation with a person of true prophetic ability would reveal a rather dire outlook. Its cave meant isolation, but insight gained in the cave might warn of unpleasant or unhappy interaction with others at a future time.

Five of Swords:

Defeat

Five of Swords: Defeat

Self-abasement, passive endurance, forcible swallowing of pride were among the meanings of the five of swords, suggesting the mandatory self-sacrifices of early god-kings in their efforts to gain or retain such feminine powers as insight, wisdom, verbal facility, or life-giving magic. A typical story was that of Odin, crucified on the World Ash Tree, while the trinity of Norns sat at the tree's root spinning the thread of his fate.

Wounded in the side by the usual spear thrust, Odin hung on the tree for nine nights, the traditional period of lying-in for parturient women, because the skills and insights he craved were formerly the exclusive property of mothers. He descended into the uterine pit of Hel, traversing "all the seven nether worlds."[1] Then he received a drink of the precious red mead from the feminine fount of wisdom, or the "wise blood" from the Cauldron in the earth's womb. Resurrected (or, reincarnated as the savior-son Balder), he then understood the magic of runes and verbal creation, and "began to be fruitful and to be fertile, to grow and to prosper."[2]

Like the card of the Hanged Man, the five of swords indicated a defeat or degradation voluntarily assumed for the sake of subsequent glory, as a martyr sought martyrdom for the sake of apotheosis (canonization or becoming god). Scandinavian kings were regularly sacrificed to enhance the fertility of the earth, up to the twelfth century A.D.[3] Apparently each was identified with the god, whose periodic deaths and resurrections were decreed by the Norns, the original female trinity, infinitely older than the sky-father Odin.[4]

In the same way, three Marys or Moerae at the foot of Jesus's cross represented the older, female-oriented sacrifices of sacred kings. So did the Gospel tradition that only women, led by Mary, could discover the pseudo-king's resurrection and announce it to his male followers, who were ignorant of the sacred tradition that he must rise again. The Bible says, "They knew not the scripture, that he must rise again from the dead" (John 20:9).

Sacred kings of the North were often identified with the sun, whose Passion took place at the midwinter solstice, the darkest day of the year, when the solar deity must die to be resurrected into a new development toward the life-giving spring and summer seasons. The sun's title, Light of the World, was also applied to Jesus.

The Golden Dawn Society named the five of swords Lord of Defeat.[5] This meant a defeat decreed by the Fates, therefore to be accepted without protest. Even kings and gods had to bow to the will of the Norns. The five of swords recalled a principle once universally recognized: that even in the face of death, which arrives in its appointed hour for every living creature, virtue lies in patient endurance and passive courage. It was also a reminder that the darkest days of winter are followed by an increase of light and the gradual onset of a new cycle.

Six of Swords:

Passage

Six of Swords: Passage

Among common interpretations of the six of swords are: a journey by water, an anxious time, a passage toward a dark, unknowable future. These and related ideas converged in ancient Greece's symbol of the river Styx, the last rite of passage and the ultimate journey, where the faceless ferryman Charon carried dead souls into the nether world. Charon was a late addition to the myth; but the Styx itself was older than the oldest gods.

Some said the waters of the Styx were black. Others said they were blood. These waters bore the same curse as menstrual blood, once represented by the Gorgon face: it was said that Styx fluid could turn men to stone. The name Styx means petrifying, a reference to its terrible taboo.[1] Yet the river was also called Alpha, the river of birth. It was said to flow from Mother Earth's genital opening, past the holy shrine of Clitor. Greek gods, born of Mother Earth, swore their most binding oaths by the Styx, as a man would swear any absolutely unbreakable vow by his mother's blood that made him.[2]

Styx was also a Goddess, called the Daughter of Ocean, possibly derived from the primitive Kali-the-Creatress called Daughter of the Ocean of Blood. The Goddess Styx married the mysterious phallic deity Pallas, and gave birth to a holy trinity known as Power, Force, and Dominance.[3]

An Egyptian form of this Goddess was Hathor, also associated with a holy river of blood (the red Nile in flood time), said to issue from a vast cavern under the Mountains of the Moon. The archaic belief was that Hathor-the-Sphinx, like Styx, carried the dead through six windings in the uterine underworld and gave them rebirth. Greek myth said King Oedipus ended the reign of Hathor-the-Sphinx in Thebes, but she went underground to assume guardianship of the dark gate. The Bible called her river Gihon, or Gehenna, which meant the river sacred to Ge, another name for Mother Earth.[4]

The dark entrance to Gehenna's headwaters, presided over by the fearsome Sphinx with her mysterious riddles, offered a telling symbol of man's fears of the veiled, unguessable future. Every rite of passage

214

was a ride into the unknown. The six swordsmen of the Tarot card were generally supposed to be moving away from danger, so the passage might not be as perilous as it seemed. Hope was a figure on the Stygian riverbank, holding up a small light. The card was sometimes said to presage success, though not immediately. Difficulties of the voyage could not be avoided. They must be faced and solved before the passage could proceed.

Seven of Swords:

Opposition

Seven of Swords: Opposition

Opposition from relentlessly hostile forces was the usual interpretation of the seven of swords, with the implication that their source would be hard to identify or to confront. Traps might be prepared by secret enemies. Slanders might be spoken behind one's back. Unknown, impersonal powers of the natural or the social environment might be aligned against one's future well-being.

Difficulties associated with this card were similar to the difficulties attributed to a witch's curse, thought to work harm in secret, therefore viewed as worse than a danger plainly seen. The standard image of a curse-laying witch, or Hag, was like paganism's divine death-dealing Crone: an elderly woman, whose "wise blood" was retained to build up irresistibly powerful magic within her.[1]

The word Hag used to mean "holy woman." It was also a synonym for "fairy."[2] Hags were the western equivalent of Indian *dakinis* or "Skywalkers," the elder priestesses who played the funerary part of the death angel.[3] The Scots called an old woman Caillech, which was also the name of their pagan Goddess of Creation, the mother of humanity, possibly derived from the Aryan Kali.[4] In the traditions of pagan Europe, Hags were once tribal rulers or "princesses" who refused to accept Christianity and continued to serve their Goddess in defiance of the church, so their title became synonymous with "witch."[5]

A witch's familiar animal-demon was supposed to help her cast spells and curses. Black cats often played this part in popular folklore, because cats were sacred to the Goddess from Scandinavia to Egypt.

215

The Scottish Queen of Witches was called "Mother of the Mawkins," because *mawkin* or *malkin* meant a cat.[6] Shakespeare named a witch's familiar Greymalkin or Grimalkin, the gray cat, which once referred to the springtime gray malkins on the pussy willow, formerly sacred to Hecate as Queen of Witches.

Witches, Valkyries, fairies, and other versions of the female "Skywalkers" were said to have the ability to turn themselves into cats, showing that the real origin of the familiar *daemon* was an animal totem, the alter ego made flesh in animal form, like the Egyptian *ba*. Pagans believed one might become an animal by wearing the animal's mask. Hence "mascot," an animal totem, came from Provençal *masco*, a witch wearing a mask. *Mascoto* meant witchcraft generally.[7]

The seven of swords is a card of *mascoto*, complete with mascot, magic signs, and the Hag whose cross-legged position denoted "sorcery."[8] Cat's eyes in the faces of both woman and cat indicate a shared soul. Seven swords facing outward reflect hostility. Being "at swords' points," curses, quarrels, difficulties, and hampering of movement are implied by the seven of swords.

Eight of Swords:

Disillusion

Eight of Swords: Disillusion

The eight of swords denoted a crisis in which conviction might suddenly show its other face, and be recognized as destructive fanaticism. Loss of faith, inner turmoil, despair, and depression were usually cited as possible consequences. A sense of such troubles might be symbolized by the legendary knight's journey to the end of the earth, Finisterre, searching for the passage to the sunset paradise, to find nothing but a lonely wasteland and a cold, impassable sea.

Seven planted swords suggest the stages of a futile journey. The eighth, stained with blood, represents the crusading warrior's disillusion when he must doubt the cause he has killed for, expecting a hero's glory. By the ancient *ius naturale* (natural law), the shadow of death hung over a killer. Classical Greek myths said he was pursued by *mias-*

ma, the Mother's Curse of spiritual pollution, sometimes personified as a Fury in the form of a black vulture following the scent of death.

In Scandinavia, the gray horse symbolized death.[1] This was the cloud-steed of Odin enroute to the land of the dead. A gray horse on the eight of swords is a soul-death or delusion, carrying a knight to his rendezvous with futility.

Other consequences of the disillusion indicated by this card were bad news, fruitless conflict, censure, and embarrassment at the discovery that formerly honored principles and beliefs proved false. The card often meant enforced isolation in retaliation for unkind acts, as imprisonment might be suffered in retribution for a crime.[2] Though much effort might be expended, as on the knight's journey to the end of the world, it would prove ultimately useless, the product of a poor decision.

Nine of Swords:

Cruelty

Nine of Swords: Cruelty

This card could mean a cruel fate, mental or physical suffering, anxiety about the imminent possibility of pain; or it could mean callous indifference to the pain of another. Violent attack and martyrdom were extreme manifestations of cruelty. Intermediate forms might be deception, worry, entrapment, or isolation from needed help and comfort.

During the period of the Tarot's appearance in Europe, and for five centuries after, the epitome of cruelty was the Inquisition, created to trap, torture, and destroy those who still clung to the old faith—mostly women. Such women were sometimes called Druidesses; or, as the Greeks said, Dryads. In ancient times, these terms meant priestesses of tree worship. Each Dryad had her own tree, a residence of her own oracular spirit. A biblical example was the seeress and tribal ruler Deborah, who lived under her own sacred tree, bearing her name (Judges 4:5). According to Homer, a Dryad would live as long as her tree lived, so she could grow wise with great age.[1] The long-lived oaks were especially prized. Tree nymphs were also known in India, where their magic brought forth their trees' blossoms and fruit because, it was said, "women are vessels of fertility, life in full sap, potential sources of new offspring."[2]

The eleventh-century scholar Michael Psellus said the Dryads or Druidesses were eternal minds in earthly bodies, capable of knowing men's thoughts and foretelling the future.[3] Churchmen naturally feared women credited with such powers. Inquisitors set out to capture and kill them, and to cut down their trees, which the country folk used to worship as divine.

Still, pagan tree spirits mysteriously appeared even in the carvings of churches themselves, in the form of tree trunks with human-like faces surrounded by leaves.[4] The druidic "Black Goddess" of Gaul was assimilated to the Virgin Mary and worshiped along with her divine child in the ancient pre-Christian crypt under Chartres Cathedral known as the Druid Grotto.[5]

Despite such syncretism, priestesses of the tree cults were branded as witches and exterminated with great cruelty. Since the Inquisition's reign of terror has never been surpassed for inhumanity, nine inquisitors aptly bear the nine swords of cruelty on this card. Other related meanings of the card were: scandal, misery, hatred, brutal neglect or abandonment, unreasoning violence.

Ten of Swords:

Ruin

Ten of Swords: Ruin

The culminating pip card in the suit of swords was probably the direst omen in the deck, which is why readers of ordinary playing cards tended to regard the ten of spades as a card of death. The ten of swords meant ruin, desolation, pain, the worst of afflictions, the nadir of fortune, some sort of martyrdom.

For Christian society, the ultimate model of martyrdom was the sacrifice of Jesus to his heavenly father, who refused to forgive humanity without his son's blood. Celtic paganism similarly viewed the death of the virgin-born savior-hero Cu Chulainn, who died bound to a sacred phallic pillar, pierced by many blades. He appeared at an ancient stone temple in Knockmay, Galway, as a young god bound to a tree and pierced by arrows.[1] Similar figures in Gaul gave rise to the legend of the martyred St. Sebastian, who was never a real Christian saint but only a new name for old statues of the dying god.[2]

Like the corresponding Christian savior, Cu Chulainn was "begotten by a man that was not a man; his father was reared by his mother as a child, a child which died and did not die."[3] Christian-like identification of the son with his divine father (the god Lug, patron deity of Lugdunum or London), and his reincarnation through the same divine mother, led some Irish scholars to insist that Cu Chulainn was an avatar of Christ. Others claimed he was an Antichrist, because his soul had entered his mother in the form of a fly, a manner of impregnation common in Celtic folklore.[4] The Bible said the devil Beelzebub was "Lord of Flies," which originally meant only that he was a psychopomp, since flies were once identified with souls.

Cu Chulainn's myth retained the element that Jesus's Gospel story left out: the anathema laid on the hero by the Crone aspect of the same Triple Goddess who gave him life and announced the season of his death. As "Queen of Phantoms," this Crone was the third of the Irish female trinity, Ana, Babd, and Macha. These three also appeared as the triple Morrigan, or the Three Sorceresses of Mab (Mabd), who sentenced Cu Chulainn to his death.[5]

The Crone was sometimes called *Bean-Sidhe*, "woman of the barrow-graves," pronounced Banshee. She emerged from the underworld through a barrow-mound and called men to their deaths. Her voice could not be resisted.[6] Her call was dreaded, but it was said, "When the Banshee loves those she calls, the song is a low, soft chant giving notice, indeed, of the proximity of death but with a tenderness that reassures the one destined to die."[7] Other traditions described her call as a blood-curdling shriek or wail. In Brittany, she was known as the Bandrhude, a "bane-druid" or Dryad of Death.[8]

Thus, the familiar Death-goddess decreed Cu Chulainn's sacrificial murder. She was the same dark deity who brought death to every man, according to pagan philosophy. She would naturally appear with the dying hero, indifferent to his fate, on the Tarot card of darkest omen. Yet, as her other aspect was periodically the mother of the same hero, a suggestion of pregnancy beneath her black robe might indicate hope for the future. As dying gods were reincarnated and rose again, and each year's sun began to wax in strength after its nadir at the winter solstice, so even the ten of swords could suggest a new birth of hope out of despair.

Princess of Swords:

Skuld

Princess of Swords:
Skuld

A princess of swords would natural-ly be a maiden mythically connected with death. Skuld was a good exam-ple. As the third Norn, Skuld repre-sented the future, where every man's death lurked in wait beyond the veil. According to the doomsday book called *Völuspá*, the Priestess's Revelation, Skuld was the leader of the Valkyries, whose name meant "choosers of the dead."[1]

Valkyries were related to Saxon *Walcyries* and Slavic Valas, Vilas, or Wilis, death-priestesses said to be able to make dying easy and pleasant.[2] Their gift was like that of Tantric *dakinis*, whose power could bless the dying with *vilasa*, "heavenly bliss."[3] The classic image of Valkyries showed them galloping over the clouds on their black horses, to carry dead heroes from the battlefield to Valhalla. They chose only men who died bravely. Valkyries were pagan psychopomps, sometimes the "celestial wives" of the heroes, like the houris of Islam.[4]

Earthly Valkyries or Valas were priestesses in charge of Norse and Icelandic temples up to the tenth century A.D., when the church began to view them as implacable enemies of Christianity, and to declare their Goddess Skuld's magic evil "skulduggery."[5] By the fourteenth century, Valkyries were equated with witches.[6] Their eastern European counter-parts, the Vilas, were also redefined as witches.[7]

Because witches were often deliberately drowned during the "water ordeal," or "ducking," the Vilas lived on in folklore as the souls of drowned women, dwelling in deep waters. On nights that marked the old pagan festivals, they came up to dance on land by moonlight. Where they danced, crops grew more abundantly and grass grew thick-er, though men feared to see them at this fertility magic.[8] They still dance in modern theaters as the Wilis of the classical ballet *Giselle*. Northern Valkyries also appear on the stage, notably in Wagner's op-eras.

As a Valkyrie leader, Skuld denoted a quick-witted, vigilant, active person, especially one used as an emissary. Like her sisters, Skuld was fearsome because she posed a stringent challenge. Her tests were dif-ficult to pass. Her formidable insight could pinpoint hidden weaknesses. Few men were heroic enough to meet her conditions, which could require nothing less than their lives. To earn the attention of a Valkyrie, a man would have to emulate the hero Ragnar Lodbrok, who composed and sang his own death-song with his last breath, declaring himself fearless: "The hours of life have glided by; I fall, but smiling shall I die."[9]

The princess of swords might be interpreted as a Valkyrie-like, sharp-minded woman of keen judgment and high spirit, who might prove dangerous to those unable to meet her challenge. She has been designated "stern and powerful." Her black horse was a common folkloric symbol of trouble. It was said that to dream of a black horse meant sorrow, loss, or death.[10] This belief descended from the image of the Valkyrie on her black horse, coming out of the whirlwind to judge and receive the souls of the dead. Like the princess of swords she was a "battle-maid," who might be propitiated but never conquered.

Prince of Swords:

Tyr

Prince of Swords: Tyr

In Norse mythology, Tyr meant war: the usual route to the paradise promised by Skuld of the Valkyries. Tyr was called the god of battles, to whom warriors should address their prayers, "without doubt the most daring and courageous" of the gods. He was never called Peacemaker.[1]

Romans identified Tyr with their own war god Mars. The weekday sacred to Mars was Tuesday, Latin *dies Martis*, French *mardi*. Its English name Tuesday came from Tiw, the Old English version of Tyr; it was Tiw's Day.[2]

Both Tyr and Mars were once "all-father" sky gods, eventually ousted from the heavenly throne by Odin and Jupiter, respectively. The elder deities became personifications of the syncretic Father's violent, vengeful, cruel side. They represented the storm, the lightning that strikes unexpectedly and brings death, the cults of the legions and the *berserkers*, and sometimes also the pestilence following in the wake of war.

Earlier Aryan versions of this formidable deity were Sama, a storm

221

king clothed in black, or Samana, "the leveller," who reaped all lives like the figure of Death with his scythe.[3] He was worshiped at the Celtic Samhain, Feast of the Dead, which became Halloween. He also appeared in the Bible as Sammael or Samuel. In Britain, his feminine counterpart was named Samothea, Death-Goddess, an alternate name for Skadi or Skuld.

The prince (or knight) of swords was always interpreted as a warlike person "inclined to dominate others and sweep them along with him like a storm-wind."[4] He could be seen as a charismatic tyrant like Hitler, spouting phrases of hatred which somehow exerted an emotional appeal on his listeners, rather than inspiring their disgust. Cruelty, or at least disregard for the feelings of others, was usually characteristic of this prince. The card could represent an impersonal force with great power to harm, such as a severe illness, accident, a natural disaster, or oppressive circumstances. The prince of swords flies the yellow flag of pestilence, suggesting injurious illness. Another interpretation of the card involved a bullying sort of person, rejoicing in his ability to cut others down. In nearly all respects the prince of swords represented, like Tyr, the spirit of war.

Queen of Swords:

Kali

Queen of Swords: Kali

The Destroyer aspect of the queen of swords was so firmly established that it even carried over into modern versions of the suit, where the queen of spades is generally accorded a dangerous character.[1] In the Western world, manifestations of the Destroyer-Crone aroused only horror, contributing to men's subconscious fear of the feminine principle; for the Terrible Mother was an archetype that couldn't be erased even by patriarchal religion.

Kali Ma personified one of the earliest, strongest expressions of the archetype.[2] Yet, Western scholars steadfastly refused to recognize her universality. The London Museum displayed her statue slightingly labeled only, "Kali—Destroying Demon."[3] The Encyclopedia Britannica gave her no more than a brief paragraph, calling her the wife of Shiva and a goddess of disease.[4]

In her home territory, Kali represented not only destruction and disease, but the culminating third of the original Holy Trinity of the Creating, Preserving, and Destroying Goddess who "giveth . . . and taketh away." Her worshiper was advised to adore her dark side. "His Goddess, his loving Mother in time, who gives him birth and loves him in the flesh, also destroys him in the flesh. His image of Her is incomplete if he does not know Her as his tearer and devourer."[5]

Conventional images of Kali showed her squatting over the corpse of her lover Shiva, with whom the male worshiper was to identify himself. She showed the most hideous of her many faces, while she drew Shiva's entrails from his belly and devoured them.[6] Her hands (sometimes, but not always, four in number) held symbols of the elements. This meant her destruction not only of each individual life in due season, but of the entire universe—which Shiva personified—when the time came for doomsday to precede another of her creations.[7] The myth was a vision of the infinite cycles of nature, "For in a profound way life and birth are always bound up with death and destruction."[8]

Kali's devotees met to worship her in the grisly atmosphere of the cremation grounds, to encounter her in the sights and smells of death, and to learn to adore even her ugliest manifestations. This may explain why medieval "witches" were said to hold their meetings in graveyards. Kali Ma was not unknown to European pagans. Finns called her Kalma, the haunter of cemeteries. Her name was translated "odor of corpses."[9] Her character contributed much to those of Cerridwen, the corpse-eating Mother of Celtic pagans; Demeter, the eater of Pelops; Isis as the vulture who devoured Osiris; Astarte and Ishtar who also devoured the dead. The epic *Beowulf* identified Kali with the Saxon earth-mother Eostre, after whom Easter was named. Eostre's first home was said to be where the waters of Ganges flowed into an unknown sea (the Indian Ocean).[10]

Though Indian patriarchal thinkers tried to replace the female trinity of Kali with a male trinity, she was not eradicated in India, as she was in the West. Kali's scriptures said the members of the male trinity were born of only a small part of Kali, and lived in relation to her as a tiny puddle of water in a cow's hoofprint in relation to the vast sea. "Just as it is impossible for a hollow made by a cow's hoof to form a notion of the unfathomable depth of a sea, so it is impossible for Brahma and other gods to have a knowledge of the nature of Kali."[11]

Archetypal fear of the incomprehensible feminine principle added to popular dread of the queen of swords, who represented a being like Kali: complex, subtle, swift-acting, given to acts apparently cruel but logically necessary in the overview. Both Kali and the queen of swords were credited with deep comprehension of truths too frightening for the average man to face. Then there was the ultimate frightening truth that all men knew, yet tried not to know: the inevitable death awaiting every self. In this sense the queen of swords stood for thinking the unthinkable, giving expression to the unspeakable. Her card also meant separation, loneliness, privation, or widowhood; for Kali was always a widow, just as she was always a bride and always a mother. She was the eternal feminine Enigma.

King of Swords:

Yama

King of Swords: Yama

The name of Yama reversed the syllables of Kali's virginal, lovable, life-giving fertility aspect, Maya. Yama was another incarnation of Shiva as the Lord of Death. His usual appearance was that of a bull-god, wearing a bull mask, dancing on the dead body of the sacrificial bull that represented himself "made flesh" on earth. Yama the Bull gave up his life to become king in the afterworld: "Yama chose death, and he found out the path for many, and he gives the souls of the dead a resting place."[1]

Vedic peoples claimed that no matter what the funerary custom, cremation or burial, all the dead went to Yama.[2] Sometimes he was benevolent. Sometimes he was a stern judge of the dead, assigning postmortem punishments like the avenging Jehovah. In fact, he was one of the prototypes of Jehovah. Early Israelites, Canaanites, and Phoenicians worshiped him as Yamm, consort of the Sea-goddess Mari (Astarte). The combined male-female deity was Mari-Yam or Meri-Yam.[3] Even now, the same androgynous deity is known in Tibet as Yamamari.[4]

Jehovah as the Gnostic Demiurge was said to have "a dark blue complexion."[5] So had Yama. Hindu artists gave most gods identified with Shiva a dark blue skin color, showing them clothed with the night sky, that is, *digambara* or "sky-clad," a reference to their holy nakedness.[6] The ancient Aryan custom appeared also among British Picts, who painted their naked bodies blue for religious ceremonies and for divine protection in battle. "Blue blood" was also a symbol of the Greek gods' immortality, bestowed on them by the Mother Goddess. Medieval alchemists identified this mysterious blue blood with the *quinta essentia* or "quintessence," an elixir of life derived from God's blood: the pagan, not the Christian god.

Like all sacrificial deities, Yama achieved eternal life by giving himself up to death and sharing his blood with worshipers. As the slain bull, he provided a model for the Sole-Created sacrificial bull of Mithraism and the cult of Attis. In Rome, bulls were slain over a grating, so their blood could pour down to baptize worshipers in the pit below. Thus washed in the blood of the sacrificial animal, like the Christian "Lamb," newly baptized pagans were pronounced "born again for eternity."[7]

Christians later developed their own version of this ceremony, the Taurobolium, which was celebrated regularly on the Vatican mount up to the fourth century A.D.[8] Tibetan festivals of atonement still have a similar Yama figure called the Holy King of Religion, who wears a bull mask, and stabs his own human effigy, pretending to extract its entrails to administer as a sacrament to the worshipers.[9]

As king of swords, Yama displays male and female symbols of sword and lotus, together with the figure-eight infinity sign signifying their union. This king was interpreted as a powerful judge, a godlike authority, an embodiment of discipline and order, like the ancient king of the underworld. On this demonic side, he could also be dangerous, inhumane, or perverse.

Though Yama was often supposed to be as terrifying as Western versions of the King of Hell, his scriptures hinted at a peculiarly Gnostic philosophy that might sum up the teachings of the Tarot symbols and the final revelations of Europe's nonorthodox religions, some of which did perceive that man creates God in his own image: "Be not terrified, do not tremble, do not fear the Lord of Death. Your body is of the nature of voidness and this Lord of Judgment and his Furies too are void: they are your own hallucinations."[10]

Like Death itself, Yama always had the last word.

Notes

For complete citations, see Bibliography following notes.

The Sacred Tarot

1. Moakley, 35.   2. Moakley, 98.   3. Cavendish, T., 17.   4. Kaplan, 24.   5. Hargrave, 101.   6. Cavendish, T., 11, 15.   7. Douglas, 20.   8. Hargrave, 224.   9. Hargrave, 27.   10. *Bardo Thodol*, 3.   11. Dumézil, 572–73.   12. Dumézil, 386, 393.   13. Potter & Sargent, 49.   14. Dumézil, 231; Kaplan, 2.   15. Dumézil, 572.   16. Funk, 54.   17. Moakley, 55.   18. Hargrave, 27.   19. Zimmer, 127.   20. Tuchman, 104, 109.   21. Coulton, 202.   22. Mâle, 270.   23. Ashe, 203, 236.   24. Bullough, 169–70.   25. Wilkins, 193.   26. Montagu, 273.   27. Tuchman, 224.   28. Lea (unabridged), 21.   29. Coulton, 44.   30. Lea (unabridged), 599.   31. Coulton, 38, 61.   32. Lea (unabridged), 489.   33. Borchardt, 272.   34. Reinach, 294.   35. Lea (unabridged), 656–60.   36. Spinka, 34.   37. Briffault 3, 487–88; H. Smith, 256–57.   38. Ravensdale & Morgan, 105.   39. Campbell, C. M., 390, 629.   40. Coulton, 20.   41. H. Smith, 292–93.   42. Lea (unabridged), 60.   43. Oxenstierna, 68–9.   44. Borchardt, 290.   45. Coulton, 27.   46. Dreifus, 4.   47. J. H. Smith, D.C.P., 238–41.   48. Borchardt, 282.   49. Leland, 142.   50. Wilkins, 81.   51. Cavendish, T., 16.   52. Keightley, 81.   53. Waite, O.S., 131.   54. Coulton, 305–6.   55. H. Smith, 253.   56. Coulton, 123.   57. Hazlitt, 89.   58. Leland, 65.   59. Tatz & Kent, 19, 32.   60. Hargrave, 247.

61. Hazlitt, 460. 62. Funk, 320. 63. Trigg, 4–8, 47.
64. *Mahanirvanatantra*, 146. 65. Elworthy, 194. 66. Lawson, 226.
67. Waddell, 467, 471. 68. Lehner, 60. 69. Avalon, 173. 70. Waddell,
468–69. 71. Vetter, 256. 72. *Bardo Thodol*, 207. 73. Hawkins, 140.
74. Briffault 2, 602. 75. Phillips, 160. 76. H. Smith, 201.
77. Turville-Petre, 227. 78. O'Flaherty, 49, 344. 79. Tatz & Kent, 18.
80. Keightley, 20. 81. Derlon, 217–21. 82. Derlon, 144, 159. 83. Trigg,
184. 84. Neumann, G.M., 152. 85. Esty, 79. 86. Derlon, 210.
87. Leland, 107. 88. Trigg, 137. 89. Derlon, 132, 135. 90. Rawson, T.,
112. 91. *Mahanirvanatantra*, 295–96. 92. Trigg, 186, 203. 93. Trigg,
47. 94. Douglas, 43. 95. *Bardo Thodol*, 3. 96. Summers, G.W.,
488–91. 97. Groome, iv, lxi. 98. Trigg, 11, 202. 99. Papus, 32 *et seq.*
100. Shirley, 31–32. 101. Douglas, 24. 102. Hargrave, 160. 103. Leland,
211. 104. Papus, 9.

Elementals

1. Campbell, M.I., 90. 2. Lindsay, O.A., 20–21. 3. Cumont, A.R.G.R.,
68. 4. Agrippa, 43. 5. d'Alviella, 240. 6. Waddell, 484.
7. *Mahanirvanatantra*, 262–63. 8. Avalon, 229, 233. 9. Rawson, T., 70.
10. *Book of the Dead*, 273. 11. Lindsay, O.A., 75, 116, 120. 12. Augstein,
209. 13. Campbell, Oc.M., 181; Agrippa, 43, 49. 14. Cavendish, P.E.,
71. 15. *Encyc. Brit.*, s.v. "Welsh Literature." 16. Gaster, 787.
17. Turville-Petre, 276. 18. Budge, G.E. 2, 103. 19. Rawson, E.A., 57.
20. Dumézil, 319. 21. Neumann, G.M., 312. 22. Waddell, 258.
23. Rawson, T., 75. 24. Malory 1, 377. 25. Gelling & Davidson, 150.
26. Davidson, 112. 27. Hollander, 26; Turville-Petre, 178. 28. Graves,
G.M. 1, 148; 2, 25. 29. Dumézil, 289. 30. Huson, 138. 31. Leland,
99. 32. Campbell, P.M., 430. 33. Potter & Sargent, 28. 34. Fodor, 290;
Larousse, 359. 35. Vermaseren, 10, 49. 36. Tacitus, 728. 37. Lederer,
22–24. 38. Hauswirth, 21. 39. Campbell, P.M., 240, 314. 40. de
Riencourt, 23. 41. Robbins, 133. 42. Lindsay, O.A., 122; Wedeck, 236.
43. *Bardo Thodol*, 15–16; Agrippa, 57. 44. Hays, 223. 45. Funk, 301.
46. Tatz & Kent, 140. 47. Douglas, 37. 48. Budge, E.M., 89.
49. Waddell, 81. 50. Lethaby, 74–75. 51. Neumann, G.M., 267,
295–96. 52. Baring-Gould, 539. 53. Lethaby, 125. 54. Lindsay, O.A.,
137. 55. Jung, P.R., 109. 56. *Bardo Thodol*, 11. 57. Budge, G.E. 1,
286. 58. *Book of the Dead*, 623. 59. Moakley, 46. 60. Menen, 93.
61. Pagels, 37. 62. Guignebert, 367–68. 63. Jung & von Franz, 137,
204. 64. Coulton, 18–20.

Wheels of Becoming

1. *Encyc. Brit.*, s.v. "Numerals." 2. Keightley, 438. 3. Avalon, 164.
4. *Assyr. & Bab. Lit.*, 420. 5. O'Flaherty, 148; *Larousse*, 371. 6. Douglas,
(frontispiece). 7. Cavendish, T., 97. 8. Jung, M.H.S., 42. 9. H. Smith,
487–88. 10. Cavendish, T., 15, 73. 11. Wedeck, 155. 12. Gettings,

87.   13. Tuchman, 41.   14. Scot, 348; Mâle, 235.   15. Wilkins, 44.
16. Campbell, P.M., 293–94.   17. *Bardo Thodol*, lxvii, 53, 188.   18 Rose,
292.   19. *Bardo Thodol*, lxvi.   20. Angus, 151–54, 202.   21. *Bardo Thodol*,
234.   22. *Waite, O.S., 195*.   23. *Waddell, 226*.   24. *Bardo Thodol*,
frontispiece.   25. Waddell, 109.   26. Graves, G.M. 2, 404.   27. Legge 1,
133.   28. Angus, 154.   29. Campbell, M.I., 388–90.   30. Huson, 71,
147.   31. Campbell, M.I., 391.   32. Dumézil, 116.   33. Goodrich, 157.
34. *Mabinogion*, 243.   35. Goodrich, 67.   36. Loomis, 315–19.   37. Pagels,
57–58.   38. H. Smith, 228.   39. Doane, 436.   40. Angus, 280.
41. Campbell, Oc.M., 455.   42. Mâle, 355.   43. de Camp, 264.   44. J. H.
Smith, D.C.P., 4.   45. Goodrich, 96.   46. Angus, vii.   47. Phillips, 152.

The Yoni Yantra

1. Simons, 141.   2. Briffault 3, 494.   3. Campbell, Oc.M., 509.   4. H.
Smith, 250; Cavendish, P.E., 27.   5. Russell, 284.   6. J. H. Smith, C.G.,
287.   7. *Mahanirvanatantra*, 127; Silberer, 170.   8. Avalon, 428.   9. *Book of
the Dead*, 204.   10. *Larousse*, 37.   11. Koch, 8–9, 54.   12. Lederer, 141.
13. Trigg, 48–49.   14. Elworthy, 407.   15. Dumézil, 94.   16. Cavendish,
P.E., 51.   17. Leland, 67; *Larousse*, 293.   18. James, 135.   19. Rawson,
A.T., 74.   20. Jung, M.H.S., 240.   21. *Encyc. Brit.*, s.v. "Magen David."
22. Silberer, 197; *Encyc. Brit.*, s.v. "Cabala."   23. Lederer, 186–88.
24. Cavendish, T., 30, 142.   25. *Mahanirvanatantra*, xxiv.   26. Brasch,
70.   27. Shah, 380.   28. Rawson, T., 32.   29. Tatz & Kent, 128–29.
30. Briffault 2, 444.   31. Bullough, 105.   32. Campbell, C.M., 159.
33. Pagels, 57.   34. Malvern, 43.   35. Legge 2, 69.   36. Malvern, 53.
37. *Larousse*, 371.   38. Knight, D.W.P., 173.   39. Guerber, L.M.A., 238.
40. Knight, D.W.P., 236.   41. Haining, 77.   42. Rawson, T., 78.
43. Wilkins, 122.   44. Baring-Gould, 652.   45. Harding, 41.   46. Briffault
3, 80–81.   47. Campbell, Oc.M., 445–46.   48. *Encyc. Brit.*, s.v.
"Templars."   49. Douglas, 21.   50. Knight, D.W.P., 193.   51. Campbell,
C.M., 168.   52. Reinach, 310.   53. Russell, 197.   54. *Encyc. Brit.*, s.v.
"Templars."   55. Coulton, 245.   56. Robbins, 208.   57. Knight, D.W.P.,
186, 202.

0. The Fool

1. Gettings, 111.   2. *Larousse*, 213.   3. Cavendish, T., 62.   4. Rose,
209.   5. Knight, D.W.P., 78.   6. Davidson, 134.   7. Campbell, Or.M.,
73.   8. Silberer, 87.   9. Waddell, 483.   10. Hazlitt, 548.   11. Graves,
G.M. 1, 283–84.   12. Shah, 223–24.   13. Cavendish, T., 66.   14. Frazer,
146.   15. de Lys, 360.   16. Campbell, M.I., 245.   17. Cavendish, T.,
64.   18. Waddell, 113.   19. Tatz & Kent, 23.   20. Gettings, 111.
21. Cavendish, T., 66.   22. *Bardo Thodol*, 234.

1. The Magician

1. Gettings, 29.   2. Cavendish, T., 68.   3. Gettings, 26.   4. Shah, 196.

5. Shumaker, 232, 242–43.   6. Maspero, 118.   7. Budge, A.T., 196–98.
8. Angus, 99, 243.   9. Angus, 102, 110, 112.   10. Campbell, C.M., 154.
11. *Encyc. Brit.*, s.v. "Hermes."   12. Graves, G.M. 1, 66–67.
13. Summers, V., 154–57.

2. *The Papess*

1. Cavendish, T., 15, 73.   2. Pagels, 22, 64.   3. Malvern, 47–49.   4. de
Voragine, 355–57.   5. Pagels, 64–65.   6. Malvern, 60.   7. *Encyc. Brit.*, s.v.
"Women in Religious Orders."   8. *Larousse*, 311.   9. Brasch, 25.
10. Briffault 3, 2.   11. Lehner, 89.   12. Huson, 148.   13. Morris, 19, 71,
142.   14. Morris, 157; Bullough, 191.   15. Bullough, 163.   16. Gettings,
33.   17. Chamberlin, 25.   18. Baring-Gould, 172–73.   19. Durrell, 11.
20. Baring-Gould, 173.   21. Chamberlin, 25.   22. *Encyc. Brit.*, s.v.
"Papacy."   23. Durrell, 8–9.   24. Simons, 116.   25. Moakley, 72–73.
26. Gettings, 33.   27. Shumaker, 183.   28. Collins, 54, 220.   29. Graves,
G.M. 2, 203.   30. Legge 2, 69.   31. Attwater, 312.   32. Brewster, 440.
33. Rose, 250.   34. Waddell, 114.

3. *The Empress*

1. Campbell, M.I., 388.   2. Bachofen, 192.   3. Summers, V., 226.
4. Gettings, 33.   5. Budge, G.E. 1, 423.   6. *Larousse*, 202.   7. Elworthy,
105.   8. James, 198.   9. Graves, W.G., 159.   10. Potter & Sargent, 185.
11. H. Smith, 127.   12. Lawson, 577.   13. Angus, 97.   14. Lawson,
563.   15. Angus, 116.   16. *Larousse*, 208.   17. *Encyc. Brit.*, s.v.
"Demeter."   18. Lawson, 79.   19. Encyc. Brit., s.v. "Demeter."
20. Graves, W.G., 159.   21. Cavendish, T., 79.   22. Kaplan, 155.

4. *The Emperor*

1. *Larousse*, 371.   2. O'Flaherty, 34.   3. Graves, G.M. 1, 73.   4. Cumont,
M.M., 95.   5. Campbell, Or.M., 202.   6. *Assyr. & Bab. Lit.*, 420.
7. O'Flaherty, 130.   8. Cavendish, T., 80.   9. Kaplan, 45.   10. Tuchman,
41.   11. Campbell, Oc.M., 334.   12. Gaster, 769.   13. Gettings, 41;
Cavendish, T., 81.   14. Cumont, M.M., 128.   15. Gettings, 41.

5. *The Pope*

1. Cavendish, T., 85.   2. Gettings, 43.   3. Kaplan, 155.   4. Cavendish,
T., 82.   5. Guerber, L.R., 206–7.   6. Gettings, 45.   7. Waite, C.M.,
275.   8. Budge, A.T., 50.   9. Frazer, 61.   10. Huson, 155.   11. Cumont,
M.M., 105, 165.   12. H. Smith, 130, 252.   13. Reinach, 240.
14. Brewster, 5.   15. Attwater, 45.   16. Attwater, 275.   17. H. Smith,
102.   18. Dumézil, 323, 583.   19. Douglas, 64.   20. Cavendish, T., 83.

21. Scott, 254. 22. Cavendish, T., 83. 23. Woods, 89. 24. Gaster, 771. 25. White 1, 386.

6. The Lovers

1. Waddell, 116. 2. Kaplan, 113. 3. Avalon, 172. 4. Waddell, 117.
5. Avalon, 466. 6. Campbell, M.I., 388. 7. Eliade, 78. 8. Briffault 3,
20. 9. O'Flaherty, 34. 10. Budge, E.L., 57–58. 11. Baring-Gould,
652. 12. Campbell, C.M., 181–82. 13. Briffault 3, 490, 494. 14. Hughes,
203. 15. Bullough, 113. 16. Lederer, 162. 17. Fielding, 82, 114.
18. Briffault 3, 248. 19. *Encyc. Brit.*, s.v. "Marriage." 20. Rose, 144.
21. Guerber, L.M.A., 240. 22. Derlon, 134; Bowness, 25; Trigg, 88.
23. Gettings, 49. 24. Douglas, 67; Cavendish, T., 86. 25. Baring-Gould,
169. 26. Goodrich, 18, 65, 69. 27. Tatz & Kent, 140. 28. Funk, 301.

7. The Chariot

1. Gettings, 52. 2. Douglas, 70. 3. Elisofon & Watts, 79. 4. *Encyc. Brit.*, s.v. "Juggernaut." 5. Dumézil, 566. 6. Cavendish, T., 90.
7. *Larousse*, 342, 369. 8. *Epic of Gilgamesh*, 27. 9. Turville-Petre, 163.
10. Oxenstierna, 214–16. 11. Dumézil, 17. 12. Lindsay, O.A., 125.
13. *Mahanirvanatantra*, cxli. 14. Menen, 70. 15. *Mahanirvanatantra*, cxii.
16. Jung, M.H.S., 174. 17. Budge, E.L., 61. 18. Rawson, T., 193.
19. Moakley, 44.

8. Justice

1. Cavendish, T., 104. 2. von Franz, 23. 3. Budge, E.L., 68.
4. *Larousse*, 41. 5. Lindsay, O.A., 277. 6. Graves, G.M. 2, 341–42.
7. Knight, S.L., 156. 8. Cavendish, T., 105. 9. *Larousse*, 84.
10. Gettings, 55. 11. Pagels, 22, 49, 64–65. 12. Malvern, 39, 47.
13. Pagels, 55–56. 14. Malvern, 82. 15. *Larousse, 54; Assyr. & Bab. Lit.*,
287. 16. *Larousse*, 86. 17. Graves, G.M. 1, 125. 18. Wainwright, 97.
19. Moakley, 111.

9. The Hermit

1. Avalon, xliii. 2. Legge 1, 133. 3. Cavendish, T., 99. 4. Silberer,
244. 5. Douglas, 76. 6. Augstein, 108. 7. Edwardes, 111–12.
8. Cavendish, T., 100. 9. Baring-Gould, 92. 10. Baring-Gould, 226.
11. Wilkins, 40. 12. Graves, W.G., 394–95. 13. *Bardo Thodol*, 204.

10. The Wheel of Fortune

1. Graves, G.M. 1, 126. 2. Cumont, M.M., 111. 3. Elworthy, 195.
4. Cumont, M.M., 95–97. 5. Rose, 228. 6. Lawson, 13. 7. *Larousse*,

29.   8. Budge, G.E. 2, 50.   9. Budge, E.L., 57.   10. Case, 123.
11. Elworthy, 183, 194.   12. Norman, 123.   13. Moakley, 86.   14. Mâle,
95.   15. von Franz, pl. 13.   16. Cavendish, T., 103.   17. Huson, 115.
18. Mâle, 95–97, 395.   19. Lehner, 60.   20. Moakley, 87.   21. Briffault 3,
366.   22. Spence, 152–153, 65.   23. Butler, 147.   24. Avalon, 40.
25. Hazlitt, 346.   26. de Riencourt, 261.   27. Douglas, 45.   28. Douglas,
40.

11. Strength

1. Branston, 87.   2. Hollander, 32.   3. Huson, 177.   4. Massa, 104; Ashe,
30.   5. Gettings, 66.   6. *Bardo Thodol*, 147.   7. Gray, 80.   8. *Larousse*, 37;
Budge, G.E. 1, 451.   9. Ashe, 31, 59.   10. Budge, D.N., 34.   11. Graves,
W.G., 405; Briffault 3, 110.   12. Knight, S.L., 130.   13. Budge, G.E. 2,
253.   14. Graves, W.G., 245; G.M. 1, 244.   15. Budge, G.E. 1, 459.
16. Cavendish, T., 105.   17. Kaplan, 272.   18. *Encyc. Brit.*, s.v.
"Illuminated Manuscripts."   19. *Larousse*, 77.   20. Cavendish, T., 98;
Kaplan, 38.

12. The Hanged Man

1. Douglas, 85.   2. Branston, 114.   3. Frazer, 412.   4. Oxenstierna,
223.   5. Butler, 154.   6. Moakley, 95.   7. Budge, E.L., 44.   8. *Book of the
Dead*, 410.   9. Ross, 32; Menen, 70.   10. *Mahanirvanatantra*, xix.
11. Pagels, 74.   12. Jung & von Franz, 100.   13. Zimmer, 205.

13. Death

1. Cavendish, T., 110.   2. Gettings, 75.   3. Guerber, L.M.A., 119.
4. *Encyc. Brit.*, s.v. "Scythians."   5. Graves, W.G., 225.   6. Steenstrup,
149.   7. Waddell, 524–25.   8. Shah, 208, 210, 218.   9. Rose, 283.
10. Pagels, 90.   11. Tennant, 189, 207.   12. H. Smith, 234, 238.
13. Mumford, 255.   14. Lindsay, A.W., 207–8.   15. Avalon, 137–38.
16. von Franz, pl. 28.   17. Kaplan, 148–50.

14. Temperance

1. Silberer, 352.   2. *Larousse*, 49.   3. Tatz & Kent, 140.   4. Zimmer, 34.
5. Neumann, G.M., 267.   6. *Assyr. & Bab. Lit.*, 249.   7. Elworthy, 187,
301.   8. Budge, E.M., 60.   9. Budge, E.L., 84.   10. Budge, D.N., 218;
Briffault 3, 314.   11. Gettings, 79.   12. Gettings, 78.   13. Funk, 301.
14. Gettings, 49.

15. The Devil

1. *Larousse*, 323.   2. *Larousse*, 317.   3. Elworthy, 384.   4. Campbell, M.I.,

388.   5. Rose, 240.   6. Briffault 2, 564.   7. Wedeck, 95, 155.
8. Campbell, Oc.M., 513.   9. Scot, 323–25.   10. Spence, 95.   11. Ashe,
15.   12. *Book of the Dead*, 544–45.   13. O'Flaherty, 274.   14. Campbell,
Or.M., 183.   15. Budge, G.E. 1, 24.   16. O'Flaherty, 348.   17. Graves,
W.G., 367.   18. Campbell, M.I., 294; Enslin, 91.   19. Robinson, 174.
20. Robinson, 175.   21. de Givry, 49.   22. Potter & Sargent, 176.
23. Cavendish, T., 118.   24. Rawson, E.A., 25.   25. Kramer & Sprenger,
167.

16. The House of God

1. Tuchman, 41.   2. Borchardt, 69.   3. Gettings, 87.   4. O'Flaherty,
130.   5. Cavendish, T., 123.   6. Rawson, E.A., 57.   7. Legge 2, 239.
8. Douglas, 100.   9. White 1, 367.   10. White 1, 364–66.   11. Mâle,
271.   12. Attwater, 57.   13. Jung & von Franz, 121.   14. Neumann,
G.M., 311.   15. Campbell, C.M., 5.   16. Kaplan, 149.

17. The Star

1. Cavendish, T., 125.   2. Budge, G.E. 2, 103.   3. *Book of the Dead*, 297.
4. Lindsay, O.A., 184, 327.   5. H. Smith, 201.   6. Briffault 1, 377.
7. Graves, G.M. 2, 405.   8. Knight, S.L., 48.   9. Graves, W.G., 124.
10. *Larousse*, 348.   11. O'Flaherty, 346.   12. Tannahill, 82.   13. Waddell,
509–10.   14. Gettings, 91.   15. Graves, G.M. 1, 86.   16. *Larousse*, 226.
17. Elworthy, 424.   18. Massa, 101.

18. The Moon

1. Douglas, 107.   2. Budge, G.E. 2, 34.   3. Briffault 2, 599; Cumont,
A.R.G.R., 19, 69.   4. Briffault 3, 78.   5. Knight, S.L., 99.   6. Hallet, 115,
152.   7. Briffault 2, 670; 3, 76.   8. Briffault 2, 601; Campbell, M.T.L.B.,
43.   9. Cumont, A.R.G.R., 107.   10. de Lys, 458.   11. Harding, 100.
12. Malvern, 121.   13. Hazlitt, 191.   14. Briffault 2, 587–89.
15. Summers, V., 238.   16. Avalon, 423.   17. Briffault 3, 132.
18. Cumont, A.R.G.R., 96, 107.   19. Gettings, 91.   20. Lindsay, O.A.,
222.   21. Douglas, 105.   22. Gettings, 95.   23. Turville-Petre, 76.
24. *Larousse*, 213, 305.   25. Spence, 126, 158.   26. Davidson, 34.
27. Eliade, 327.   28. Zimmer, 60.   29. Cumont, A.R.G.R., 186; Agrippa,
217.   30. Briffault 2, 605.   31. Douglas, 106.   32. Budge, G.E. 1, 19.
33. Lethaby, 193–94.   34. O'Flaherty, 352.   35. Robertson, 115.
36. Sturluson, 39.   37. *Book of the Dead*, 182.   38. *Mahanirvanatantra*, 113.
39. Graves, W.G., 406–7.   40. Graves, G.M. 2, 385.   41. Gettings, 95.
42. Campbell, M.I., 149.   43. Gifford, 31.

19. The Sun

1. Branston, 290; Sturluson, 92.   2. Legge 2, 63.   3. Cavendish, T., 135.
4. Gettings, 100.   5. Knight, S.L., 98; Baring-Gould, 286.   6. Graves,
W.G., 309.   7. Hawkins, 139–40.   8. Graves, W.G., 310.   9. Hitching,
213.   10. Graves, W.G., 144.   11. Baring-Gould, 201.   12. Wilkins,
119.   13. Baring-Gould, 539–40.   14. Gettings, 100.
15. *Mahanirvanatantra*, xl.   16. Cavendish, T., 133.   17. Douglas, 109.

20. Judgment

1. H. Smith, 176.   2. Pfeifer, 133.   3. Black, 3.   4. O'Flaherty, 339,
349.   5. Barret, 97.   6. H. Smith, 129–30.   7. Turville-Petre, 147–48, 150,
154.   8. *Encyc. Brit.*, s.v. "Dalai Lama."   9. Turville-Petre, 164, 284.
10. *Mahanirvanatantra*, 49–50, 295–96.   11. Douglas, 112; Cavendish, T., 136.

21. The World

1. Gettings, 109.   2. *Bardo Thodol*, xxxv.   3. Campbell, C.M., 488.
4. *Mahanirvanatantra*, xxxi.   5. Zimmer, 25, 178.   6. Avalon, 27, 31.
7. Campbell, C.M., 347.   8. Shirley, 42.   9. Collins, 113.   10. *Encyc. Brit.*,
s.v. "Plotinus."   11. Angus, 71.   12. Budge, G.E. 1, 519.   13. Angus, 71,
119, 240.   14. Shirley, 46.   15. Agrippa, 65.   16. Douglas, 113.
17. Waddell, 359, 435.   18. Graves W.G., 64.   19. Menen, 149.
20. Douglas, 114.   21. Neumann, G.M., 233.

The Suit of Cups

Ace of Cups: Love

1. Briffault 3, 494.   2. Jung & von Franz, 75, 114, 121.   3. Neumann, A.P.,
6.   4. Campbell, C.M., 13.   5. Erman, 252.

Two of Cups: Romance

1. Turville-Petre, 76.   2. Guerber, L.M.A., 26.   3. H. Smith, 266; Hughes,
211.   4. Shah, 121.   5. Campbell, C.M., 44.   6. Silberer, 212.   7. Shah,
98; Wilkins, 128.   8. Loomis, 251, 276.

Three of Cups: Grace

1. Dumézil, 166.   2. Graves, G.M. 1, 53–55.   3. Elisofon & Watts, 118.
4. Lindsay, O.A., 391.   5. Pagels, 50.   6. *Larousse*, 132, 138.   7. Guerber,
L.M.A., 267.

Four of Cups: Decline

1. Neumann, A.P., 87.   2. Briffault 3, 94.   3. Neumann, A.P., 31.
4. Angus, 251.   5. Reinach, 77.   6. Harrison, 174.   7. Graves, W.G., 75.

Five of Cups: Regret

1. Budge, E.L., 75.   2. Douglas, 174.

Six of Cups: Childhood

1. *Mahanirvanatantra*, xlvii–xlviii.   2. Tennant, 134.   3. Turville-Petre, 144,
231.   4. Cavendish, T., 134.   5. *Larousse*, 83.   6. *Larousse*, 85.
7. *Larousse*, 170.

Seven of Cups: Dream

1. Graves, G.M. 1, 55; 2, 401.   2. Avalon, 164; Campbell, Or.M., 202–3.
3. Rawson, E.A., 255.   4. Ross, 141.   5. Malory 1, xxi.   6. Baring-Gould,
620; Briffault 3, 451.   7. Pepper & Wilcock, 258.   8. *Larousse*, 208.
9. Leland, 206.   10. Douglas, 176.

Eight of Cups: Loss

1. Graves, G.M. 1, 115.   2. Graves, W.G., 230, 392.   3. Merivale, 64, 72,
119.

Nine of Cups: Happiness

1. Wilkins, 128.   2. Spence, 78.   3. Piggott, 72.

Ten of Cups: Salvation

1. Guerber, L.M.A., 185, 200.   2. *Mabinogion*, 243.   3. Goodrich, 64.
4. Goodrich, 81.   5. Tuchman, 177.

Princess of Cups: Elaine

1. Malory 2, 130.   2. Campbell, C.M., 535–36.   3. *Larousse*, 234;
Cavendish, V.H.H., 49.   4. Loomis, 209–11.   5. Jung & von Franz, 114,
181.   6. Russell, 69.   7. Keightley, 295.

Prince of Cups: Galahad

1. Malory 1, 91; 2, 171.   2. Malory 2, 199, 268.   3. Graves, G.M. 2, 136.
4. Frazer, 387.

Queen of Cups: Virginal

1. *Larousse*, 333.   2. Briffault 2, 391–96.   3. Guerber, L.M.A., 115.
4. Neumann, G.M., 152.   5. Jung, M.H.S., 189.   6. de Riencourt, 250–51.

King of Cups: Dewi

1. Attwater, 102–3.   2. Brewster, 121.   3. Spence, 158.   4. Rees, 47.
5. Baring-Gould, 619.   6. Guerber, L.M.A., 182–83.

The Suit of Wands

Ace of Wands: Power

1. O'Flaherty, 348.   2. Graves, W.G., 367.   3. *Assyr. & Bab. Lit.*, 4.
4. O'Flaherty, 274, 131.   5. *Encyc. Brit.*, s.v. "Precession of the
Equinoxes."   6. Hitching, 242.   7. Brandon, 360.   8. Graves, G.M. 1, 27.

Two of Wands: Alliance

1. Hays, 339.   2. Graves, G.M. 1, 55–57.   3. Baring-Gould, 57.
4. Graves, G.M. 1, 113.   5. Groome, 131–32.

Three of Wands: Fate

1. Campbell, C.M., 121–22; Goodrich, 32.   2. Waddell, 169.   3. Avalon,
328–29.   4. Rawson, E.A., 160; *Mahanirvanatantra*, xxxiv.   5. Wedeck,
66.   6. Graves, W.G., 61.   7. Goodrich, 65.   8. Silberer, 280.   9. Budge,
E.M., 121.   10. *Book of the Dead*, 205.   11. Graves, G.M. 1, 52.
12. Malvern, 39.   13. Ashe, 76, 135.   14. Briffault 2, 625.   15. Hazlitt,
379.   16. Briffault 3, 160; Trigg, 80.

Four of Wands: Success

1. *Book of the Dead*, 427.   2. Briffault 1, 374.   3. de Riencourt, 187.
4. Angus, 183.   5. Daly, 99.   6. *Mabinogion*, 90.   7. Briffault 3, 406.
8. *Larousse*, 335.   9. Hollander, 39.   10. Turville-Petre, 187.   11. Lawson,
563, 586.   12. Graves, G.M. 2, 277.   13. Groome, xlviii, lxvii.

Five of Wands: Impasse

1. *Larousse*, 335.   2. Wilkins, 113–14, 124.   3. Wilkins, 106–8.   4. Tatz &
Kent, 84.   5. Wilkins, 81.   6. Frazer, 671.

Six of Wands: Glory

1. Waddell, 497.   2. *Bardo Thodol*, 70.   3. Graves, G.M. 2, 202.
4. Lindsay, O.A., 333.   5. H. Smith, 183.   6. Knight, S.L., 98.   7. H.
Smith, 135–36.   8. Campbell, Or.M., 73.

Seven of Wands: Challenge

1. Graves, G.M. 1, 114.   2. *Encyc. Brit.*, s.v. "Damocles."   3. Frazer, 328.

Eight of Wands: Fall

1. Graves, G.M. 1, 254–55.   2. Graves, G.M. 1, 239.   3. Budge, D.N.,
276.   4. Budge, G.E. 2, 158.   5. Lindsay, O.A., 191–92.

Nine of Wands: Defense

1. Budge, G.E. 1, 504.   2. *Larousse*, 63.   3. Edwardes, 23.   4. Budge,
E.M., 84; *Book of the Dead*, 145, 194, 205.   5. James, 135–39.   6. Douglas,
168.   7. Kaplan, 333.

Ten of Wands: Oppression

1. Albright, 232.   2. Lindsay, O.A., 24, 29.   3. Douglas, 169.

Princess of Wands: Atargatis

1. Potter & Sargent, 180.   2. *Assyr. & Bab. Lit.*, 338–39.   3. Chagnon,
47.   4. Neumann, G.M., 174.   5. Rawson, E.A., 260.   6. Farb, 93.
7. Spence, 95–96.   8. Stone, 164.

Prince of Wands: Dagon

1. Waddell, 364.   2. Ashe, 48.   3. Campbell, M.I., 294.

Queen of Wands: Hel

1. Turville-Petre, 55.   2. Johnson, 165.   3. Wainwright, 113.   4. Rank,
73.   5. Potter & Sargent, 52, 73.   6. Oxenstierna, 191; Baring-Gould,
579.   7. Keightley, 93.   8. Frazer, 3.   9. Turville-Petre, 202.   10. Graves,
G.M. 1, 229.   11. Campbell, Oc.M., 398.   12. Neumann, G.M., 286.

King of Wands: Valraven

1. Hays, 412.   2. Graves, W.G., 87.   3. Turville-Petre, 58.   4. Guerber,

L.M.A., 274–75.　5. Campbell, M.I., 389.　6. Rose, 289.　7. Lethaby, 244–45.　8. Koch, 74.

The Suit of Pentacles

Ace of Pentacles: Reward

1. Budge, E.L., 75.　2. Brewster, 343.　3. Hooke, 112; d'Alviella, 153; Campbell, Oc.M., 210.　4. d'Alviella, 166–67; Graves, G.M. 2, 277; Lindsay, O.A., 54.　5. Pagels, 30–31.　6. Turville-Petre, 187.　7. Groome, 18, 28.　8. O'Flaherty, 196.　9. Groome, xlviii; Derlon, 157.　10. Waddell, 245.　11. Koch, 6; Hornung, 212.

Two of Pentacles: Change

1. Hazlitt, 176.　2. Kramer & Sprenger, 25.　3. de Givry (frontispiece). 4. Silberer, 128–29.　5. Maspero, 123–25.　6. Tatz & Kent, 79.

Three of Pentacles: Work

1. Cavendish, T., 168.　2. *Larousse*, 220, 224.　3. Malory 1, 115.

Four of Pentacles: Avarice

1. *Larousse*, 204.　2. Frazer, 229.　3. Briffault 3, 276.

Five of Pentacles: Hardship

1. Coulton, 42.　2. Lea, 599.　3. Guerber, L.R., 255.

Six of Pentacles: Charity

1. Malvern, 49.　2. Briffault 3, 169.　3. Avalon, 175.　4. Dumézil, 94. 5. Lindsay, A.W., 33.　6. *Mahanirvanatantra*, 328.

Seven of Pentacles: Failure

1. Campbell, C.M., 388, 394.　2. Jung & von Franz, 75, 202.　3. Graves, W.G., 194.

Eight of Pentacles: Learning

1. Avalon, 203; Shah, 389.　2. *Mahanirvanatantra*, 88.　3. Wilkins, 110.

4. Shah, 108.   5. Lederer, 181.   6. Campbell, Oc.M., 445.   7. Wilkins,
42.   8. Campbell, M.I., 235.   9. *Mahanirvanatantra*, 360.

Nine of Pentacles: Accomplishment

1. Lederer, 137.   2. Campbell, Or.M., 307.   3. H.Smith, 227.   4. Briffault
2, 447–48; Graves, W.G., 179.   5. Rose, 229.

Ten of Pentacles: Protection

1. Wedeck, 50.   2. Graves, G.M. 2, 374–75, 404.   3. Campbell, P.M., 101;
Ashe, 201.   4. Gifford, 87–88.

Princess of Pentacles: Nimue

1. Piggott, 72.   2. Baring-Gould, 539.   3. Spence, 57.   4. Graves, W.G.,
491–92.   5. Loomis, 107, 324–42.

Prince of Pentacles: Merlin

1. Turville-Petre, 147–48.   2. Rees, 193, 293.   3. Potter & Sargent, 89.
4. Guerber, L.M.A., 205–8.   5. *Encyc. Brit.*, s.v. "Merlin."   6. Rose,
209.   7. Jung & von Franz, 367.

Queen of Pentacles: Erda

1. Neumann, G.M., 85.   2. Graves, G.M. 1, 11.   3. Neumann, G.M.,
94.   4. Campbell, C.M., 121; Turville-Petre, 150.   5. *Larousse*, 89.
6. Campbell, P.M., 240.

King of Pentacles: Baal

1. Briffault 3, 106.   2. Gray, 108.

The Suit of Swords

Ace of Swords: Doom

1. Keightley, 45.   2. Guerber, L.M.A., 138.   3. Loomis, 387; Malory 1,
8.   4. Loomis, 342.   5. Graves, G.M. 2, 76.   6. Goodrich, 217.
7. Guerber, L.R., 219.

Two of Swords: Balance

1. Wainwright, 97.   2. Bachofen, 186, 189.   3. Erman, 121.   4. Avalon, 93.   5. *Bardo Thodol*, 236.

Three of Swords: Sorrow

1. Campbell, Or.M., 272.   2. Rose, 40.   3. Herodotus, 270.   4. Lederer, 126–27.   5. Cavendish, T., 165.

Four of Swords: Seclusion

1. Agrippa, 159.   2. *Larousse*, 208.   3. Cavendish, T., 165.   4. Graves, G.M. 1, 80.

Five of Swords: Defeat

1. Baring-Gould, 247.   2. Turville-Petre, 42, 48, 115.   3. Turville-Petre, 40, 46.   4. Branston, 208.   5. Cavendish, T., 165.

Six of Swords: Passage

1. Harrison, 73.   2. Graves, W.G., 405–7.   3. Harrison, 72–73.   4. Hallet, 401.

Seven of Swords: Opposition

1. Gifford, 26.   2. Scot, 550.   3. Tatz & Kent, 148; Waddell, 129.
4. Rees, 41; Frazer, 467.   5. Keightley, 431–32.   6. Potter & Sargent, 71.
7. de Lys, 94.   8. Agrippa, 159.

Eight of Swords: Disillusion

1. Turville-Petre, 48.   2. Douglas, 187.

Nine of Swords: Cruelty

1. Keightley, 446.   2. Zimmer, 69.   3. Scot, 417.   4. Knight, D.W.P., 221, 229.   5. Derlon, 210.

Ten of Swords: Ruin

1. Spence, 85.   2. Attwater, 304.   3. Rees, 235.   4. Spence, 95–96.
5. *Larousse*, 233.   6. Goodrich, 177, 192.   7. Pepper & Wilcock, 275.
8. Baring-Gould, 493.

Princess of Swords: Skuld

1. Branston, 184–85. 2. Woods, 156; *Larousse*, 293. 3. Avalon, 199.
4. Eliade, 381–82. 5. Turville-Petre, 227, 261. 6. Branston, 191.
7. Leland, 143. 8. *Larousse*, 292–93. 9. Guerber, L.M.A., 266.
10. Hazlitt, 191.

Prince of Swords: Tyr

1. Branston, 135. 2. Branston, 109, 136. 3. Frazer, 78; *Larousse*, 346.
4. Cavendish, T., 166.

Queen of Swords: Kali

1. Cavendish, T., 166. 2. Neumann, G.M., 149–53. 3. Wilson, 257.
4. *Encyc. Brit.*, s.v. "Kali." 5. Rawson, T., 112. 6. Neumann, G.M., pl.
66. 7. *Mahanirvanatantra*, 49–50, 295–96. 8. Neumann, G.M., 153.
9. *Larousse*, 306. 10. Goodrich, 18. 11. Rawson, T., 184.

King of Swords: Yama

1. Rees, 108. 2. Dumézil, 63. 3. Ashe, 48. 4. Waddell, 364.
5. Lindsay, O.A., 137. 6. Campbell, Or.M., 219. 7. Angus, 239.
8. Clodd, 79. 9. Waddell, 531. 10. Campbell, M.I., 408–9.

Bibliography

Agrippa, Henry Cornelius. *The Philosophy of Natural Magic*. Secaucus, N.J.: University Books, 1974.

Albright, William Powell. *Yahweh and the Gods of Canaan*. New York: Doubleday & Co., 1968.

Angus, S. *The Mystery-Religions*. New York: Dover Publications Inc., 1975.

Ashe, Geoffrey. *The Virgin*. London: Routledge & Kegan Paul, 1976.

Assyrian and Babylonian Literature: Selected Translations. New York: D. Appleton & Co., 1901.

Attwater, Donald. *The Penguin Dictionary of Saints*. Baltimore, Md.: Penguin Books Inc., 1965.

Augstein, Rudolf. *Jesus Son of Man*. New York: Urizen Books, 1977.

Avalon, Arthur. *Shakti and Shakta*. New York: Dover Publications Inc., 1978.

Bachofen, J. J. *Myth, Religion and Mother-Right*. Princeton, N.J.: Princeton University Press, 1967.

Bardo Thodol (Tibetan Book of the Dead). London: Oxford University Press, 1927.

Baring-Gould, Sabine. *Curious Myths of the Middle Ages*. New York: University Books, 1967.

Barrett, C. K. *The New Testament Background*. New York: Harper & Row, 1961.

Black, Matthew. *The Scrolls and Christian Origins*. New York: Charles Scribner's Sons, 1961.

Book of the Dead. New York: Bell Publishing Co.

Borchardt, Frank. *German Antiquity in Renaissance Myth*. Baltimore, Md.: Johns Hopkins Press, 1971.

Bowness, Charles. *Romany Magic*. New York: Samuel Weiser Inc., 1973.

243

Brandon, S. G. F. *Religion in Ancient History*. New York: Charles Scribner's Sons, 1969.

Branston, Brian. *Gods of the North*. London: Thames & Hudson, 1955.

Brasch, R. *How Did Sex Begin?*. New York: David McKay Co., 1973.

Brewster, H. Pomeroy. *Saints and Festivals of the Christian Church*. New York: Frederick A. Stokes Co., 1904.

Briffault, Robert. *The Mothers*. 3 vols. New York: Macmillan, 1927.

Budge, Sir E. A. Wallis. *Amulets and Talismans*. New York: University Books Inc., 1968.

———. *Gods of the Egyptians*. 2 vols. New York: Dover Publications Inc., 1969.

———. *Egyptian Magic*. New York: Dover Publications Inc., 1971.

———. *Dwellers on the Nile*. New York: Dover Publications Inc., 1977.

———. *Egyptian Language*. New York: Dover Publications Inc., 1977.

Bullough, Vern L. *The Subordinate Sex*. Chicago: University of Illinois Press, 1973.

Butler, Bill. *Dictionary of the Tarot*. New York: Schocken Books, 1975.

Campbell, Joseph. *The Masks of God: Primitive Mythology*. New York: Viking Press, 1959.

———. *The Masks of God: Oriental Mythology*. New York: Viking Press, 1962.

———. *The Masks of God: Occidental Mythology*. New York: Viking Press, 1964.

———. *The Masks of God: Creative Mythology*. New York: Viking Press, 1970.

———. *Myths To Live By*. New York: Viking Press, 1972.

———. *The Mythic Image*. Princeton, N.J.: Princeton University Press, 1974.

Case, Paul Foster. *The Tarot*. Richmond, Va.: Maccy Publishing Co., 1947.

Cavendish, Richard. *Visions of Heaven and Hell*. New York: Harmony Books, 1977.

———. *The Tarot*. New York: Harper & Row, 1975.

———. *The Powers of Evil*. New York: G. P. Putnam's Sons, 1975.

Chagnon, Napoleon A. *Yanomamo: The Fierce People*. New York: Holt, Rinehart & Winston, 1968.

Chamberlin, E. R. *The Bad Popes*. New York: Dial Press, 1969.

Clodd, Edward. *Magic in Names and in Other Things*. London: Chapman & Hall, Ltd., 1920.

Collins, Joseph B. *Christian Mysticism in the Elizabethan Age*. New York: Octagon Books, 1971.

Coulton, G. G. *Inquisition and Liberty*. Boston, Mass.: Beacon Press, 1959.

Cumont, Franz. *The Mysteries of Mithra*. New York: Dover Publications Inc., 1956.

———. *Astrology and Religion among the Greeks and Romans*. New York: Dover Publications Inc., 1960.

d'Alviella, Count Goblet. *The Migration of Symbols*. New York: University Books, 1956.

Daly, Mary. *Beyond God the Father*. Boston, Mass.: Beacon Press, 1973.

Davidson, H. R. Ellis. *Pagan Scandinavia*. New York: Frederick A. Praeger, 1967.

de Camp, L. Sprague. *The Ancient Engineers*. New York: Ballantine Books, 1960.

de Givry, Grillot. *Witchcraft, Magic and Alchemy*. New York: Dover Publications Inc., 1971.

de Lys, Claudia. *The Giant Book of Superstitions*. Secaucus, N.J.: Citadel Press, 1979.

de Riencourt, Amaury. *Sex and Power in History*. New York: Dell Publishing Co., 1974.

Derlon, Pierre. *Secrets of the Gypsies*. New York: Ballantine Books, 1977.

de Voragine, Jacobus. *The Golden Legend*. New York: Longmans, Green & Co., 1941.

Doane, T. W. *Bible Myths and Their Parallels in Other Religions*. New York: University Books, 1971.

Douglas, Alfred. *The Tarot*. New York: Taplinger Publishing Co., 1972.

Dreifus, Claudia., ed. *Seizing Our Bodies*. New York: Vintage Books, 1978.

Dumézil, Georges. *Archaic Roman Religion*. 2 vols. Chicago, Ill.: University of Chicago Press, 1970.

Durrell, Lawrence. *Pope Joan*. London: Derek Verschoyle, 1954.

Ebon, Martin. *Witchcraft Today*. New York: New American Library, 1971.

Edwardes, Allen. *The Jewel in the Lotus*. New York: Lancer Books, 1965.

Eliade, Mircea. *Shamanism*. Princeton, N.J.: Bollingen Series, 1964.

Elisofon, Eliot, and Watts, Alan. *Erotic Spirituality*. New York: Macmillan, 1971.

Elworthy, Frederick. *The Evil Eye*. New York: Julian Press Inc., 1958.

Encyclopedia Britannica, 1970 edition.

Enslin, Morton Scott. *Christian Beginnings*. New York: Harper & Bros., 1938.

Epic of Gilgamesh. Harmondsworth, England: Penguin Books Ltd., 1960.

Erman, Adolf. *The Literature of the Ancient Egyptians*. New York: Benjamin Blom Inc., 1971.

Esty, Katharine. *The Gypsies, Wanderers in Time*. New York: Meredith Press, 1969.

Farb, Peter. *Word Play*. New York: Alfred A. Knopf, 1974.

Fielding, W. J. *Strange Customs of Courtship and Marriage*. New York: Garden City Co., 1942.

Fodor, Nandor. *The Search for the Beloved*. New York: University Books Inc., 1949.

Frazer, Sir James. *The Golden Bough*. New York: Macmillan, 1922.

Funk, Wilfred. *Word Origins and Their Romantic Stories*. New York: Bell Publishing Co., 1978.

Gaster, Theodor. *Myth, Legend and Custom in the Old Testament*. New York: Harper & Row, 1969.

Gelling, Peter, and Davidson, Hilda Ellis. *The Chariot of the Sun*. New York: Frederick A. Praeger, 1969.

Gettings, Fred. *The Book of Tarot*. London: Triune Books, 1973.

Gifford, Edward S., Jr. *The Evil Eye*. New York: Macmillan, 1958.

Goodrich, Norma Lorre. *Medieval Myths*. New York: New American Library, 1977.

Graves, Robert. *The Greek Myths*. 2 vols. New York: Penguin Books Inc., 1955.

———. *The White Goddess*. New York: Vintage Books, 1958.

Gray, John. *Near Eastern Mythology*. London: Hamlyn Publishing Group Ltd., 1963.

Groome, Francis Hindes. *Gypsy Folk Tales*. London: Herbert Jenkins, 1963.

Guerber, H. A. *Legends of the Rhine*. New York: A. S. Barnes & Co., 1895.

———. *Legends of the Middle Ages.* New York: American Book Co., 1924.

Guignebert, Charles. *Ancient, Medieval and Modern Christianity.* New York: University Books, 1961.

Haining, Peter. *Witchcraft and Black Magic.* New York: Grosset & Dunlap, 1972.

Hallet, Jean-Pierre. *Pygmy Kitabu.* New York: Random House, 1973.

Harding, M. Esther. *Woman's Mysteries, Ancient and Modern.* New York: G. P. Putnam's Sons, 1971.

Hargrave, Catherine Perry. *A History of Playing Cards.* New York: Dover Publications, 1966.

Harrison, Jane Ellen. *Epilegomena to the Study of Greek Religion.* New York: University Books, 1962.

Hauswirth, Frieda. *Purdah: The Status of Indian Women.* New York: Vanguard Press, 1932.

Hawkins, Gerald S. *Stonehenge Decoded.* New York: Dell Publishing Co., Inc., 1965.

Hays, H. R. *In the Beginnings.* New York: G. P. Putnam's Sons, 1963.

Hazlitt, W. Carew. *Faiths and Folklore of the British Isles.* 2 vols. New York: Benjamin Blom, 1965.

Herodotus. *The Histories.* New York: D. Appleton & Co., 1899.

Hitching, Francis. *Earth Magic.* New York: Pocket Books Inc., 1978.

Hollander, Lee M. *The Skalds.* Ann Arbor, Mich.: University of Michigan Press, 1968.

Hooke, S. H. *Middle Eastern Mythology.* Harmondsworth, England: Penguin Books Ltd., 1963.

Hornung, Clarence P. *Hornung's Handbook of Designs and Devices.* New York: Dover Publications Inc., 1959.

Hughes, Robert. *Heaven and Hell in Western Art.* New York: Stein & Day, 1968.

Huson, Paul. *The Devil's Picturebook.* New York: G. P. Putnam's Sons, 1971.

Huxley, Francis. *The Way of the Sacred.* New York: Doubleday & Co., 1974.

James, E. O. *The Ancient Gods.* New York: G. P. Putnam's Sons, 1960.

Johnson, Walter. *Folk-Memory.* New York: Arno Press, 1980.

Jung, Carl Gustav. *Psychology and Religion.* Yale University Press, 1938.

———. *Man and His Symbols.* New York: Doubleday & Co., 1964.

Jung, Emma, and von Franz, Marie-Louise. *The Grail Legend.* New York: G. P. Putnam's Sons, 1970.

Kaplan, Stuart R. *The Encyclopedia of Tarot.* New York: U.S. Games Systems Inc., 1978.

Keightley, Thomas. *The World Guide to Gnomes, Fairies, Elves and Other Little People.* New York: Avenel Books, 1978.

Knight, Richard Payne. *The Symbolical Language of Ancient Art and Mythology.* New York: J. W. Bouton, 1892.

———. *A Discourse on the Worship of Priapus.* Secaucus, N.J.: University Books Inc., 1974.

Koch, Rudolf. *The Book of Signs.* New York: Dover Publications Inc., 1955.

Kramer, Heinrich, and Sprenger, James. *Malleus Maleficarum.* New York: Dover Publications Inc., 1971.

Larousse Encyclopedia of Mythology. London: Hamlyn Publishing Group Ltd., 1968.

Lawson, John Cuthbert. *Modern Greek Folklore and Ancient Greek Religion.* New York: University Books, Inc., 1964.

Lea, Henry Charles. *The Inquisition of the Middle Ages.* New York: Citadel Press, 1954. New York: Macmillan, 1961 (unabridged version).

Lederer, Wolfgang. *The Fear of Women.* New York: Harcourt Brace Jovanovich, 1968.

Legge, Francis. *Forerunners and Rivals of Christianity.* 2 vols. New York: University Books Inc., 1964.

Lehner, Ernst. *Symbols, Signs and Signets.* New York: Dover Publications Inc., 1969.

Leland, Charles Godfrey. *Gypsy Sorcery and Fortune Telling.* New York: University Books, 1962.

Lethaby, W. R. *Architecture, Mysticism and Myth.* New York: George Braziller, 1975.

Lindsay, Jack. *The Ancient World.* New York: G. P. Putnam's Sons, 1968.

_____. *The Origins of Astrology.* New York: Barnes & Noble, Inc., 1971.

Loomis, Roger S. and Laura H. *Medieval Romances.* New York: Modern Library, 1957.

Mabinogion. London: Everyman's Library, J. M. Dent & Sons, 1970.

Mahanirvanatantra. New York: Dover Publications Inc., 1972.

Mâle, Emile. *The Gothic Image.* New York: Harper & Row, 1958.

Malory, Sir Thomas. *Le Morte d'Arthur.* 2 vols. London: J. M. Dent & Sons Ltd., 1961.

Malvern, Marjorie. *Venus in Sackcloth.* Carbondale, Ill.: Southern Illinois University Press, 1975.

Maspero, Gaston. *Popular Stories of Ancient Egypt.* New York: University Books, 1967.

Massa, Aldo. *The Phoenicians.* Geneva: Editions Minerva, 1977.

Menen, Aubrey. *The Mystics.* New York: Dial Press, 1974.

Merivale, Patricia. *Pan the Goat-God.* Cambridge, Mass.: Harvard University Press, 1969.

Moakley, Gertrude. *The Tarot Cards Painted by Bembo.* New York: New York Public Library, 1966.

Montagu, Ashley. *Touching.* New York: Columbia University Press, 1971.

Morris, Joan. *The Lady Was a Bishop.* New York: Macmillan, 1973.

Mumford, Lewis. *Interpretations and Forecasts.* New York: Harcourt Brace Jovanovich, 1973.

Neumann, Erich. *Amor and Psyche.* New York: Harper & Row, 1956.

_____. *The Great Mother: An Analysis of the Archetype.* Princeton, N.J.: Princeton University Press, 1963.

Norman, Dorothy. *The Hero.* New York: World Publishing Co., 1969.

O'Flaherty, Wendy Doniger. *Hindu Myths.* Middlesex, England: Penguin Books Ltd., 1975.

Oxenstierna, Eric. *The Norsemen.* Greenwich, Conn.: New York Graphic Society, 1965.

Pagels, Elaine. *The Gnostic Gospels.* New York: Random House, 1979.

Papus. *The Tarot of the Bohemians.* New York: Arcanum Books, 1958.

Pepper, Elizabeth, and Wilcock, John. *Magical and Mystical Sites*. New York: Harper & Row, 1977.

Pfeifer, Charles F. *The Dead Sea Scrolls and the Bible*. New York: Weathervane Books, 1969.

Phillips, Guy Ragland. *Brigantia*. London: Routledge & Kegan Paul, 1976.

Piggott, Stuart. *The Druids*. New York: Frederick A. Praeger, 1968.

Potter, Stephen, and Sargent, Laurens. *Pedigree*. New York: Taplinger Publishing Co., 1974.

Rank, Otto. *The Myth of the Birth of the Hero*. New York: Vintage Books, 1959.

Ravensdale, T., and Morgan, J. *The Psychology of Witchcraft*. New York: Arco Publishing, 1974.

Rawson, Philip. *Erotic Art of the East*. New York: G. P. Putnam's Sons, 1968.

––––––. *The Art of Tantra*. Greenwich, Conn.: New York Graphic Society, 1973.

Rees, Alwyn and Brinley. *Celtic Heritage*. New York: Grove Press Inc., 1961.

Reinach, Salomon. *Orpheus*. Horace Liveright, Inc., 1930.

Robbins, Rossell Hope. *Encyclopedia of Witchcraft and Demonology*. New York: Crown Publishers, 1959.

Robertson, J. M. *Pagan Christs*. New York: University Books Inc., 1967.

Robinson, J. M., genl. ed. *The Nag Hammadi Library in English*. San Francisco: Harper & Row, 1977.

Rose, H. J. *Religion in Greece and Rome*. New York: Harper & Bros., 1959.

Ross, Nancy Wilson. *Three Ways of Asian Wisdom*. New York: Simon & Schuster, 1966.

Russell, J. B. *Witchcraft in the Middle Ages*. Ithaca, N.Y.: Cornell University Press, 1972.

Scot, Reginald. *Discoverie of Witchcraft*. Yorkshire, England: Rowman & Littlefield, 1973.

Scott, George Ryley. *Phallic Worship*. Westport, Conn.: Associated Booksellers.

Shah, Idris. *The Sufis*. London: Octagon Press, 1964.

Shirley, Ralph. *Occultists and Mystics of All Ages*. New York: University Books Inc., 1972.

Shumaker, Wayne. *The Occult Sciences in the Renaissance*. Berkeley: University of California Press, 1972.

Silberer, Herbert. *Hidden Symbolism of Alchemy and the Occult Arts*. New York: Dover Publications, 1971.

Simons, G. L. *Sex and Superstition*. New York: Harper & Row, 1973.

Smith, Homer. *Man and His Gods*. Boston, Mass.: Little, Brown & Co., 1952.

Smith, John Holland. *Constantine The Great*. New York: Charles Scribner's Sons, 1971.

––––––. *The Death of Classical Paganism*. New York: Charles Scribner's Sons, 1976.

Spence, Lewis. *The History and Origins of Druidism*. New York: Samuel Weiser Inc., 1971.

Spinka, Matthew. *A History of Christianity in the Balkans*. Archon Books, 1968.

Steenstrup, Johannes C. H. R. *The Medieval Popular Ballad*. Seattle, Wash.: University of Washington Press, 1968.

Stone, Merlin. *When God Was a Woman*. New York: Dial Press, 1976.

Sturluson, Snorri. *The Prose Edda*. Berkeley: University of California Press, 1954.

Summers, Montague. *The Geography of Witchcraft*. New York: University Books, 1958.

_____. *The Vampire, His Kith and Kin*. New York: University Books Inc., 1960.

Tacitus. *Complete Works*. New York: Modern Library, 1942.

Tannahill, Reay. *Flesh and Blood: A History of the Cannibal Complex*. New York: Stein & Day, 1975.

Tatz, Mark, and Kent, Jody. *Rebirth*. New York: Anchor Press/Doubleday, 1977.

Tennant, F. R. *The Sources of the Doctrines of the Fall and Original Sin*. New York: Schocken Books, 1968.

Trigg, Elwood B. *Gypsy Demons and Divinities*. Secaucus, N.J.: Citadel Press, 1973.

Tuchman, Barbara. *A Distant Mirror*. New York: Alfred A. Knopf, 1978.

Turville-Petre, E. O. G. *Myth And Religion of the North*. New York: Holt, Rinehart & Winston, 1964.

Vermaseren, Maarten J. *Cybele and Attis*. London: Thames & Hudson, 1977.

Vetter, George B. *Magic and Religion*. New York: Philosophical Library, 1973.

von Franz, Marie-Louise. *Time, Rhythm and Repose*. New York: Thames & Hudson, 1978.

Waddell, L. Austine. *Tibetan Buddhism*. New York: Dover Publications Inc., 1972.

Wainwright, F. T. *Scandinavian England*. Sussex, England: Phillimore & Co., Ltd., 1975.

Waite, Arthur Edward. *The Book of Ceremonial Magic*. New York: Bell Publishing Co., 1969.

_____. *The Occult Sciences*. Secaucus, N.J.: University Books Inc., 1974.

Wedeck, Harry E. *A Treasury of Witchcraft*. Secaucus, N.J.: Citadel Press, 1975.

White, Andrew D. *A History of the Warfare of Science with Theology in Christendom*. 2 vols. New York: George Braziller, 1955.

Wilkins, Eithne. *The Rose-Garden Game*. London: Victor Gallancz Ltd., 1969.

Wilson, Colin. *The Outsider*. Boston, Mass.: Houghton Mifflin Co., 1956.

Woods, William. *A History of the Devil*. New York: G. P. Putnam's Sons, 1974.

Zimmer, Heinrich. *Myths and Symbols in Indian Art and Civilization*. Princeton, N.J.: Bollingen/Princeton, 1946.

Index